Reminiscence Theatre

of related interest

Storymaking and Creative Groupwork with Older People
Paula Crimmens
ISBN 978 1 85302 440 5

Introduction to Dramatherapy
Theatre and Healing – Ariadne's Ball of Thread
Sue Jennings
Foreword by Clare Higgins
ISBN 978 1 85302 251 7

Practical Approaches to Dramatherapy
The Shield of Perseus
Madeline Andersen-Warren and Roger Grainger
Preface by Anna Seymour
ISBN 978 1 85302 660 7

Discovering the Self through Drama and Movement
The Sesame Approach
Edited by Jenny Pearson
ISBN 978 1 85302 384 2

Social Cognition Through Drama And Literature
for People with Learning Disabilities
Macbeth in Mind
Nicola Grove and Keith Park
ISBN 978 1 85302 908 0

Healing Arts Therapies and Person-Centred Dementia Care
Edited by Anthea Innes and Karen Hatfield
Bradford Dementia Group Series
ISBN 978 1 84310 038 6

Reminiscence Theatre
Making Theatre from Memories

Pam Schweitzer

Foreword by Glenda Jackson MP

Jessica Kingsley Publishers
London and Philadelphia

All extracts from play scripts and books published by Age Exchange used by kind
permission of Age Exchange Theatre Trust.
Lyrics from 'Let's Do It' by Cole Porter used in Chapter 13
by kind permission of Alfred Publishing Co., Inc.

Every reasonable effort has been made to trace all copyright holders of quoted material. The author apologises
for any omissions and is happy to receive amendments from copyright holders.

First published in 2007
by Jessica Kingsley Publishers
116 Pentonville Road
London N1 9JB, UK
and
400 Market Street, Suite 400
Philadelphia, PA 19106, USA

www.jkp.com

Library of Congress Cataloging in Publication Data
Schweitzer, Pam.
Reminiscence theatre : making theatre from memories / Pam Schweitzer ; foreword by Glenda Jackson.
p. cm.
Includes bibliographical references and index.
ISBN-13: 978-1-84310-430-8 (pbk. : alk. paper)
ISBN-10: 1-84310-430-X (pbk. : alk. paper) 1. Amateur theater. 2. Theater and older people. 3. Playwriting.
4. Oral history. I. Title.
PN3156.S38 2007
792'.0222--dc22

2006030777

British Library Cataloguing in Publication Data
A CIP catalogue record for this book is available from the British Library

ISBN 978 1 84310 430 8

Printed and bound in Great Britain by
Athenaeum Press, Gateshead, Tyne and Wear

Contents

Part 1: Reminiscence Theatre: Process and Product

Part 2: Participatory and Inter-generational Projects

Part 3: Older People Dramatising and Performing their Memories

Foreword

A great theatre director once said that all drama begins with 'an empty space'. This book, written by a valued and inspirational friend, details how theatre can help fill some of our personal empty spaces: spaces made by loss – loss of family, community, country or memory.

The value of theatre in education, in its widest sense, has been recognised for decades, but Pam has taken her original work in this field to new and, without her, probably unexplored heights.

As a Patron of Age Exchange, over the years I've watched, with awe and fascination, the benefits, experienced by so many, of Pam's constant pursuit of her belief that theatre can make the seemingly impossible a reality. Through her work, people meet and speak to each other and work creatively together across all external boundaries of colour, creed, gender and generation. They find that our common humanity is infinitely more similar than our differences. And, via theatre, Pam has discovered ways in which, even with memory loss, we can speak to and for ourselves, when all communication seems lost.

When I became an MP, I was told not infrequently that I had merely exchanged one form of theatre for another. My reply now, as then, is that Parliament is remarkably under-rehearsed, very badly lit and the acoustics are appalling. This book, however, is not under-rehearsed by virtue of Pam's long and dedicated experience. She sheds new light on complex human issues and the message is loud and clear: reminiscence and reminiscence theatre can make a profound improvement in real people's real lives.

Incidentally, it is clear that a great time was had by all.

Glenda Jackson MP

Preface

I am writing this book at the end of a 23-year exploration of reminiscence theatre through practice as Artistic Director of Age Exchange Theatre Trust, a charitable organisation I founded in 1983. It had not been part of my thinking at that time to spend a working life in the reminiscence field. However, the initial project opened up a very rich seam full of exciting artistic possibilities and I wanted to dig deeper. It is a testimony to the enormous interest and variety within the field of reminiscence work, and reminiscence theatre and drama in particular, that it has held me in its grip so long and indeed continues to do so.

I am extremely grateful to the Bridge House Trust for funding the writing as part of a project managed by Age Exchange Theatre Trust. This is not, however, an Age Exchange publication and it does not attempt to represent the organisation's current work. The views expressed herein are entirely my own and what follows is a personal retrospective. I wish to express my thanks to Jessica Kingsley Publishers for giving me the opportunity, at the point of my retirement, to share my experience of reminiscence theatre with a wider readership and for their support through the editorial process.

Over the years I have worked on 30 original reminiscence theatre productions and as many publications of memories and three-dimensional reminiscence exhibitions. It has been very difficult to select from so many projects a handful of examples which will demonstrate methods and approaches suited to different audiences and interest groups. Each project I have worked on holds special memories for me, both of the original story-tellers, and of the many wonderful writers, actors, musical directors, designers and project workers who have helped me bring the many and varied productions into reality.

In the course of developing these projects, I began to see the need to develop new ways of working through reminiscence with specific groups of older people. These included small group work in the context of health and social care, inter-cultural and inter-generational projects in the community, and therapeutic reminiscence projects in the area of mental health. Reminiscence affords a meeting place for workers from disciplines which are usually very separate, so I have been privileged to work as a theatre practitioner with psychologists, health and social care workers, artists, museum and gallery staff and teachers, to name but a few. It has been immensely stimulating developing new projects which combine our different skills in the hope of contributing to the quality of life of communities, and especially of older members of those communities.

Though not exactly a 'how to do it' book, I hope the examples of plays and other drama-based reminiscence projects described and analysed herein will enable readers to apply these creative approaches readily to their own work fields and interests. I have drawn readers' attention to the work of other theatre companies and reminiscence drama projects and referred to many articles and books which lead deeper into the field, showing the range of disciplines which can be fruitfully connected through reminiscence.

In writing this book, I have used the traditional reminiscence method of working through interview, transcribing and then editing the resulting tapes. I am very grateful to Clare Summerskill, a long-standing colleague and friend, who conducted and transcribed the interviews and then helped me through the process of organising the material. Clare has offered me invaluable feedback and encouraged me to continue with the sometimes overwhelming task of distilling the last 23 years of practice in these pages.

I also wish to thank those who have read part or all of this book in manuscript and encouraged me in the writing of it: Joanna Bornat, Errollyn Bruce, Craig Fees, Sue Heiser, Sally Knocker, Jen Lunn, Helena Platt, Frances Rifkin, Micheline Steinberg and of course Faith Gibson, who has also been a most important mentor to me over the years, and for whose generous introduction I am most grateful.

Special thanks are due too to my husband Alex, who has put up with my reminiscence mania over so many years and supported me, both emotionally and practically, through all the ups and downs of getting an organisation off the ground and fighting to keep it going and growing over the years. Without his tireless work on the Age Exchange buildings there would not have been a Reminiscence Centre to function as a creative hub for reminiscence work nationally and internationally, to house all the projects, training days and festivals and to showcase all the productions before they went out on the road.

Finally I wish to acknowledge my tremendous debt to the thousands of older people with whom I have had the pleasure to work over the years for generously and openly sharing their lives and for participating in a thousand different ways in the reminiscence work described in the following chapters.

Pam Schweitzer

Introduction

The indomitable spirit, boundless energy and crusading conviction that has always characterised Pam Schweitzer's commitment to reminiscence and reminiscence theatre shine through this account of her 23 years at the Age Exchange Reminiscence Centre. More than a personal memoir, her book illustrates and illuminates the essential elements of reminiscence theatre in which the universal components of people's remembered personal past are transformed into accessible dramatic representations despite differences of age, culture, ethnicity and language.

Based on recorded transcripts, the book mirrors the methods employed in the process of creating reminiscence theatre. Personal memories are first recorded, transcribed and then reformed and transformed by thinking and thinking again. The exercise of memory, accessed by reminiscence and recall and the interplay of imagination, provides the basis for creating theatrical and musical representations as well as exhibitions of individuals' and groups' lived experience. Through improvisation, dynamic scripting, linked singing and dramatic re-presentation, actors stimulate the memories of the audience. In turn through after-show discussions with the performers, members of the audience are stimulated and energised to engage in their own remembering, reviewing and reconstructing memories, a process which encourages them to develop life scripts with which they can bear to live.

Reminiscence Theatre serves as a review of Pam Schweitzer's remarkably productive life as pioneer, energiser, researcher, writer, artistic director and business manager. It passes lightly over the relentless, recurring search for funds, the prodigious workload and the versatility required to work with older and younger volunteers, professional and non-professional actors, musicians, teachers, artists and health and social care staff of varying abilities, ambitions, talents and temperaments.

Those of us who have been privileged to know Pam and share in aspects of her work throughout the United Kingdom and in the European Network owe her a great debt. We have enjoyed immensely and learned much from the performances of the professional company, the Youth Theatre, the Good Companions, the exhibitions, the international conferences and the Remembering Yesterday, Caring Today projects. We too have experienced the excitement, the rush of adrenaline and the immense pleasure and stimulation associated with reminiscence theatre whose benefits are by no means limited to older audiences deprived of artistic stimulation.

The vast scope of the work recounted in this book as well as the detailed guidance it provides will become an invaluable resource for anyone who wishes to mine the riches of reminiscence work and to transform the spoken word into tangible artistic forms. This book bears witness to the resilience of the human spirit; it testifies to the enduring creativity of older people, even those overtaken by frailties of body or mind, and it demonstrates the transforming power of memories made accessible through reminiscence theatre.

Faith Gibson
Emeritus Professor of Social Work, University of Ulster

About This Book

In this book I explore different ways of dramatising and making theatre from memories. I aim to cover a range of work where the content is generated through interviews and discussions with older people and where the playing back of the stories in theatre form acts as a spur to memory, communication, empathy and imagination.

The 'Background to the Development of Reminiscence Theatre' section will set the work in a personal, cultural and social context. Thereafter, I have divided the book into three main sections, though there will be much fruitful overlap between them.

Part 1 is concerned with fully scripted pieces of reminiscence theatre performed by actors to many different audiences, but predominantly to older people themselves. It covers all the processes involved in creating a reminiscence play, from the original concept through interviews, scripting, rehearsal, production and performance. It focuses on using the authentic voices of the interviewees in the scripts and gives examples from certain productions to illustrate the method. Two chapters in this section are specifically devoted to theatre around the memories of minority ethnic elders and feature a more imagistic approach to reminiscence theatre.

Part 2 explores participatory and inter-generational reminiscence, from professionally performed Theatre in Education projects presented in specially created environments, to play-making by younger people in classrooms and in community contexts from the memories shared with them by older people. Again, there is specific reference to multicultural reminiscence drama work involving old and young performing together.

Part 3 explores direct creative involvement by groups of older people in reminiscence performance. This includes the creation, with professional support, of original plays around stories from their own lives, which are then played to audiences of contemporaries or younger people. It also demonstrates the use of spontaneous dramatic enactments and group improvisations in creative reminiscence projects in residential homes and day centres. Finally it explores the use of drama as a valuable means of recapturing memories to support people with dementia and their family members in the present.

Background to the Development
of Reminiscence Theatre

Personal and cultural influences

Given that reminiscence theatre might be thought of as a rather specialised approach both to play-making and to working with older people, I would like to say something about what led me into it in the first place, as well as what has held me there so long. Many influences, personal, cultural and social, have contributed to the idea of making professional theatre from older people's memories and using creative drama approaches with groups of older people as a way of awakening and exploring memories.

The oral tradition

Throughout the 1960s, when I was growing up, the oral tradition was starting to be valued again with the rebirth of interest in folk song. As a semi-professional singer, this was my great love for many years. It was the power of the story in the song which drew me, the respectful listening of the groups to individual voices and the blending of these voices in spontaneous harmony which enchanted me.

Recording people's lives

The growth of oral history around the same time, with its special emphasis on recording working people's voices and vanishing ways of life, was another powerful influence (Thompson 1978). For some years, my father, for his own interest, had been recording people speaking to him about their lives on a reel-to-reel Uher tape machine, and on the rare occasions when I was allowed to listen to the results, I found the interviewees' extraordinary stories, their quirkiness and individuality, endlessly intriguing. As the technology for such recordings was becoming ever more affordable, portable and efficient, I made my own tapes, including travelling in Iceland and recording the songs and stories of the old people I met there. When Charles Parker created his magnificent *Radio Ballads* for the BBC (MacColl, Parker and Seeger 1958–1964), this seemed to me the perfect combination of recorded spoken words of working people and songs, both traditional and specially written, illustrating the detail of their lives.[1] Since that time, far more radio and television broadcasts have featured first-hand testimony from eye-witnesses at 'ground level', as well as from the educated and the privileged. I remember being heavily influenced by the work of Stephen Peet who created the *Yesterday's Witness* series for BBC television in the 1970s. In these films older people spoke directly to the camera without interpretation by an all-knowing commentator and Peet allowed us to hear the authentic voice relating lived history in a uniquely personal way.

People's theatre

The 'people's voice' was also being heard in Joan Littlewood and Ewan MacColl's Theatre Workshop (Coren 1984) and in the social documentaries mounted at Peter Cheeseman's Theatre Royal in Stoke. By incorporating the particular speech rhythms, idioms and dialects of many different working people whose lives and views the shows reflected, these innovators built a dynamic relationship between the sources, the players and the audience, different in feel from the more passive conventional performer/audience relationship. The influence of Bertolt Brecht in creating this more socially and politically aware theatre was palpable, but the British version was more stylistically eclectic, combining the speech of 'ordinary people' with documentary sources, official pronouncements and live music, both traditional and specially composed. For me as a young theatre practitioner, these experiments in social documentary theatre, often focusing on the stories of local industries in crisis as perceived by the workforce who depended on them for their livelihoods, and playing to audiences closely involved with the issues, were a significant influence pushing me towards reminiscence theatre.

Theatre in Education

Theatre in Education (TIE) was at its most experimental and challenging in the 1970s and early 1980s, with some very fine minds and committed performers being drawn to the idea of theatre as an agent of change. The leading teams attached to repertory theatres in Coventry, Bolton, Leeds and London conceived their original programmes, devised for performance in classrooms, as a means of raising fundamental issues, social, moral, political and historical, with young people. They demonstrated that children could grapple with these complex issues if they were presented through character, situation and action, far better than if they were taught from a book or blackboard. These interactive Theatre in Education programmes presented the children with apparently 'real' situations in which conflicting characters sought their support and in which they were required to participate directly and responsibly. It was a far cry from run-of-the-mill children's theatre with its emphasis on illogical fantasy, exaggerated zany characters and token participation, performed by would-be professional actors who were biding their time and hoping for 'proper' theatre work. In the 1970s I had the good fortune to observe the work of the leading TIE companies on behalf of the Arts Council and became convinced of the importance of their work (Schweitzer 1975). I collected and edited some of their most effective scripts and arranged their publication so that others could learn the approach and the method (Schweitzer

1980a, 1980b, 1980c). Years later, as Artistic Director of Age Exchange, I was very excited to revisit this area and create a reminiscence-based version of the TIE form.

Educational drama

Educational drama too was becoming a valued part of education in the 1960s and 1970s, as a discipline in its own right and as a way of learning which could be useful across the curriculum (Fines and Verrier 1974; Nixon 1982). Working with school students developing original pieces of drama drawn from their own experience and other sources, and performing them in improvised or scripted form, was becoming as widely accepted as mounting more traditional school productions of existing plays. I chose to spend many years teaching educational drama in secondary schools in London and, when I saw the effect on young people in drama classes of dramatising the issues in their own lives, I became convinced of its immense social and psychological value. As far as I know, no schools at that time were developing plays from memories of local older people, but if anyone had thought to do so, it would certainly have been in keeping with the educational drama movement's thinking. The work reflected in the second and third parts of this book calls very heavily on my earlier experience as an educational drama teacher and adviser, but with the added dimension of community-building by encouraging different generations to work creatively together.

The wider social and demographic context

More representation for older people

An important social factor in the development of reminiscence theatre over the last quarter of the twentieth century was the ongoing demographic change, with an increasing proportion of the population retired and a falling birth rate (Phillipson 1982, 1998). For this reason, and because of their ever-rising expectations of length and quality of life, older people were more and more visible. They were also becoming more vocal, with pensioners' lobbies speaking more confidently as they realised their potential to influence events and policies. In the early 1980s I became much more alert to the issues facing older people when I went to work for Task Force, later known as Pensioners' Link, one of the more radical voluntary sector organisations set up to work 'with pensioners, not for them'. Funding bodies at that time were increasingly aware of their failure to support cultural projects aimed at this sector and were therefore more willing to give favourable consideration to applications addressing this vacuum in provision. This was undoubtedly an influence in securing funding from the Greater London Council for the new Age Exchange Theatre Trust in 1983, especially as the request was strongly backed by the then mighty Transport and General Workers Union, who valued the involvement of their retired workers in generating theatre reflecting and celebrating their lives.

A multicultural society

A further significant demographic change in London was that a high proportion of the Commonwealth immigrants who had come to Britain in the post-war years were now reaching retirement age (Phillips and Phillips 1998) and seeking to meet up with fellow countrymen and women, to eat traditional food together and to enjoy familiar craft and cultural activities. Part of this drive was led by the desire of many minority ethnic elders to talk together about their shared memories, singing songs from 'home'. This activity led to these elders putting increasing value on their first-generation immigrant experience and wishing to record and preserve their unique life journeys for posterity.

As so many of the younger generation in the local schools were from minority ethnic backgrounds, elders became more motivated to transmit their own migration history and stories about their countries of origin, with the intention of increasing the children's sense of self-worth and identity (Hewitt and Harris 1992; Schweitzer 1993, 2004a). This was in line with thinking embodied in the new National Curriculum, encouraging use of first-hand testimony, especially in the study of recent and local history and of migration. From very early on, I felt that if Age Exchange was to reflect the views, concerns and life experience of older Londoners, then a significant space must be provided for minority elders whose voices were so rarely heard by the majority.

Growth in community education

There was increasing recognition too that older people's minds needed nourishment. An ever-growing range of day classes was offered in the 1970s and 1980s to community and education centres. Reminiscence discussion and writing groups often began under the umbrella of adult or community education classes and this was true of the Age Exchange project. Some of the older people I worked with in such classes in the years just before starting Age Exchange stayed loyal to the idea and became active volunteers, remaining in the organisation for many years. They found participating in the various projects and the day-to-day life of the Reminiscence Centre to be a source of stimulation, social exchange, psychological support and personal satisfaction. Many of these long-serving volunteers have told me that having creative contact with others of their own age group and younger people has helped them to avoid loneliness, depression and consequent decline into ill health, an abiding if unspoken priority for all of us.

The Freedom Pass

The advent of the Freedom Pass, the universal free travel offered to London's pensioners in 1984, has been a very significant factor in allowing older people to participate in arts and educational projects outside their own homes. By taking the financial worry out of travel and enabling older people to explore new places and revisit old favourites, the Freedom Pass, so aptly named, has transformed countless lives. The Age Exchange Reminiscence Centre, with its carefully located base right beside bus and train links, has benefited immensely from this concession, and it is probably true to say that, without it, many London community projects for older people started during the last 25 years would have been twice as hard to get off the ground.

Quality of life issues in care homes and day centres

Parallel with the adult and community education developments already mentioned was the growing awareness in the 1970s and 1980s that those frail older people who were being taken care of in residential homes also deserved stimulus and opportunities for social and creative communal activity. Increasingly, local authorities supported freelance community arts practitioners and part-time teachers to run sessions for these house-bound older people under their adult and community education programmes. Although some of these opportunities were short-lived because of financial cut-backs, they gave considerable impetus to reminiscence work in many parts of the country and this initiative was supported by the development of reminiscence aids for use in such settings. The Department of Health and Help the Aged created an invaluable tape/slide resource pack entitled 'Recall', which enabled people who were just starting out in reminiscence to run structured sessions supported by carefully chosen audio and visual prompts (Help the Aged Education Department 1981). This also gave reminiscence work an official stamp of approval and made it much easier for care managers to introduce the activity in their homes and day centres, and to encourage their staff to participate (Bornat 1994).

Training for professional carers

The need for training to support care staff was increasingly recognised during the 1980s and 1990s, and experience of reminiscence work was acknowledged as a relevant part of this training (Burnside 1990). There was growing evidence that when care workers had a chance to get to know more about their clients' past lives their own job satisfaction in taking care of them in the present was increased (Gibson 2000, 2004, 2006; Petrukowicz and Johnson 1991). Furthermore, reminiscence work encouraged a more respectful approach generally since, however frail, the older people were clearly the experts on their own lives and could engage in reminiscence groups as active, authoritative and competent participants. Touring reminiscence theatre and related arts-based projects complemented all these developments in the social care sector.

Person-centred dementia care

The number of older people with dementia became more and more significant with each decade and voluntary organisations were growing up during the early 1980s to help people in the community to care for their relatives at home. Clearly, they could not all be housed by local authorities, which were increasingly contracting out their residential facilities, and the concept of Community Care was in the ascendant as it became clear that more and more aged people would become dependent on a wide range of domiciliary health and social services. The medical advances in treating dementia and related disorders have been slow, although there have been some drugs produced which retard the damaging effects for a while, extending the capacity of families to cope with the situation and increasing the independence of the person with dementia.

The emphasis has been gradually shifting to treatment of the person rather than the illness, and interventions designed to improve quality of life for people with dementia and their carers are increasingly seen to be effective as part of an overall strategy (Kitwood 1997). Groups where both can speak and be listened to have been set up to meet this need and are in keeping with other support group movements, mainly run by ex-carers. There has been a growing recognition in the field of professional dementia care that life review (a series of structured one-to-one sessions going through key life stages with a therapist, and closely related to reminiscence work in its person-centred philosophy) can also make an important contribution to the sense of identity and worth of the person with dementia (Haight 1998; Haight and Webster 1995). This shift in emphasis towards psycho-social interventions has also favoured the incorporation of structured reminiscence work as described in the final chapter of this book.

A favourable environment

It is no coincidence then that the reminiscence theatre and drama projects described in the following pages happened when they did and in the ways that they did. All the factors mentioned above, personal, cultural, educational, social and demographic, have provided a favourable context for development.

Part 1

Reminiscence Theatre: Process and Product

The following chapters are concerned with reminiscence theatre performed by actors to many different audiences, but predominantly to older people themselves. They cover the processes involved in creating a reminiscence play, from the original concept through interviews, scripting, production and performance. They focus on using the authentic voices from recorded and transcribed interviews in the scripts and give examples from certain productions to illustrate the method.

Starting with a case study of the collaboration between a group of older women and a group of senior school drama students in making a play, the first chapter moves on to trace the development of a professional company dedicated to further exploration of the reminiscence theatre method. It describes how the contributors participated in the rehearsal process, how the company developed individual scenes and the overall structure, and finally how the audiences of this first touring show responded. It lays down the blueprint for future shows, including the involvement of the audience through post-show discussions.

The second chapter explores the verbatim approach to scripting the memories of older people recorded in groups and through individual interviews. It takes the reader through all the necessary steps of interviewing, transcribing, identifying important stories, finding a structure in the assembled material and incorporating many stories into a coherent piece.

Chapter 3 takes the reader briefly through several productions, showing how the verbatim approach was adapted to suit particular projects and how different writers interpreted the task of creating a script from the interview material.

The next two chapters in this section are specifically devoted to theatre around the memories of minority ethnic elders, including working in more than one language. The two shows featured in Chapter 4 show how an imagistic approach with music and dance can compliment the spoken word and enable productions to reach audiences outside the cultural and language group they represent. Chapter 5 explores the importance of finding a way to celebrate the memories of less visible minority groups who nevertheless seek to preserve their identity and transmit their experience to younger generations.

Chapter 6 gives examples of themes and structures for shows which have been successful in different ways and which could be useful models for other groups who seek to dramatise memories related to their locality.

Chapter 7 considers some of the more practical aspects of staging and touring reminiscence theatre productions.

Setting Up a Reminiscence Theatre Company

In this chapter I shall describe my discovery of the value of reminiscence work, my first experience of making reminiscence theatre and the setting up of Age Exchange in 1983 as a professional theatre company dedicated to this work.

In the early 1980s, after ten years of teaching drama and humanities in secondary schools, I was appointed Education Officer in a voluntary organisation called Task Force working with pensioners, with a brief to explore potential learning opportunities in inter-generational co-operation. Up to that time, the work between old and young had always been seen as the children *doing something for* the old people, such as decorating their kitchens or digging their gardens, things at which incidentally the young people were not particularly skilled. It concerned me that the older people were always seen as passive recipients of the young people's 'good works'. This confirmed the idea of an unequal relationship, wherein young people were effective and older people were without resources of their own.

Sharing the past in the present

Reminiscence: a new idea

Reminiscence was a relatively new idea in the early 1980s (Bornat 1989). Talking about the past was still generally seen as something not to be encouraged amongst older people, since it implied that they were also living in the past and bordering on senility (Coleman 1986, 1994). My introduction to reminiscence was visiting Minnie Bennett House, a sheltered housing unit in Greenwich, to observe a facilitated session for a group of elderly ladies, in their 80s.[2] There were about half a dozen of them and they were all completely lucid, if a little hard of hearing. They were reminiscing in a group about their younger days and they were very lively and animated, reminding one another of things they had done and places they had been. Some of these memories were coming back very vividly after a long time and I was surprised that the older people could recall experiences from another era with such clarity. I found what they were remembering fascinating and rich in detail, and was eager to hear more. I felt myself to be in a very privileged position listening to these stories, and was sure they would be of interest to many more people, young and old.

Renewed energy and new connections

As the older people reminisced, they were bringing the remembered energy of their younger days into the present, so that I could see the 17-year-old girls inside these 90-year-old story-tellers. The old people were apparently making new connections with one another as they told their stories, discovering things from the past which they had in common. In a sheltered housing unit it is often difficult for older people to make new friends and the reminiscence sessions seemed to be providing a basis for developing new but strong relationships founded on shared experience.

Remembering in dialogue

I noticed that they were telling a lot of their memories in the form of dialogue, and almost performing their stories as though they were happening in the present. For example, one lady might say, 'My Mum, she says to me, "You'd better be in by nine or your Dad'll be after you." And I says, "Yes Mum, I will." And then when I come back, it's "Sorry Mum, I couldn't help it. I missed the bus. Don't tell Dad." Cos if Dad found out, well…' Being someone with a background in theatre, I could immediately see the stories they told as dramatised scenes. The switches they made between narration and approximately remembered dialogue were so natural that I could readily imagine transforming the two types of recalling into a performable play text, with story-telling and enactment side by side. It was obvious that this material, collected and edited, could form the basis for a piece of theatre in a style of its own, mirroring the way in which the original speakers remembered the past.

An Age Exchange

Old and young agreeing to work together

It also struck me that the young people in schools with whom I was working could learn a great deal from hearing the older people's stories. If they were then to undertake curriculum work based on these memories, they might have a more equal and dynamic relationship with the old people who had related them, who would, in effect, be the experts. I decided to ask the older people in this group if they would be willing to talk to a group of 'A' level Theatre Arts students, aged 16 to 17, in a local girls' comprehensive school to put this idea to the test. They agreed to have the students visit them in the sheltered housing unit and, together with their drama teacher, these students agreed to try to make a play from the memories they would hear and submit the resulting play as their examination piece.

Asking and telling

At the first session there were six old people and six 17-year-old girls. The students had prepared some questions and came equipped with tape recorders. They asked the older people about what life was like when they were their age, what they had worn, where they had gone for entertainment, how they met boys, how they learned to dance and what music they liked to dance to, how they got their first jobs and what they were paid. Because the young people knew they were going to have to perform these memories they listened intently and their questioning had a certain urgency. They had to get enough information to enter into the period and the specific experiences of the old people. Recognition of the students' needs made the old people much more willing to go into detail. They could see that the students were not just asking for the information out of politeness, but because their stories were going to be used in a project that was crucial to their studies.

Processing the information

The young people recorded the stories on tape and they then worked as a group in subsequent weeks to develop scenes through improvisation from the material. Their task was somehow to transmute those stories into something which had a theatrical life and structure of its own. They had to make sense of the memories they had heard and shape them so that they could convey them dramatically to an audience. Each girl took on the part of one of the older ladies, so they had to try to empathise with that person's experience and imaginatively identify with it, however different it was from their own, in order to perform it, to make it theirs, to own it.

Valuing the experts

Checking with the sources

As part of their scripting and rehearsal process, the students then took these scenes back to the old people, who watched with great interest, occasionally interjecting with comments like, 'No, no. You'd never have spoken like that to your mother in those days.' Or, 'We wouldn't have been allowed to do that.' Basically they were the experts, the sources, and they were providing a service for the young people. The relationship was reciprocal in the sense that the students were preparing to give back an original piece of theatre that celebrated the stories they had collected.

Performance as stimulus

After some rehearsal back at their school, during which the comments and further memories of the elders were incorporated into their script, the students then performed the play at the sheltered housing unit, not just for the half dozen older ladies who had given the original stories, but also to a larger audience, including all the other residents. There was a great sense of occasion as they all came down from their rooms to see what had been going on. The performance itself triggered many

memories amongst people who had not originally been involved in the reminiscence sessions. After the play, there was a buzz of conversation between the tenants,
stimulated by the stories of work, leisure and pleasure amongst the young in the
days before 'teenagers' were invented.

Pride and ownership

There was evident pleasure and pride on the part of the contributors, who at certain
points would turn round to the rest of the audience and say: 'That's my story. That
bit was mine.' So they had a sense of ownership of the stories as performed by the
students. The presence and vitality of the young people had had an energising
effect on all those involved and had created a rare sense of occasion in the
communal lounge. 'The value of reminiscence theatre lies in the past becoming not
just the property of the old person himself but being involved in and related to
problem-solving in the present' (Witkin 1982, p.34).

A few days later, the students performed the play as part of their 'A' level drama
examination, and they all achieved excellent results. This was partly because they
had co-operated well with one another in producing the piece, but also because
their integrity and commitment to this project shone through their work and the
material had yielded an original and effective piece of theatre, showing sensitivity
towards their intended audience.

A valid experiment

I found this whole experience most enlightening and encouraging. I had seen the
power of reminiscence to revitalise older people, to put them in touch with their
own past and with one another. From the work with the students, I also saw that
the young people had gained artistically, educationally and socially. They had
taken something from the old people, worked with it, shaped it and given it back in
a form through which it achieved a higher profile. The wider audience of residents
in the sheltered unit had clearly been very stimulated by seeing stories performed
to which they could relate, and that, in turn, had triggered their own memories and
involved many more old people in the reminiscence process.

The only drawback was that, because the students were strapped to a rigid
timetable, and were involved in a heavy schedule of exam work, their show could
only be performed once for the residents and once for their own Theatre Arts
examination. At that point, I realised how valuable it would be to have young professional actors involved in creating such a show, as they could do 30 or 40 performances of the finished product, taking the show to thousands of other older
people who had not been involved in the original creative process.

And that was how the idea came about to set up a professional theatre
company. I wanted to continue the fundamental idea of a partnership across generations based on mutual respect and creativity and, with this in mind, I decided to
call the new theatre company Age Exchange Theatre.

Setting up a professional theatre company: Age Exchange

A target audience

From the outset I decided that all the productions of the new company would be based on the memories of older people and that the performances were not going to happen in conventional theatre spaces. We would take the shows to day centres, pensioners' clubs and community centres, sheltered housing units, care homes and hospitals: all places where people had very little entertainment, or stimulus of any kind. The shows could act as an important trigger to stimulate exchange of memories between older people and to remind them that they had lived through the same period, experienced the same major events, social changes, advances in technology and changes in society's attitudes on key social issues. Our efforts in researching the plays would be focused on working people's memories, since their voices were rarely heard and they were the least likely, for educational and social reasons, to record their lives in writing. In reflecting their experience, we were most likely to relate effectively with our intended audience in local authority-owned venues, who were also predominantly from a working class background.

Free performances

I felt strongly that no older person should be expected to pay for a ticket. It would not have felt right to have people staying away from a performance because they were worried about the cost, when the purpose was essentially to enhance the quality of life of all the older people in the culturally deprived environments where they spent most of their time. For this reason it was crucial to find funding to cover the full cost of employing professional performers, and for the first show the Greater London Council generously agreed to provide this. I auditioned professional actors and recruited five talented players with musical skills, who demonstrated a particular interest in being involved in this area of work.

Deciding content

And then the question was: what should be the subject of the first play? In the year I set up the company, 1983, there was a lot of anxiety about unemployment, with three million unemployed. I discovered that in 1933 there had also been three million unemployed, so I decided to use the subject of how people had coped with unemployment during that time as the theme of the new play, which would be called *The Fifty Years Ago Show*. The choice of subject ensured that, during the research phase of the play, the older people would be the experts, that their many individual tales would contribute to a more general portrayal of the period, and that the resulting production would have meaning in the present for younger audiences and the younger performers.

Researching the first professional play

Group reminiscence sessions

In order to introduce the actors to the reminiscence process, I invited them to attend and participate in a series of group reminiscence sessions in four local sheltered housing units. There were as many as 20 or 25 people in each group, and the hope was that a smaller number of individuals would emerge who had strong recall of their daily lives during the period in question and who could then be privately interviewed in their own flats by the actors.

Stimulus

As a way into the period, and a means of focusing the older people's memories, our pianist played favourite songs from the 1920s and 1930s. The older people remembered the words of the songs, the artists who had originally performed them, the circumstances in which they had first heard them, and what was happening in their lives at that time. Then we darkened the room and projected slides taken from copy-shots of items from local newspapers of 1933 to stimulate the older people to remember what life was like for them around that time and to create a local context for their stories.

Common memories

In the 1930s, some of the residents, now in their 80s, had been setting up home as 'young marrieds'. They remembered buying furniture on the HP (Hire Purchase) and struggling to keep up the payments as wages fluctuated. They remembered the Relieving Officer coming round to their homes and telling them they would need to sell everything of value before they could claim any benefits, and that this often included highly treasured pieces of china handed down over generations or the piano that had been in the family for years as the focus of family celebrations. They remembered haggling with the money-lenders, taking in washing from the more well-to-do houses, and seeing the Jarrow Marchers go by on their great unemployment protest. Some had been involved directly in fights with the British Union of Fascists and had been influenced by key figures in the labour movement at a local level. Everyone remembered the plight of Edward VIII around the time of his abdication and their reaction to it. As they were recalling these events, they were in fact tapping into a communal identity (Buchanan 1996). As the detail of their own lives came back and they listened in the group to one another's stories, they were able to see their own personal experience against the wider historical backcloth of what was happening in Britain in the 1930s, the inter-war period and the economic depression.

Sad memories shared in the group

Many of the memories were very sad. There were people who had lost children to malnutrition and disease, and there were people who had coped with very difficult family, housing and work situations. By telling those stories in the group they found that they were not alone, that other people had similar stories and that there was a groundswell of sympathy and mutual understanding. Although the older people we were working with were living in the same sheltered unit, they did not necessarily know the other residents very well, so the group sessions enabled them to learn more about one another and to find past experience in common.

Building older people's confidence as story-tellers

Many of those attending these group reminiscence sessions were not used to being asked anything about themselves and they said very little at first. There were comments such as: 'I don't remember anything. It's all so long ago.' Or women in particular would say things like, 'Nothing much happened to me; you would find my life rather boring really.' But as other people's stories suddenly reminded them of incidents they had not called to mind for 50 years, these normally reticent people blossomed. The older people stimulated and entertained one another, as well as giving us invaluable material. Once they could see that we relished the details they were recalling from their own long lives, they gained confidence, saying: 'Oh is *that* the sort of thing you want? Oh, right, I can tell you all about that.'

In a relaxed atmosphere the sessions began to feel less like a means of gathering historical information and more like social events. We often had to say: 'Please don't all talk at once because we're going to transcribe this tape, so you've got to take it in turns. But just let us know if you've got a story that you've suddenly been reminded of.' During the sessions, there was much laughter and animation. The older people seemed surprised and delighted by what they *could* remember and also by how highly it was being valued by our company. The majority of the older people had left school at 14 and, although some of them were very bright, they were mostly not confident about speaking about themselves in public. Very few of them had thought of committing part or all of their life stories to paper, so our process of witnessing and recording their memories felt special, important and even necessary.

Individual follow-up interviews

After the initial group sessions, the actors then went into the flats in the sheltered housing units and interviewed individuals. We agreed beforehand the kinds of questions we were going to ask (concerning family life and working life) but allowed the interviewees to determine the direction of the sessions according to what they were spontaneously recalling. (A more extensive discussion about interviewing individually and in groups appears in the next chapter.) The actors' close involvement with the interviewees increased their commitment to the project and their emotional investment in the show's creation. In fact we all began to feel concerned that these older people's memories would disappear after the theatre production, so everyone wrote up the best of the stories they had recorded and these were included in a book we published to accompany the show (Schweitzer 1983a).

Leaving behind in book form the stories and photos collected for the show

Devising the play from the stories

Assessing the assembled material

Working from the taped interviews, the actors wrote down from the tapes the stories that they liked most. We met up to talk about what they'd found, and on huge pieces of wallpaper lining paper, we all noted down the stories we thought would make the strongest scenes. The actors played a very important role in suggesting ideas and scenes for the show. That company was full of intelligent and creative actors who all had their own ideas as to how the show should be developed. In fact, every actor had written the show in his or her own head as he or she wanted it, in styles varying from Brecht to Lloyd Webber!

Finding the story

We finally agreed to focus the chosen stories around one particular family coping with the anger and humiliation of unemployment and we built in a love story which centred on the son, his flirtation with fascism and his courting days at the cinema and dance halls. Into this framework, we could fit the best stories we had collected, find a through-line with characters and plot, varying the mood and pace to include moments of exuberance, bitterness, contentment, despair, love and hilarity.

Drafting a script from the scenario

The agreed scenario formed the basis for more in-depth exploration of each possible scene through improvisation. The actors called on their written records of what people had said, and phrases they remembered from the interviews they had conducted, to inform the improvisations. Scene by scene, we developed the story-line and the characters, recording the improvisations and noting down the strongest versions to form a draft script. A mixture of scripting styles began to emerge, from naturalistic scenes played between the characters to monologues giving one person's perspective addressed direct to the audience, with much intertwining of these styles.

A collaborative rehearsal period

A continuing relationship with the sources

We prepared three or four scenes and arranged to play them back to residents in the sheltered housing units, including the individuals who had given the particular stories in the first place. This would enable us to test our dramatic approach and to gain further authenticating detail from the story-tellers to bring the scenes to life for other audiences. We also wanted to include the older people as far as possible in our creative process. It was our way of saying, 'Thank you for your stories. We value them. Here's how we are working with them. What do you think?' There was a very positive response to this initiative. Contributors became increasingly enthusiastic about our process the more they understood it and they expressed much interest in seeing the resulting show.

Corroboration and further detail

One story that we wanted to use in the play concerned a woman who had been a seamstress in a tailoring factory in the East End of London. She had told us how she had to work all hours of the day and night, including Sundays, which was strictly against the law. Her mother had finally gone to the factory to complain about this. However, when we arrived, the woman who had given us this story was not present. We were told that she was feeling unwell and rather miserable and did not want to attend. I went to her room with the warden and said to her, 'If you could possibly come down just for a few minutes, it would be wonderful because we've worked on your story and we'd like you to see it.' Very reluctantly she came and watched it.

Seeing the health value in playing back memories

Seeing her reaction was like witnessing a medical miracle! This depressed, rather sickly woman just came to life as she saw her own memories being acted out before her. When she saw our representation of the story, she remembered the whole event much more clearly than when we had interviewed her first, and added many details she had not recollected for 50 years. As she recalled, she repeatedly brushed her hand in front of her face, almost as if she were brushing aside the cobwebs which had obscured the sharp detail. The interchange with the actors and the development of the story had an extraordinary physical effect on this woman. She sparked to life and became the 'star' of the place! The whole incident was, for me, a very significant indicator that reminiscence work of this kind was not just serving the artistic process and giving the actors valuable additional material to work with; it was also promoting health and personal re-orientation and could be a means of recovering past identity in the present.

Role play by the older people

Another memorable occasion from the same week, but in a different sheltered unit, was when the actors played out a scene prepared in rehearsal about the arrival of the Relieving Officer at the family home. I wanted to know if the scene felt accurate to them. In fact, some people pointed out that the actor playing the Relieving Officer was far too courteous, and the family too quick to answer back, and that this did not tally with their memory of similar events. We persuaded two residents, albeit a little reluctantly at first, to take on the roles of the mother and father to show us exactly how the scene might have been while the officer was there and once he had gone. Two very old people, well into their 80s, acted out the scene for the company, building the tension, saying little until pushed beyond endurance, and then exploding into anger and injured pride, as a result of which they lost their claim. They stepped into their roles and achieved absolute authenticity of tone because they were doing what they remembered and they did it in the spirit and language which was right for the time.

The actors were very touched by this experience and one of them commented that it was quite humbling to watch the old people reliving the painful situation to show us how it was for them. The older people who acted rose to the occasion and were enthusiastically applauded by the other tenants. It was clear that they had really enjoyed participating and had apparently never shown that outgoing side of their personalities before.

Relocating remembered energy in the present

The woman who had performed said to me, 'Oh I enjoyed that. I'll do anything if they ask me. I will really.' I assumed this was true and congratulated the warden on having such a lively and confident tenant. I said, 'She's a natural, isn't she? She's exceptional! How wonderful that she's willing to do this and that she's got the style and she's got the feeling for it.' The warden then told me that this came as a total surprise to her and the other tenants, because this woman was often depressed and rarely came out of her room.[3]

I thought that we had witnessed something very powerful; that the dramatising of the older people's lives by the actors had enabled them to tap into an energy and confidence from their younger days that had been dormant for a long time. Their involvement in the dramatising process demonstrated for them that their story, which perhaps they did not initially think was very interesting, was actually being worked on, that they were the experts on it and that something very effective was going to be made from it, which would be seen and appreciated by many others.

Deciding the form

Separate scenes interspersed with participatory discussion

Around the time of establishing the Age Exchange Theatre Company, I became aware of a theatre group called Fair Old Times, working in Dartington, Devon, under the direction of Bazz Kershaw and performing in old people's homes (Langley and Kershaw 1982). They had been developing programmes of short theatrical scenes, using reminiscence objects and back-projected images as visual stimuli, and interspersing these scenes with facilitated reminiscence sessions with the audience. Their guides in this work had been Gordon Langley, an old age psychiatrist, and his wife, Dorothy, a drama therapist, who together had extensive experience of working with older people and understood the potential value of reminiscence as a means of stimulating feelings of self-worth. The project was well grounded in the locale and used memories of places and events which had meaning for many of the residents and which were particularly effective in evoking further memories, so that the process was cyclical. The company's brief was to use theatre to stimulate reminiscence to meet the social and emotional needs of older people in residential homes and hospitals, so there was a much stronger therapeutic direction to their work than to the fledgling artistic policy of Age Exchange.

Performance followed by discussion

There was some discussion with the cast of *The Fifty Years Ago Show* as to whether we too should intersperse the scenes with reminiscence with the audience, rather than perform the show straight through and then hold informal conversations with the audience afterwards. Our feeling at the time was that the power and tension of the play would lose its impact if constantly interrupted, and that there would be many logistical problems around the older people switching focus and hearing one another's stories, especially when the seating was arranged 'theatre style' to help them see the performers. It seems that such concerns were aired in the Fair Old Times Company too. Jacolyn Corder, their administrator/researcher, wrote: 'The actors seriously questioned whether the stimulation of immediate feedback should be the main objective... They sought to raise the intellectual pitch and depth of response beyond that of simple recognition and factual recall' (Langley and Kershaw 1982, p.19).

   In the event, we all felt that the play should be a free-standing artistic event, especially as it would be performed to a wide range of audiences and levels of understanding, and that we should not sacrifice the potential emotional and aesthetic impact by breaks for a very different kind of engagement. (Chapter 8 will detail an Age Exchange production by Clare Summerskill based on a variation on the Fair Old Times approach, exploring the advantages and disadvantages of this approach.) However, we did all recognise the value and importance of exchange with the audience around the issues the play raised and their personal experience of comparable situations. So, built into the touring schedule of this first show and every subsequent production was a minimum of half an hour's audience discussion time at the end of the performance. This would normally be informal in style, with the actors sitting with audience members and talking to them over a cup of tea, but it could be offered as a more formal facilitated discussion if that was the preferred format of the venue, and this would normally be led either by the director, if present, or by one or more of the actors.

The central role of music

It had already become very clear in the initial group sessions that music was a highly effective agent in stimulating reminiscence. When the older people were talking, they would often remember the songs, sing them quietly together and be transported back in time to the age they were when they first heard them. It seemed clear that any show we did would need to have a great deal of music in it, so that when the actors performed it they could trigger memories of favourite singers, films, dance halls and shows from their younger days and associated memories. In a dramatic context, the use of music could also accentuate an emotion or atmosphere, or enable a change of mood or pace, especially when we touched on painful memories.

We built intensive music sessions into the rehearsal period, locating music of the period to complement the scenes, with the actors singing full harmonies accompanied by piano and violin. We were guided in the choice of songs by the older people's suggestions during our initial group reminiscence sessions. Many of the songs we used in the show were from the well-known musicals of stage and screen, including numbers such as 'We're in the Money', 'Lullaby of Broadway', 'Pennies from Heaven' and 'On the Other Side of the Hill'. They were all songs of the period, many of them expressing, with gentle irony, the fundamental hopes and anxieties of that era.

The actors' relationship with the older people in performance

An 'out-front' playing style

Following our experience of improvising with the older people during the rehearsal period, we decided very early on that the actors would 'play out' to the audience, even in more naturalistic scenes where the characters were relating to one another, as well as, more obviously, in their narrated monologues. This would enable people who were hard of hearing to see their faces and read their lips. Equally importantly, we wanted the audience to receive the stories and experience the play as a dialogue between them and the actors, even if they were not invited to respond vocally there and then, but rather when the performance was over.

The cast of The Fifty Years Ago Show *in full song: (left to right) Dianne Hancock, John Patrick Deery, Anna Philpott, Tom Austin*

Responding to spontaneous reactions from the audience

This very direct form of address to the audience did sometimes produce unexpected, personal and spontaneous responses from audience members, caught up in the reality of the play. For example, an actor was performing a soliloquy along the lines of 'I've been up since five o'clock this morning looking for work. I've been all over town trying to get a job…' when a lady from the audience called out: 'You look exhausted, darling, come and sit down by me before you go off again.' Of course the actors with experience of performing in cabaret and community venues where they had to respond to audience heckling were far better adapted to the unpredictable environments of reminiscence theatre than those schooled in Stanislavskian immersion in character!

A visible and audible audience

The actors' experience of the first few performances was a very positive one. It was a new style of work for most of them, relating so closely to the audience. None of the rules of more conventional theatre performance applied. Instead of the audience being in the dark and the actors brightly lit, the actors in our show could see the audience clearly and witness their responses to the scenes. And instead of a silence, interrupted by occasional laughs from the audience, our players could hear a constant, if quiet, undertow of vocalised reaction, much of it expressed in phrases like 'Yes, that's right' or 'I remember that' and 'That was me'.

The actors were all moved by playing real people whom they had met and talked to. They felt a continuing responsibility to the particular individuals whom they had originally interviewed or improvised with, and whose lives they were now portraying. One of the actors in the show, Dianne Hancock, said, 'I found the whole experience humbling really. The old people know it, they have lived the stories themselves. We are representing them.'[4]

Connecting with the audience in post-show discussions

During the performances, the actors were so close to the audience that they could see when they had struck a chord for an individual, and when particular people were responding strongly to particular scenes. In the post-show discussion period, the actors could pick up on these signals, and talk quietly with the individuals concerned. This opportunity for personal exchange elicited many more memories and gave to every new audience a sense that they also had a contribution to make. It also showed the actors that the play on tour was reaching out way beyond the original story-tellers, and was triggering spontaneous reminiscence exchanges which would never have taken place without this theatrical stimulus.

Playing for 'special needs' audiences

In some venues where we performed, there was a preponderance of people with dementia, and for them it was obviously more difficult to stay focused for the duration of the play. In these places, the songs provided little pauses from the dramatic action and a chance for these audience members to reconnect with the story, or, at the least, to engage with the mood and to enjoy feeling part of the event. However, it was clear from very early in the life of the company that it would be desirable to develop special projects geared to the specific needs of these people, with smaller numbers participating and a more flexible framework for involving them directly in the reminiscence process, while still offering the stimulus of music, role play and strong visual images. (This approach will be explored further in Chapter 14.)

Production issues on tour

Problematic performance spaces

The venues on our tour of *The Fifty Years Ago Show* were often far from easy for the actors to set up and perform in. Many had high-backed chairs, which impeded vision, and we sometimes had people unwilling to move, saying: 'I always sit in that space!' The staff were not used to the idea of providing a proper changing area for the actors to get into costume and apply the necessary period make-up. Sometimes the company were not even expected, as the information provided by our administrator had not been fed to the particular staff on duty that day. It was quite a new idea, taking professional performances into homes and day centres, and I remember one terrible time when the cast performed to five people while 50 others who were the intended audience played Bingo in an upstairs room, furious about having to move out of their usual place! (See Chapter 7 for more discussion about playing in non-theatrical venues.)

Involving the staff

During that first tour, there were several care staff who used the performance time as an opportunity to take a break and maybe have a cup of tea in their staff rooms, leaving the actors to cope with whatever went on amongst the residents. This was a pity for the staff as well as for the performers, in that they missed all the potential cues that their clients were giving in their spontaneous responses to the stories in the show, and which they could have fruitfully followed up after the actors had gone. In those early days, the therapeutic value of reminiscence had not been widely recognised and staff were not encouraged by their managers to maximise the impact of any structured or spontaneous reminiscence input or to undertake such work themselves. Later, staff at all touring venues were notified by the company administrator of reminiscence training services and many built success-fully on the input provided by the performance in their home or day centre.

Audience reaction

Strong identification

The vast majority of the audiences were extremely moved and delighted by the play in performance. They expressed their gratitude very warmly, sharing the long-forgotten memories it had evoked for them. Sometimes there were tears in the audience, but there was also a lot of singing along, a lot of laughing and a lot of vocalised corroboration from the audience. I sometimes felt as though what we were doing was creating a special kind of 'time-jumping mirror', and holding that mirror up for the audience to see themselves as they were when young. They suddenly had all their former vitality and resilience reflected back to them in the truthful performances of their stories by the actors. Paradoxically, exploring the past theatrically had a rejuvenating effect on our extremely elderly audience members, generating present-day energy and present-day engagement with one another.

We had obviously hit a very rich seam, so that people we had never met before would come up and say things like 'That was my story, how did you know my story?', showing how strongly they had identified with the content. This had been our hope at the outset and it had governed our choice of material to go into the play; it had to reflect the specific original story, but it also had to be typical and rep-resentative if it was to have reverberations across the lives of the thousands of people to whom we were playing.[5] Older people and staff bought the book of stories and photos we had prepared and this proved useful as a starting point for small reminiscence groups which sprang up in venues after the performances.

We did a couple of performances for young people in secondary schools on that first tour to see how they would relate to the story and the particular form of telling it. The music clearly presented an aesthetic barrier, being quite alien to them, but there was an obvious educational value in the content. The play was an effective means of introducing key topics in the social history of the 1930s, especially when the performance was followed by discussion with some of the contributors. However, although we kept the idea of doing a small number of performances for local schools, we all felt it to be important that the target audience had to remain the older people who were getting so little by way of stimulus and whose own lives the play reflected.

The blueprint emerges

And that was essentially the way our first production, *The Fifty Years Ago Show*, emerged. It came about through listening to the stories, working the stories through improvisation, showing them back to the sources and modifying them in the light of additional material and comments, and then scripting.

The key elements to emerge from this first professional production were the following:

- the value of stimulating the older people to share memories in a group, and then in individual interviews
- the importance of locating a subject with wide appeal to which working people could relate and contribute
- the value of creative engagement between the actors and the older people during the whole dramatising process
- the desirability of exploring a full range of emotions during the course of the play
- the recognition of live music as an essential element in the form
- the need for a conversational, inclusive playing style on the part of the performers
- the importance of the older people's involvement and participation in post-performance discussion
- the value of collecting the stories and photos gathered during the research period into a book, or other lasting form, for posterity
- leaving behind a stimulus for discussion to help the audience to remember the show and the staff to continue the reminiscence work.

The blueprint was there, and all these elements were retained in future productions over the next 20 years, even though each show was unique and specific with particular challenges in its creation and performance.

Summary

This chapter has traced the development of an idea, from the point of first recognising the value of reminiscence as an enjoyable and stimulating activity for older people to the creation of a dedicated reminiscence theatre company. It has described the inter-generational origins of the work through the pilot production by school students based on older people's memories and shown how this led to the setting up of a professional touring company. The evolution of a working method and the creation of a blueprint for future reminiscence shows was explored through the devising, rehearsal and performance periods of *The Fifty Years Ago Show*.

CHAPTER 2

From Interviews to Verbatim Script

Since reminiscence theatre was very much a new theatrical form, all those involved with the theatre company had much to learn, experimenting by trial and error with several different approaches to this work. Some of the following chapters will detail the varied production methods we tried, and describe the form and content of several productions, in the hope that this information will provide ideas for others seeking to work in this field. However, underlying all the different and varied productions, the general principles outlined in the previous chapter continued to underpin the work, as we gradually evolved a methodology for creating a piece of reminiscence theatre. More detailed explanations of the processes involved in the various stages, from deciding the production's theme, through methods of gathering interview material, relations with interviewees, and transcription through to the scripting process itself, are now described.

Research for reminiscence theatre

Choosing the theme

The creation of a piece of reminiscence theatre begins with the selection of a topic or theme or an area of experience. It must be one which is of interest and significance for the theatre company and one to which the intended audience will relate. The choice involves selecting a particular time, a particular geographical locality and its changes over time, or a significant event in living memory which has reverberations and relevance for the present day.

Background research

Background research around the subject is necessary before making visits to individual or group interviewees, so that the interviewer has a context, historical and geographical, for the information to be given by the elders. Interviewers who have done no 'homework' can feel foolish when they do not understand any of the references in an interviewee's testimony, and their lack of preparedness can cause their interviewees to be sceptical about their commitment to the enterprise.

However, it is unnecessary, and even off-putting, to display encyclopaedic knowledge, as this will undermine the confidence and motivation of interviewees.

For detailed information concerning preparation for interviewing, equipment, sound checks and informed consent to use interview material, see the Oral History Society's excellent practical advice and copyright sections on their website, www.ohs.org.uk, and the information sheets issued by the East Midlands Oral History Archive.

Ways of gathering stories for reminiscence theatre

There are two main ways of gathering stories from older people for reminiscence theatre: the one-to-one interview and the group discussion. The one-to-one interview can feel like a slightly daunting prospect for a less confident informant, who may worry that his or her testimony will be found wanting in some way. For this reason, it is often desirable to start with a group discussion, wherein the flow of remembering and discussing becomes more of a shared responsibility, supported by one or more of the interviewing team. The group session also allows the interviewers to identify individuals with particularly strong recall or an especially lively way of telling a story, and these identified speakers can then be invited to give individual interviews on a separate occasion.

Group interviews

Practical considerations

When setting up a reminiscence group discussion, it is important to attend to practical arrangements at the outset. The room should be relatively free of disturbance and the people should be seated where they can see and hear one another as well as the interviewers, so a circular arrangement is the most desirable. Ideally there should be some relevant objects and images to stimulate informal discussion early in the session, perhaps while waiting for the group to assemble. The atmosphere should be informal, but there needs to be a sense of order to give the group confidence that the interviewers have planned the session and are in control of its smooth running (Gibson 2006).

Recording group sessions

It is almost always desirable to record a reminiscence session when it is conducted in connection with a piece of reminiscence theatre. The speakers must therefore be asked to say their names before speaking, and it should be explained that this is to help the transcriber and to ensure that all contributions are properly attributed. When people forget to say who they are, perhaps because the discussion is racing ahead, or perhaps because stating their own name may feel rather uncomfortable or unnatural, then the discussion leader can state who the speaker is, so that comments are correctly ascribed in any transcript.

Conducting the group reminiscence session

In a group interview, it is often the case that, after a slow beginning, perhaps domi-
nated by the most confident speakers, the conversation suddenly gathers
momentum. This is a positive response, but whoever is leading the discussion will
need to orchestrate the individual contributions so that only one person speaks at a
time and so that the time is shared reasonably equally between group members. It is
important to draw everyone's attention to the connections between what individuals have offered and to restore a sense of direction to the discussion if the group
loses focus (Osborn 1993).

A highly sociable affair

The most successful group reminiscence sessions feel like a social event for the participants, with people sparking one another off. Someone might tell a story involving some detail of place or time, or a well-known local name, and this will trigger a
long-forgotten memory for somebody else, who will then tell that newly remembered story with exceptional spontaneity and colour. There is always an element of
surprise and delight in retrieving a long-lost piece of the past, and contemplating it
afresh in the present.

'A community of memory'

In a group discussion, the verbal contributions will very often start with phrases
such as 'Wasn't it around then that...' or 'Then there was...' or 'Oh, and what
about...?' or 'That reminds me of something too...' This informal approach allows
quieter, less confident people to nod and affirm while others tell their stories. In
this way, they can feel linked in to the collective memory of the group as it emerges,
until they feel confident enough to interject themselves with their own contribution. This kind of tentative spontaneous contribution will perhaps begin with
'What about the...' or 'In our house, it was always...', and end with a request for
confirmation through phrases like 'wasn't it?' or 'Does anyone else remember
that?'

Through this kind of exchange, an increased sense of group historical identity,
a 'community of memory', can emerge, in which people speak of 'we' rather than
'I' (Buchanan 1997). Through group reminiscence, participants start to see themselves as makers of, and participants in, history. They are communally recreating
the time they lived through, remember and know about. This sense of ownership
of the past can arise, even when the experiences which the group are recalling are
about feeling like passive recipients, or even victims of history. When each person's
memory is heard in the context of others' related experience, the process is inclusive and cumulative. Between them, the group members conjure up the essence of a
period of socio-economic history, with themselves as part of it.

One-to-one interviews

In-depth exploration

In individual interviews, the interviewee will often be much more willing to divulge personal experiences and difficult memories. The one-to-one interview can yield particularly rich story-telling because the flow of the reminiscence is not interrupted by others, and the person telling the story will have no fear of talking too much or dominating a group discussion and therefore risking unpopularity within that group. With an individual interview, there can be a much more detailed factual account and an in-depth exploration of feelings connected with the incident or period remembered.

A rare opportunity to speak to an attentive listener

Interviewees will very often relish the opportunity to be listened to and recorded for posterity on a subject close to their hearts. Being consulted as expert witnesses, and knowing that their insights and experience are likely to feature in a piece of theatre to be seen by many people of all ages, affords them some measure of recognition and acknowledges them as authorities.

The experience of the one-to-one interview can be genuinely empowering for the individuals involved, since it may well be the first time they have had an opportunity to reflect on their experience with a listener who clearly has a very sincere interest in what they have to say and a very direct need to hear and record it. Joyce Holliday, who wrote several shows for Age Exchange, said:

> An awful lot of people have no voice. They have valid reactions and thoughts, but no one listens, not even their own families. People suddenly say, in the middle of interviews, 'You don't want to hear this', because they've been told that all their lives, that no one wants to hear. (Television History Workshop 1985)

Attentive and purposeful listening

If the interviewer sits up, looks attentive, reflects back some of what has been said from time to time to show that he or she is really listening, and asks additional questions eliciting more detail, these will all be strong signals to the interviewee that their contribution is valid and valued and that their efforts are appreciated. This expression of interest in the details of a story has the effect of slowing down the interviewee and legitimising a more in-depth version of the remembered experience, which might otherwise be held back for fear of boring the interviewer. It is also effective in situations where the interviewee has told his or her story many times before, because the detailed and specific questioning, such as might be required for the purposes of creating a scene from the story, can lead the speaker down new avenues of memory and give the experience of remembering a new dimension.

The need for detail to bring the story to life

The writer, director or performer can justify asking for as much supplementary detail as possible, without becoming intrusive, on the grounds that they will be using the information gathered to make the play come alive for the audience. They can say things like, 'I don't feel I have enough information to do justice to this story on stage. What was your response when that happened? Do you remember what you actually said? Where were you standing in relation to him? What happened then?' This approach of requesting more detail for the purpose of visualising the scene, which could then be made into play-script, can also help the interviewees to see their contribution as an important element in a creative process. The interviewee should of course be invited to see the show and to attend the launch of any related publication, as well as receiving a copy of any such publication.

Transcription for reminiscence theatre

Hard labour, rich rewards

In the creation of a reminiscence theatre script, the starting point is usually an accurate transcription of all the interview material. Transcription is an extremely time-consuming process, but the effort required is rewarded by a sense of being on top of the material and having it available in a form where it can quickly be retrieved and used in more or less its original form. With a group discussion it is very helpful for the person who conducted the session to do the transcription and to complete it as soon after the event as possible, while the identities of the individual speakers, who said what and where they sat, are still reasonably clear in the mind's eye. At times, it may be necessary to limit the amount that is transcribed to the most memorable exchanges in every recorded session and produce a log of other topics covered for later reference.

A body of research

A great advantage of transcribing material when making reminiscence theatre is that everyone working on the production then has access to the body of research which has been generated. Obviously each member of the creative team will have clearest recall of the memories given by people they have interviewed directly, but a more democratic devising and writing process is possible where all the transcript is visible and accessible. Material generated for a theatre piece has other longer-term value, perhaps in book form or for selective quotations in a printed programme which becomes a souvenir and reminder of the performance to be enjoyed in a more leisurely way by the audience members, and in this case, the fuller the original transcription, the better.

Authenticity of language and tone

When transcribing interviews for theatre, it is not necessary to tidy up the grammar of the speakers. The stories in their original form will have a resonance with the majority of the audience who are listening to them. As Sandra Kerr, one of Age Exchange's musical directors, commented in an interview for Channel 4 Television on verbatim theatre: 'With oral history for reminiscence theatre, we're mainly talking about working class speech' (Television History Workshop 1985). For example, many of the London contributors we interview say 'We was' (rather than 'We were') and if you keep to the special nuances and the turns of phrase, then the audience feel the original speaker in the language and also relate very strongly to that material. If using the same material in a written form, for example in a book of memories, this sort of decision needs to be discussed and agreed with the contributors, who may have strong feelings about what appears in their name in print.

Scripting reminiscence theatre

Assemble the content and seek the form

The most obvious way of starting the scripting process of a piece of reminiscence theatre is to assemble and read through all the stories in transcribed form, noting those that you think are important, the ones you want to use and, only then, looking for a structure to bind them together. As Joyce Holliday commented: 'You collect memories from all sorts of people... You have them all transcribed...and you end up with a great wodge of papers and somehow out of that you've got to make a show' (Television History Workshop 1985). The creative team must avoid writing the show in their heads before conducting the interviews. This does unfortunately happen occasionally, especially when a writer or director has a strong view and is using the vehicle of reminiscence theatre to promulgate it. Such an approach, where the testimony is reduced to confirmatory material, seriously undermines and compromises the interview process.

Scripting from improvisation

Reminiscence theatre can also be created through improvisation without writing down any of the interview material, and instead loosely interpreting what has been learned from the sources during the research period. (See Chapter 1 for examples of this approach.) Where the time to put a show together is very short, this may be the only viable approach. Where a group of artists are using the 'sources' as inspiration for an interpretive piece, especially one relying more on dance and music than speech, a looser link with the interview material can of course be justified. In this case, it is up to the creators to make clear for interviewees what their relationship is with the finished product to be performed so there are no disappointments and misunderstandings.

Scripting verbatim reminiscence theatre

In their own words

In verbatim theatre all the text in the script comes from the interview material and everything spoken on stage is in the words of the sources, augmented by documentary material, song, dance and visual props. It is about using people's direct experience and the way they recall it, using their own words directly in the finished play.

Verbatim theatre is not about the writer or the players finding stories in their imaginations. Neither is it about the writers listening to people's stories and writing what they imagine it would have been like for those people to live through those experiences. Of course there must be empathy between the artistic creator and the source, and an imaginative approach to representing their experience in an effective performance, but the sources should always speak for themselves and interpret their own experience, both individually and as a group.

Artistic interpretation

The collection of transcribed interviews is the raw material and the art lies in the imaginative structuring, editing, sifting and shaping of this material into a coherent and performable script. It also lies in the interpretation of this script during the subsequent move into theatrical production by directors, designers, musical directors and of course performers.

Letting the audience hear the voices

In scripting verbatim reminiscence theatre, it must be very clear that these are real stories that have happened to real people. Each person whose story is used has an individual form of expression, often with a distinct regional accent and sometimes with quite an idiosyncratic turn of phrase. Consequently, when the original language of the interviews is spoken from the stage, the audience will be reminded that they are hearing the authentic voices of the story-tellers and that their stories are true, rather than inventions of the theatre company.

Because many transcribed stories start with phrases such as 'We always used to' and 'I remember when' there is a potential danger of repetition in the scripting. A few of these 'remembering mode' phrases should be kept in the text however to remind the audience of the reminiscence process underlying the play and to encourage a natural transition into participation in informal discussion following the performance.

Language in time and place

Language changes over time, and when a group of people of a particular age record their memories, they tend to describe past events in a way that is specific to their generation. There are idiomatic expressions popular at a particular time, turns of phrase and even adjectives which have a period flavour to them. The contributors will use words which might not have been heard for a long time, and they might mention activities, places, trade names and products which will have a particular resonance for others of their age group, including of course the intended audience of the show. Hearing those references can quickly transport the listeners back to another era, about which they have their own stock of memories.

Remembering in direct speech

Very often people who have had limited access to education, and for whom writing is not the main means of communication, have a very particular way of telling stories. They will often remember in the form of direct speech and their narration will be interspersed with fragments of dialogue. These recalled exchanges, though not necessarily exact representations of what was said, are likely to be good approximations. Such passages can be lifted from the transcript and inserted in the play-script verbatim, to be spoken as dialogue by the actors, reinforced by physical enactment. In this way, the writer is able to achieve an absolute authenticity of tone.

Performable dialogue from recorded group discussion

When group remembering is transcribed, it is often a gift for the writer of reminiscence theatre, since the dialogue generated in this way can seem particularly immediate and fresh. The cascade of related memories given by the group members in turn can readily be transformed into a seamlessly flowing script for a group of performers. If they play it in a way which recreates that pleasurable sense of sudden recovery of an individual memory in the original group discussion, it will be particularly effective in eliciting many more previously forgotten fragments of memory from the eventual audience.

Combining different versions of a story

If several of the interviewees have spoken about a particular event or experience for example, even if it is not one with obvious dramatic appeal, it should probably be included, on the grounds that it will have meaning for many audience members. Where there are three or four tellings of the same, or a very similar, story, the writer or devising group may choose to use extracts from more than one source in piecing the scripted version together, as long as the story continues to flow. If there is a particularly rich phrase to describe something in one of the versions, but perhaps it misses something else, which is there in another person's version, two or more versions can be merged to produce a definitive version.

Monologues in reminiscence theatre

Sometimes a very effective use of verbatim speech is simply to have a piece of monologue in which a whole story is told by one performer in character direct to the audience. When this happens, the audience settles into a different, more intent mode of listening where they feel they are important witnesses to the event being recounted. In fact they can sense that this story is being told to them in the same way that it was given by the original individual interviewee.

Another advantage of using this form of direct story-telling to the audience is that, because stories are often remembered out of sequence, the enacted drama too can move backwards and forwards in time, the action following the impulse of the spoken narrative. The original telling of the story will often bring together events which in fact occurred a long way apart in terms of where and when they happened, and this genuine remembering process can help in shifting the story to a different period or mood.

Escaping naturalism

The kind of set-piece story-telling described above is one of the many methods the reminiscence theatre writer can use to escape from the limits of naturalism. Songs, or even full-scale choreographed ensemble 'numbers', can be inserted at relevant moments of emotion, such as celebration, hope or sorrow, without any feeling of incongruity or discontinuity for the audience. The writer can also work with 'flash backs' and switch between times and locations almost like a film director and is not trapped into the consecutive or contiguous. In fact, the writer of reminiscence theatre has the same freedom to explore where the memories lead as the original interviewee had when the recording was made.

Incorporating written contributions

Older people sometimes submit written stories about their experiences, and often such contributors have given a lot of thought to what they want to say. Their offerings feel more formal in style and more ambitious in the vocabulary they use and they do not yield the same amount of direct speech as the more informal group interviews or the spontaneity of the individual spoken interviews. However, they can be effectively inserted as 'set pieces', noticeably different from what surrounds them, which can effectively slow down the pace, encouraging concentration and empathy and reminding the audience that many people have contributed their experience in different ways to the making of the show they are watching.

The writer's own preferences

Over the years, I have invited different writers to join the company for particular productions and all have had their own particular way of creating verbatim scripts. Occasionally writers have used the transcribed interviews very selectively to give colour to a more freely written script of their own, whereas others have limited their scripts to the exact recorded words of the contributors, even to the point of recording and transcribing additional telephone calls made during the writing period to clarify points of detail.

Some writers move rapidly into dialogue, breaking up the continuous stories that have been transcribed into smaller segments with a 'naturalistic feel', whilst others tend to keep whole stories with one speaker, supported by concurrent visual enactment by the rest of the cast. Writers coming from a documentary background might add text from contemporary advertisements, government propaganda or legal documents as 'stiffening' material to support and contextualise what is being remembered at a personal level, and there is tremendous potential for irony in juxtaposing the 'official' and 'unofficial' versions of history in a theatre script. For me personally, discovering the effectiveness of using the verbatim transcripts to construct a play was so powerful that it determined the direction of my own theatre writing for several years to come.

Incorporating music into the script

Music is such a powerful reminiscence tool and can be a highly effective trigger of memories and associations. Audience members who initially seem unable to engage with the drama, often start to relate to it through the songs. In a typical reminiscence theatre show, musical content will constitute up to a quarter of the play, so it is important to incorporate songs into the scripting process from early on, rather than simply add them in at the end. Music can underline the emotion of a scene or be used to break a mood and link one part of the story to the next.

Songs and costumes of the period trigger memories and associations. The cast of What Did You Do in the War, Mum?*: (left to right) Melanie Walters, Anna Philpott, Sheila Tait, Anna Skye, Susan Betts*

Songs of the period

The vast majority of the songs in reminiscence theatre are songs from the period covered in the show, and the most fruitful source of suggestions for suitable songs are the older people who have given their memories. The intention in using period songs is to stimulate the audience to remember the circumstances in which they heard or sang these numbers, the people they had been with and the places where they danced, courted, went hiking or worked. A song can also be chosen because of its lyrical content and its close relation to specific themes in the play.

The actors in their performances can evoke popular performance styles of the past such as barber shop or crooning, and can remind the audience of popular artists such as Al Bowley, the Andrews Sisters or George Formby. Sometimes it is desirable to write songs especially for a show and these can be written in period style to achieve a particular effect. Very often the musical directors will conduct musical research and find appropriate additional songs in BBC archives and from their own knowledge to suggest to the writer and director. (See Chapter 7 for further discussion of this topic.)

Summary

In summary, verbatim theatre celebrates the richness of direct story-telling, the distinct and unique way people tell their own memories. It is not about the writer crafting a phrase, but rather the writer recognising the special quality in what the source has given and putting it prominently in the script. Of course the professional writer must then sharpen the impact of the chosen material by pruning, selecting, editing and shaping what has been said, and supporting it with appropriate songs, but it should be clear to the audience that the sources are the real authors. The audience are hearing older individuals like themselves remembering ordinary and extraordinary matters in day-to-day speech with which they feel familiarity and empathy. This gives them the feeling that they could join in and tell their stories in a similar idiom in the post-show discussion, and that their experience would be equally valued.

A note on the wider world and verbatim theatre

During the last decade, the use of verbatim transcript as the basis for theatre has become more recognised by mainstream companies, including the National Theatre, with documentary pieces such as *The Permanent Way* (Hare 2003) about the Potters Bar rail crash and *Stuff Happens* (Hare 2004) about the Iraq war. Mainly used to highlight political causes célèbres, such as the treatment of West Indian ex-servicemen in post-war Britain in *Black Poppies* (Theatre Royal, Stratford East 1991) or *Bloody Sunday* (Kent 2005) in Northern Ireland and *Guantanamo* (Brittain and Slovo 2004) at the Tricycle Theatre, these pieces by established writers have pulled together and shaped testimony which is then 'performed' for a theatre audience.

An even more recent development of the use of verbatim in the theatre has come from certain experimental groups who have taken words recorded on minidisc, and used twin or multiple earphones to enable actors to relay verbatim what is coming though their headphones one milli-second after hearing it. An example is *Strawberry Fields* (Blythe 2005) at Pentabus Theatre. This causes the audience to listen acutely to what is said, be it a trivial conversation in a doctor's waiting room or an exchange on a more weighty matter, because it is now theatre text performed by actors.

The consciousness-raising nature of these theatrical presentations is similar in some ways to the use of verbatim in reminiscence theatre, in that one is constantly reminded that the actor is a channel linking the source to the audience and this form serves both to give weight to the original utterance and allow the writer to emphasise an irony by juxtaposing it with contrary statements.

CHAPTER 3

Developing the Practice of Verbatim Theatre

In this chapter, I aim to show how verbatim scripting has been developed in specific productions and how a wide range of topics have lent themselves to dramatisation in this way. The plays I have chosen to illustrate the use of verbatim scripting in this chapter include the 'big themes' of work, war and health. These productions reflect the mainstream of the company's work, dramatising the lives of 'ordinary' older people and playing them to others from a similar background, inviting them to add their own 'take' on the events and situations portrayed.

Of Whole Heart Cometh Hope

Reminiscence theatre as celebration

Anniversaries have been the starting points for the creation of many commemorative projects and programmes. Practically speaking, anniversaries alert researchers and community artists and historians to the need to capture, while they are still accessible, the memories of an often dwindling group of older witnesses. An anniversary can trigger a review of the significance of certain historical events or a reassessment of the achievements of organisations which have contributed to public and community life. Often a centenary or other anniversary provides the incentive for releasing special funding to celebrate previously unrecorded or uncelebrated collective and individual achievement.

Vanishing history

Of Whole Heart Cometh Hope, a piece celebrating the centenary of the Co-operative Women's Guild, was the first Age Exchange show to be produced entirely from verbatim transcript. In this instance, the Co-operative Retail Society (CRS, the trading arm of the co-operative movement) commissioned the researching and writing of a new play to be performed at Central Hall Westminster to mark the occasion, and then to play to Guilds across the south-east of England, especially at local celebrations of the organisation's one-hundredth birthday. The commission included the production of an illustrated book of edited memories collected during the research period (Salt, Schweitzer and Wilson 1983). The broader aim was to record for posterity the memories of the mainly elderly Guild members and to remind the wider world that, although now declining in numbers and vigour, the Guild had played a key role in promoting the health and education of Britain's working class women, especially in the first half of the twentieth century.

Grass roots support

The branches of the Guild helped us by setting up group reminiscence sessions and introducing individuals who were willing to be interviewed. The play was to be made from personal memories about the Co-op as an institution and the way it had impacted on people's lives as individuals and families. The scope of the play was, however, much wider than the organisational history of the Guild, as the members had played such an active part in key struggles of the twentieth century. They had campaigned through the Guild for women's rights, especially on matters of maternity and birth control, they had embraced internationalism, been part of the peace movement, supported the hunger marches of the 1930s and taken care of the Basque children who escaped as refugees from the Spanish Civil War.

At a more local level, they had run free adult education classes for working class women, campaigned for high quality food geared to the limited budgets of poorer families and tried to imbue their children with the high moral values and ideals of the co-operative movement. So the memories and specialised knowledge of the Co-operative Women's Guild members made them important witnesses to the changes in pre- and post-war Britain.

Using the interviews in the script

Chrys Salt, a writer who was very convinced of the potential of scripting from the recorded interviews, took on the scripting task and produced a very pure version of the verbatim approach, with the cast speaking text taken directly from recorded memories. In addition there were insertions in the script of some documentary material taken from the history of the Co-operative Women's Guild and from speeches written by its then current leading lights. The following extract shows how a recorded story was converted into performable script, with remembered direct speech becoming dialogue.

Interview extract

The most embarrassing thing I ever did in my life, if anybody asks me what is the most embarrassing thing in your life…I was sent to a meeting for the Guild and somebody moved a resolution you see and somebody said, 'Well, I'll second it!' And I jumped up on my feet and said, 'I'll third it!' The chairman put me at my ease straight away and she said: 'Don't worry, dear, it shows you're awake which is more than can be said for some of them here!' I felt terrible. I felt really terrible. I was so full of enthusiasm you see.

Play extract

> ANNIE: The most embarrassing thing I ever did in my life. If anybody asks me what is the most embarrassing thing I ever did in my life…somebody moved a resolution you see and somebody said:

> JESSIE: I'll second it.

> ANNIE: And I jumped to my feet (*She does so*) and I said, 'I'll third it!'

Other cast members giggle.

> ANNIE: I felt terrible, really terrible.

> ALICE: Don't worry, dear, it shows you're awake, which is more than can be said for some of them here!

> ANNIE: (*To audience*) I was so full of enthusiasm, you see.

The production mirrored the simplicity of the speaking style and also reflected the rather Spartan conditions of the local halls in which meetings of the Guild traditionally took place. However, most of the Guilds we played to had wonderful banners, all made in velvet and silk, hand-stitched by past members, so these were used as part of the scenery wherever they were available.

Of Whole Heart Cometh Hope: *(left to right) Catherine Charlton, Cryss Healey, Jessica Higgs*

Raising the profile

The professional production gave the Guild a higher profile in the community, which included younger people who heard about the history of the movement for the first time. The older women who contributed to the play, as well as those who saw it on the anniversary, took great pride and pleasure in it and felt uplifted by its message, just as they had in the past.

For the theatre company, however, the original brief and its fulfilment on the tour was somewhat limiting in that, despite the breadth of subject matter it encompassed, it was for and about a specific organisation and reflected only the views of its members. I therefore felt strongly that the next shows we were to produce should have a more universal appeal, with memories recruited from, and playing to, older audiences in lunch clubs, day centres, sheltered housing units, hospitals and care homes, as these were the audiences least provided for.

All Our Christmases

A subject with a broader appeal

Christmas memories provided a more-or-less universal theme for the next show we were to produce and a chance to interview and play for these priority audiences. At that time of year, local authorities and other funders such as Help the Aged and the Midland Bank, were willing to make goodwill payments to the company so we could ensure that all performances would be free to the older people themselves, something which we felt was of the utmost importance. We also undertook to make a book of the stories. I was now wedded to the idea of giving a more permanent life through publications to the wealth of material generated by all our theatre projects (Schweitzer 1983b).

Unity of time and place

Initially I was not sure how the verbatim form would work on the subject of Christmas which, for most people, is associated with a family-based and private event. How could the many personal testimonies of individual contributors from such different situations be welded into a satisfactory whole? I invited Chrys Salt to work with me again, co-researching and writing this new show in order that, together, we could test the verbatim method further. We decided to link the stories around a generic south London family over the 24 hours of their Christmas celebration and all the incidental characters of neighbours, relatives (living and remembered) and tradesmen connected with it. We chose to set the action during the inter-war period as this was a time in their childhood or young adulthood remembered particularly sharply by our informants. It was also a time of financial uncertainty for many, so the play reflecting this background would be much more than a Christmas romp.

Group sessions provide the material

Most of the research that we undertook for this project was in the form of group reminiscence sessions in day centres, sheltered units and pensioners' clubs where the eventual shows would be performed. The participants in the group sessions were in their 70s, 80s and older, and we explained that the stories they gave might well find their way onto the stage. Perhaps because of the festive nature of the subject, or perhaps because so many stories were surfacing effortlessly in the group, as one person's memory triggered another, there was often a general feeling of spontaneity and hilarity in these sessions. People told stories of errant fathers, eccentric neighbours, culinary disasters and dreaded party-turns and, as these tales were related, the spirits of the participants were greatly improved and of course the stories also made wonderful dramatic material.

The regular reminiscence group sharing memories of Christmas past

Creative involvement of the sources

Other interviews were conducted with a regular reminiscence group that I had started through the local Adult Education Institute in Greenwich and, over the next few years, this group continued to provide invaluable reminiscences. The members were all well over 60 and they developed a real interest in sharing memories in a small group and seeing how these memories were incorporated into the rehearsal period and the final production of the plays. Two of the group commented on the experience in an interview in 1984 for ITV's *Help* programme.

Margaret Kippin said:

> We started talking about our memories and then the actors came down and did a run-through of the script and we helped by giving ideas and suggestions for songs. There's a mixture of pain and comedy in the process. The little bits of tragedy are there, but you're able to look back and laugh at them.

Joan Welch commented:

> For us pensioners these days, life is quite a strain. It's great to look back in our group, and even though they were hard times, we had lots of fun talking about them.

About eight of these people prepared written memories as well, which often provided a starting point for the group discussions. Some of these were inserted as 'set pieces' in the show and all of them found their way into the eventual Christmas memories book and launched to coincide with the start of the tour.

Ordering the stories

The structuring of the stories into a play-script turned out to be surprisingly simple. Christmas had its own relentless chronology, starting with savings clubs and planning, preparing the cakes and puddings, shopping and bargain hunting. The play moved on through descriptions of making decorations, carol singing, midnight Mass and the day itself, complete with the ritual present opening, pre-dinner tipple, consequent marital rows over a late meal, the King's speech, the much-needed brief period of post-prandial nap, and then the party, with speciality turns by all the family. The stories we had recorded fitted quite easily into this sequence, and key family roles were allotted to the cast of four who, between them, told all the stories and also played all the incidental characters involved.

In the following extract, the story is told in the past of the early 1900s, when the mother was a child, and the present of the 1930s. The monologue from the mother (delivered direct to the audience) is inter-cut with animated action from the children, whom she watches with satisfaction:

> MUM: I remember when I was little my father was out of work, and when we came down, well, none of us had anything. I was in a family – one of eight – I got downstairs and looked. 'I've got nothing in my stocking!' And I can remember my mother with tears in her eyes and she said, 'No, there is no Father Christmas, it's your mother and father, and your father's out of work.' So we had stew for dinner. And that's something that always stands out in my mind when I see what goes on now.

> *Mum watches children playing with presents.*

> BERT: We spent Christmas morning playing with our presents – boys always had Meccano.[6]

> CISSIE: I might have a skipping rope with wooden handles.

> BERT: You could build the Forth Bridge with one of those.

CISSIE: (*Meeting friend*) We'd be skipping out in the streets – showing them off to other children in the street.

BERT: Or a steam-driven crane.

CISSIE: (*Skipping*) All skip together girls,
In the frosty weather girls
I saw a pistol hanging out the window
Shoot! Bang! Fire!

(*Breathless*) We used to skip up and down, show off our skipping ropes. By that time quite often our knickers was down our legs. They used to fall down when we was skipping. It used to slide them down, but we didn't stop!

MUM: When I had a family of my own – I always had one thing in my mind – to let your kids have something better than you had yourself. Never let your kids put up with what you had to put up with. They had things which we'd never heard of.

CISSIE: (*Skipping*) Redcurrant, blackcurrant, strawberry tart,
Tell me the name of your sweetheart.

A more elaborate production

This play seemed to require a very different visual treatment from the Co-operative Women's Guild show. We decided to go to town on the set so that we could reflect the paraphernalia of Christmas, even to the extent of touring an old bedstead for the 'children' to leap in and out of, a table and chairs and all the necessary props including a turkey and a giant Christmas pudding! A piano was a central feature of the play as so many people's memory of Christmas was 'round the piano', but this was the last time we relied on the venues providing a workable instrument. The homes and day centres were shedding their pianos at that time and those that remained were extremely neglected and unpredictable. The backcloth was a painted domestic interior of the period on three separate stage-flats which could be decorated by the characters during the play, with suspended curtains between them for backstage space. Most costume changes, however, still happened on stage, facilitated by the ubiquitous hat stands.

The context for the performances of *All Our Christmases* was often a Christmas party for the older people in the audiences in the residential homes or community centres where the play was being performed, which of course led to tremendous logistical problems in importing the set and props into the performing spaces. The advantage was that audiences were very attuned to the subject matter and the post-show discussions could often happen in a very natural way over sherry and mince pies or even full-scale Christmas dinners.[7]

Consolidating the company and the touring circuit

This Christmas production enabled the company to consolidate relationships with older people's venues previously visited with *The Fifty Years Ago Show* and to create the beginnings of a regular touring circuit. It also produced some multi-skilled actor-musicians who were attuned to the work and committed to developing it further. The actors were keen to conduct some of the interviews for the next show themselves and to have a hand in the structuring of the verbatim material. We decided upon the broad theme of starting work at the age of 14 in the 1910s, 1920s and 1930s and the play was to be called *My First Job*.

My First Job

Everyone we approached had an interesting story to tell on this theme, many featuring outrageous exploitation recalled with much bitterness, but many told with humour and philosophical acceptance. There were tales of apprenticeships which kept young people in firms for several years with only token payments on the basis that they were learning a trade for life, and stories of dismissal at 16 when employers were required to pay National Insurance on their young workers. There were stories of long hours and meaningless tasks, domestic work under dragon-like housekeepers, shop work with 60-hour weeks and hapless adventures of naïve lads in the building trade falling for the practical jokes played on them by old timers (Schweitzer 1984a).

Four people play a cast of thousands

The cast portrayed a huge number of different work situations in a series of short, sharp scenes, switching gender and age at a tremendous rate. The musical director on this show, Marilyn Gordon, wrote link music and special songs to connect the scenes and help the audience to move from one character's story to another.

LUCY: (*Singing, supported by the cast*)

> I started off in a factory
> I didn't know what to do
> 'Lucy do this, fetch that, go there'
> Got meself in a stew
> It wasn't the greatest job in the world
> But still it paid me a wage
> You've got no choice at 14 years of age

LUCY: We had to take any job we could get. My first job, I worked at Deans at the Elephant. The rag people. They used to make rag dolls and books. My job was general dogsbody. (*Lucy dons overall and hairnet, as do the rest of cast, including men.*) Didn't know what I was letting myself in for.

Whirring machines (sound effects produced vocally by actors) with mimed sewing and cutting by 'the girls'

PHYLLIS: Lucy, just go and do this.

MABEL: Lucy just go there.

Lucy runs around at their beck and call

LUCY: I'd be waiting on them, you know.

MABEL: I said jasmine.

LUCY: If I got the wrong thing, I used to be well in the cut.

MABEL: Call this lilac?

LUCY: All unusual colours, you know. By the time I got there I forgot what colour I was supposed to be looking for. (*She grabs one and looks at it*) I remember lettuce was a yellowy colour. Ever seen a yellow lettuce?

MABEL: Lucy, you're to go on to pressing.

LUCY: Pressing the dolls' frocks. (*She mimes this*) This was all for five shillings a week and Saturdays till one o'clock.

PHYLLIS: Will you just go and fetch…

MABEL: Where's that box I asked for?

Lucy leaves the iron on and goes off to run errands. Then she smells the burning clothes. Mabel and Phyllis are horrified and freeze in furious positions. Lucy runs home.

LUCY: My mum, she said:

MUM: You wanna tell them.

LUCY: I was getting all headaches you see.

MUM: Tell 'em you haven't got a dozen pair of 'ands.

Chorus of calls of 'Lucy'

LUCY: (*Shouting at supervisor suddenly*) I want a rise.

Everyone freezes, then statuesque supervisor reaches for cards.

SUPERVISOR: Here's your cards, Miss.

LUCY: (*Wryly*) You got your cards. You never even got an envelope for them, did you?

Introducing a documentary image element

The play gained variety of pace, mood and subject from the arrangement of different memories. The set and costumes for the show echoed the decision to move quickly from one job and location to another, mirroring the youthful employment record of many of our sources. We experimented with displaying back-projected photographs for each story onto a screen set into the scenery. These images were taken from the contributors' collections and from the archives of the workplaces they remembered. The back-projected slides gave a strong visual cue and a sense of period to each story. However, because we required blackout for this device to work, there were some daytime venues where we could not show these images to full effect.

The actors wore basic period costumes and they added extra items for each scene in full view of the audience, often helping one another into overalls, hairnets and hats, as they stepped into new work situations. These 'over-costumes' were arrayed on hooks in a line attached to the set so that it looked like a works changing room, but it was also painted with authentic advertisements of the time. This open approach to moving into new characters and situations was very liberating and the resulting play had the feel of an animated tour of all the varied workplaces.

Back-projected images support the stories in My First Job*: (left to right) Philip Judge, Angela Bain, Amanda Carlton*

What Did You Do in the War, Mum?

A time to remember

The fortieth anniversary of the end of World War II in 1985 was a very significant event for our now regular audiences, which were largely composed of older women. Women's contribution to the war effort was rarely recorded and poorly documented, so it made sense to create a new piece of reminiscence theatre specifically about women's war work with an all-female cast. Two researchers were hired to help conduct the interviews. In this instance, we advertised in the local papers for women who had a story to tell around this specific area, and many people came forward, anxious to achieve some belated recognition for their wartime efforts. Fifty individual interviews were recorded, and some group interviews were held in addition (Schweitzer, Hilton and Moss 1985; Summerfield 1998). All were fully transcribed before they were handed over to the writer, Joyce Holliday. Joyce had worked for many years at the Theatre Royal, Stoke-on-Trent, with her then husband Peter Cheeseman, on social documentary scripts around important local industries and events and she had agreed enthusiastically to work on producing a verbatim play text from the research we had amassed.

Combining the stories within a chronological framework

The wartime stories came from women who had served in the forces, in the Land Army and on munitions, and Joyce's task was to bring together these many individual stories and fit them into a chronological progression from the outbreak of war to its ending. For example, it would be desirable to show how the calling up of women moved from semi-voluntary in the early years to compulsory later on, including older women who were dragged back into the labour market as the war progressed. The play would attempt to show how the acquisition of new money and new skills affected the lives and attitudes of the women workers.

Documentary material supporting verbatim memories

Joyce's instinct was to draw heavily on documentary sources to help the progression of the story. This proved particularly effective, since the government announcements were often unintentionally comical, especially when delivered by posh do-gooders over the radio. By performing these documentary extracts in the style of the time and juxtaposing them with the real life experience of the women we had recorded, some moments of high comedy were achieved.

Officials enter and distribute forms.

OFFICIAL: Every household will receive a form. Householders must fill in this form on a given night stating who is living there and whether they are living there temporarily or permanently.

The women bring their forms back to the officials individually.

RUTH: I had a problem with this temporary or permanent business.

OFFICIAL: Well, permanent means 'intending to remain there indefinitely'.

RUTH: I know what it *means*. It's my mother-in-law. She's just moved in with us. She thinks she's moved in permanent. But I think she's only moved in temporary.

HELEN: My two boys were evacuated and the people where they went
    thought they was there indefinite, but I missed 'em. So I had 'em back.
    So they *were* permanent there, but now they're permanent here.

JEAN: My husband filled this in.

OFFICIAL: But I see your husband's in the army.

JEAN: He did it when he was home on leave.

OFFICIAL: Then he shouldn't be down as permanent.

JEAN: He'd better be permanent, or I'll have something to say about it!

The popular songs of the time, reflecting the problems of wartime rationing, were
offset, with considerable irony, against the official voice of government and the
struggles of hard-pressed housewives to make the rations last:

OFFICIAL: Nearly half our food comes across the sea. The U-boats attack our
    ships. Now, here is *your* part in the fight for Victory. When a particular
    food is not available, cheerfully accept something else – home-
    produced if possible.

Officials distribute recipe leaflets.

HELEN: I used to make my kids bananas out of parsnips. I used to boil them
    and put this banana essence in them. My kids used to think they had
    bananas. We did a lot of things like that.

SONG: Yes, we have no bananas.
    We have no bananas today.
    We've broad beans and bunions,
    Cabbages and onions,
    And all sorts of fruits and, say!
    We have nice juicy tomatoes,
    And old-fashioned potatoes.
    But, yes, we have no bananas.
    We have no bananas today.

OFFICIAL: Keep loyally to the rationing regulations. Above all whether you
    are shopping, cooking, or eating – remember, food is a munition of
    war, don't waste it!

JEAN: If you had meat one week, you couldn't have it the next, cos you
    wouldn't have enough coupons, and you could only have one egg on
    the book. We used to have to make cakes without eggs.

SONG: Hey, little hen, when, when, when
    Will you lay me an egg for my tea?

OFFICIAL: Imitation Eggs: Make a batter. Cut a tomato in two and put it
    into the batter. Lift each half out with a spoon, keeping the round side

up, and put it into hot fat. The tomato shines through, looking like the yolk of an egg. If cooked in bacon fat you can almost imagine that you have the bacon as well.

SONG: Hey, little hen, when, when, when
Will you lay me an egg for my tea?

OFFICIAL 2: Four Fruit Jam: Wash and peel four ounces of cooked beetroot and carrot. Chop finely. Add strawberry jelly and blackcurrrant jelly. Leave to set. Eat within three days.

OFFICIAL 3: Shoot Straight Lady! You've got a fighting job on hand, too. These are significant days, and anyone – man, woman, or child – who is less than fighting fit is a pull-back on the total war effort. Food is your munition of war!

Inviting contributors to rehearsals

Because many of the women were fiercely proud of their wartime service, it felt necessary to check every last detail with them before putting the play out on tour. So, with the actors' consent, I invited the key contributors to attend rehearsals. This gave them a far greater stake in the play and a feeling of having their experience valued.

A GENUINE COLLABORATION BETWEEN SOURCES AND PERFORMERS

It has always been fruitful to have the original story-tellers present when their scene is being worked by the director and actors. They often became 'directors' themselves, putting flesh on performances and helping the actors to get in touch with the reality of the situation and the feelings it evoked at the time. Many older people found it a real pleasure to get to know the actors and help with the portrayal. Iris Gange commented on this process in an interview with Greg Giesekam from the University of Glasgow:

I was reading the local paper one day and I saw an article in it and they were asking for anyone who had done anything in the war as regards women's work. And as I was involved in the Women's Auxiliary Air Force, I phoned the organiser, Mrs Pam Schweitzer, and she came and interviewed me. I've always written comical poetry and Pam saw this poem in my scrap book called 'Plugger up of holes', based on a Jack Warner wartime number 'I'm a bunger up of holes'. It went like this.

I do my duty every day, I'm a plugger up of calls.
I sit at my board and push my plugs in all the little holes.
Group Captains, Pilots, all come up to hear me speak my mind,
And if I hand wrong numbers out, 'tis then they start to bind.
It's, 'Have you got my number, Miss? For goodness sake, be quick.
It's strictly a priority call.' That man I'd like to kick,
For having cut off other calls in order to do his bidding,
His opening words are, 'Hello my sweet.' I know then he's been kidding.

Other verses here, ending with:

So the next time you pick up the phone and have to wait at all,
Just think of me, the little WAAF who plugs in all the holes.
Don't think I'm knitting 'comforts' or drinking canteen tea,
For if you could but see me, I'm as busy as can be.

Well, to my delight, I attended the rehearsal one day in Blackheath, and they'd put my poem to music and they were singing it just like the old Andrews sisters. I just stood back and laughed. I've not been involved in anything like this since I belonged to a dancing group as a girl. I'm getting interested in it again now and I'd like to be involved if I can be of any help.

Rehearsing Iris Gange's poem set to music in What Did You Do in the War, Mum?: *(standing left to right) Anna Philpott, Melanie Walters, Susan Betts, Sheila Tait; (seated) Iris Gange and Anna Skye*

It was very exciting to see it, the final show, and I only wish my mother and my grand-mother were both alive to see it. They showed it at my grand-daughter's school, which is my old school (Prendergast School for Girls in Catford), and my grand-daughter and her friends thought it very interesting and humorous. They didn't realise ladies did that during the war.

For the actors, the direct involvement of the older people was extremely important in helping them understand the often quite complex tasks undertaken by women as part of their wartime work. For example, when developing the scene about the

Women's Land Army, an area on which there was very little documentation, it was crucial to have the older women present in the rehearsal to advise us. We invited Frances Crane, a woman who had recorded her story with us, to describe for the actors the complex working of the dangerous threshing machine which she and her friend had been asked to operate.

Breaking up verbatim text for dramatic effect

Rather than use the recorded interview as a complete narrative, words and phrases have been extracted by the writer and reconstructed as a staccato sequence of shouts and responses (underscored by a screaming violin) mirroring the action of the machine and the nightmarish fear it invoked in the young women. The resulting scene was frightening and felt very real because it had been choreographed by the woman herself, who knew the movements and the sounds and could convey them exactly to the actors. This is how it was finally scripted:

BOSS: Threshing machine. (*Indicating table, which will represent threshing machine. Sound of throbbing engine made vocally by the cast.*)

FRAN: It was like a council dustcart.

BOSS: (*Prodding Fran*) You. Get up there.

FRAN: On top of that?

BOSS: Bloody get up.

Fran climbs on top of table. Boss mimes lifting up the sheaf which is tied with twine.

BOSS: Use knife. Cut twine. Into drum.

Boss mimes cutting the twine and throwing the sheaf down.

FRAN: Shouldn't there be a guard up? What happens if I fall in?

Boss laughs and draws the knife across his throat before handing it to her. He climbs down.

BOSS: (*To Maud*) You. Rake the chaff out the bottom.

Maud rakes. Fran struggles to cut the twine.

BOSS: Get it in!

The machine hum changes to a whine, produced on violin.

BOSS: Hear that whine? Bloody get it in!

Fran throws the sheaf down. The whine changes back to a hum. Boss throws another sheaf. Fran catches it better but cannot cut it.

BOSS: Bugger me! Cut it. Cut it!

FRAN: I can't!

The hum changes back to the whine.

BOSS: You're wasting time.

FRAN: I can't cut it!

BOSS: You're losing me money.

Fran cuts it and drops it in. Whine turns back to hum. The whine and the hum alternate and the actors' movements become mechanical and accelerate through a further sequence concluding...

FRAN: Straw sticks in hair. Dust gets in eyes. Barley spikes in skin. Bladder going to burst. Arms ache. Back aches. Eyes sting. Feet slip. I must not slip!

Boss turns the engine off.

BOSS: All right. Dinner.

FRAN: It's a filthy job. Where can we wash our hands?

BOSS: Bloody hell! Townies!

The power of remembered songs

The war years generated some of the most moving and well-loved songs of the last century, well remembered by our target audience and full of associations. The musical director on this show, Paula Gardiner, who was to stay with the company for some years, arranged these songs around the many and varied instruments played by the actors. Having electronic keyboard, violin, flute, clarinet and saxophone in the show brought back memories of a time when live music was more commonly enjoyed than it is today. Paula was also very inventive with the domestic implements used as props in the show, so buckets, basins and scrubbing brushes made excellent percussion instruments. Songs which were so very well known and so closely associated with personal relationships and events of that time in the minds of our audiences provided a perfect vehicle for the moods and emotions of the show. The actors were often moved by the sound of quiet gravelly voices of 80-year-olds singing along to their very well-polished harmonising.

Visual prompts

The scenery too was designed to evoke memories of the war years, with recruiting posters for the women's services, the Women's Auxiliary Ait Force (WAAF), the women's Royal Navy (WRNS) and the Auxikiary Territorial Service (ATS), displayed alongside propaganda posters telling mothers to evacuate their children to safety in the countryside. The main element of the set was the front half of a corrugated iron Nissen hut (a pre-fabricated pressed steel building widely used in World War II by all services). I feel sure it would not have been allowed under the more stringent health and safety requirements of today, but having the authentic corrugated iron material on stage was itself a potent reminder for our audiences of that period. At times when the play moved into musical mode, flashing light bulbs in red, white and blue, which were built into the set, reminded the audience both of warning lights and of the live entertainment in those years. The mixture of the hardship of living in the shelters and the enjoyment of the lively musical entertainment of the time was therefore effectively evoked by the set. It was designed to be erected in half an hour in the 100 venues we played to, and for the elderly audiences, who often arrived early, watching the set go up was an added bonus to the main event and enabled their memories to start flooding back, even before the show had begun.

'Dangerous subjects'

In a few cases, there had been a certain amount of concern by managers of residential homes that our play would distress the elderly residents and that war was potentially a 'dangerous subject'. We reassured them that we would not convey any violent action or extreme emotion on stage, and in fact very little of either was relayed to us during the interviews, though of course there were many sad stories, such as fathers and brothers not returning from the front. In fact, these anxieties about raising emotions proved to be misplaced and we did not encounter any resistance to remembering and discussing the war from the older people, either during the period of collecting the memories or during the eventual tour. Many people remembered the war years with a certain degree of fondness as a time when they were at their most active and energised and when they had many close friendships and a great sense of purpose. Tears were often shed by members of the audience in the course of the performances, but these were mainly during the songs, when people were moved by the power of the music and the memories of people and places from their past which it evoked.

Can We Afford The Doctor?

The professionalism and the universal appeal of *What Did You Do in the War, Mum?* won the company many new supporters and a wider touring circuit, including venues in the south-west of England, Wales, Scotland, Manchester, Liverpool and Yorkshire. By 1985, the theatre company was well enough established and highly enough valued to be the subject of a 90-minute documentary programme by Television History Workshop for Channel 4 Television, which had a particularly lively documentary department at the time. The film tracked the next production, *Can We Afford The Doctor?*, through every stage from interviews through rehearsal to performance (Television History Workshop 1985).

The company's reputation was now well established, with funding coming in from regional arts boards, charitable trusts and, in this instance, area health authorities. At this point, there was a growing pressure to increase the number of performances in 'proper' theatres to more general audiences, with groups of older people bussed in to see the plays. However, although I recognised the desirability of building in some such public performances in prestigious 'gigs' for every touring show, I felt strongly that we should stick to the kinds of venues for which the company had been set up and which were not being served by anyone else. We were offering a unique cultural service by taking theatre of a particularly relevant kind to older people in homes, who would never have been taken out to a theatre because of the logistical and financial problems involved.

Choosing topics of major concern to older people

Following the success of our relationship with Joyce Holliday, we commissioned her to write a new verbatim play and this time to conduct many of the interviews herself. The subject was health care in the days before the National Health Service and the play was entitled *Can We Afford The Doctor?* (Schweitzer 1985). This topic was chosen because, for most of our audiences, health was (and had always been) a major concern. Many were worrying that, at a time when they most needed the NHS, it seemed to be under threat. This was the 1980s when there was an increasing level of anxiety about the sustainability of the free health care offered at the time. The Conservative government was introducing certain limits and restrictions on national health care expenditure, and many hospitals were closing down as part of a massive rationalisation programme. This included some hospitals for which the older people remembered making house-to-house collections in the pre-war years for donations to their building funds, and others which had been in the forefront of nursing for women and children just a few decades before.

A political subtext

The play was not going to be a direct political campaigning piece, but rather an opportunity to remind everyone what life was like for mothers in the days when they looked at their sickly children and asked themselves: 'Can we afford the doctor?' This production with its political subtext led to some very lively discussion with older audiences concerning their desire to protect what they felt they had fought for, and how anxious they were about the future of their local hospitals. *Can We Afford The Doctor?* toured nationally and, although we made reference to particular London hospitals and to local situations in the play, the material was readily transferable to all the places where we performed, where older people shared the concerns of London's pensioners.

Contributors re-enact their stories in rehearsal

Again, the contributors were invited to attend the rehearsals, including those retired doctors and nurses who had answered our advertisements for interviewees. A memorable rehearsal was when two elderly nurses (trained in 1923 and 1939 respectively) converted the rehearsal room into a hospital ward with the actors as patients and showed us how they would care for sick children with diphtheria or pneumonia at the time. Sarah Ferres, one of the retired nurses, told us how fierce her Ward Sister could be: 'If Sister was in a good mood you were on top of the world, but if not, it was "Up, up, up", and you'd have to redo all the beds and there were thirty beds on a ward' (Television History Workshop 1985). The following extract, taken from the televised recording of the improvised rehearsal, is of Sarah, acting in role as the Ward Sister, talking to Bertha Barrett, the other contributor, who is playing the part of Sarah herself as a young nurse.

> Can you step aside, Nurse Ferres? I don't like the way you've come to this bedside. You've rushed on duty this morning. Your cap is not correct and your apron…the crosses aren't correct. The navy is showing below your white apron and you've got something in your pocket, which you know you ought not to have. I'd like you to go and see Matron in the morning, because if I can't instil in your brain after 18 months of training just how you should wear your uniform, then I think Matron is the right one for you. (Television History Workshop 1985)

The actors learn from the elders

Watching such improvisations was both funny and entertaining for the actors, but it also conveyed to them the pride the nurses had taken in their profession, the all-round care they provided and also the harsh discipline to which they had been subjected.

> We worked ten hours a day and we got the large sum of £40 for the first year and £45 in the next. Sometimes we got extra for working with fevers because of the danger of infection. You'd be in your element if you had a really ill patient, say with pneumonia, and to get that patient well was the biggest thrill.

In the play, memories from the nurses and patients in hospital are juxtaposed, with the lines distributed amongst the cast as seen in the following script extract:

EDWARD: I was taken to the Brook Hospital. That was an isolation hospital. Twelve wards for scarlet fever, ten wards for diphtheria. Huge wards they were, and the ceiling seemed miles away. It was the first time I'd been away from home and I was desperately frightened.

NURSE: There now, what is it?

Edward whispers to the nurse who nods, and exits.

EDWARD: I was frightened of wetting the bed.

Nurse returns with a bedpan.

NURSE: Part of our work as a nurse in those days was to talk to the patient. You had to really care for them. There weren't any antibiotics, no miracle cures, your only hope was to nurse them through.

EDWARD: It was mainly bed rest. Bed rest and gargling with permanganate of potash.

NURSE: First job in the morning was to pull all the beds out to the middle of the ward, sweep all around, damp dust at the back of the beds and push them all back again. We had to dust the patients' lockers, change the water and do the flowers. But while you were doing that you could chat to the person in the bed. There was this contact. You got to know the patients and they got to know you. They were in hospital for weeks and weeks and you were with them all that time until they got better.

A child's long stay in hospital with diphtheria played by Steve Fortune and Sarah Parks in Can We Afford The Doctor?

A song for every topic

Subjects such as home remedies and children's ignorance at the time of the facts of life provided much humour in the play and awakened many memories to share in the post-show discussions. Songs like 'Doctor Quack' (whose patent remedies would 'cure you of any attack') and 'Don't have any more Mrs Moore' (on the desirability and impossibility of contraception) were fitted between pieces of first-hand testimony, and the audience sang along enthusiastically, remembering the times these songs had been popular and relevant. It was a pleasant surprise to find that there was a song for every subject in the show. The musical director, Sandra Kerr, an expert on folk and music hall traditions, had dug around in the BBC archives for long-forgotten songs with a health-related theme, as well as com-posing some new numbers in traditional styles using the words of the contributors.

Sandra Kerr commented on the role of music in the show:

> Music plays such an important part in people's lives, especially when dealing with this period [1920s]. Songs can change the focus of attention in the theatrical presentation, break tension and alter the mood. If they're good songs, and songs directly related both to the subject matter and to the style of delivery, they will enlighten us about the

social conditions underlying the scene we've just seen. Songs should, as far as possible, be contemporary with the reminiscences, and it's best to use existing music. Up to 1929 there are songs on everything, every subject. After that, composers discovered 'lurve' and the songs after that are all about love! (Television History Workshop 1985)

The cast of Can We Afford The Doctor? *work with Sandra Kerr (Musical Director): Howard Leader to her left, Steve Fortune, Nicky Goldie, Sarah Parks and Anne Haydn to her right. (Set design by Sarah-Jane Ash)*

Performance implications in verbatim scripting

A particular playing style

The verbatim approach to script writing has a radical effect on the playing style of the performers. While it is vitally important to have genuine recognisable interaction occurring between the characters on stage, the actors are encouraged by the verbatim script to 'play out', to tell the stories directly to the audience. This way of scripting militates against a 'fourth wall' playing style, in which the actors perform to one another as though the audience are not there. This 'fourth wall' style would, in any case, not be appropriate for the target audience, many of whom were in their 70s and 80s. They need every assistance in hearing what is going on, which includes seeing the actors' faces, watching their lips and, if possible, having the stage illuminated with theatre lights so they can focus on the action.

The style of playing out direct to the audience also feels very familiar to many older audiences who remember the music hall tradition and the variety shows where the performers aimed everything 'out front' as though talking to a large group of friends, before breaking into song or dance with live musical accompaniment. Joyce Holliday, who wrote three very strong shows for the company, commented on writing from verbatim for older audiences:

> They are an exciting audience to write for as they haven't been to the theatre for ages. They may be familiar with music hall or pantomime conventions, which is where the songs come in, but they haven't got expectations or preconceptions, so you can do anything. (Television History Workshop 1985)

Actors grapple with the form

Some actors were wary about performing verbatim scripts, fearing that the style might limit the power of the drama and cut down on what they could achieve in performance. Angela Bain, who was to perform in many Age Exchange shows over the years, commented:

> Sometimes the reminiscences you are re-telling may or may not have a dramatic arc or 'punchline'. As a performer, your instinct is to tell a riveting story, so it is a balancing act between honouring the reminiscence, and making a piece of narrative theatre that takes the audience along with it.

Most actors come to see the form's unique value as a means of engaging with an older audience, who then give audible and visible evidence of their involvement. They might call out approval, urge caution or show sympathy for the characters in a way which would startle performers on a conventional theatre stage, and the actors in verbatim reminiscence theatre shows need to respond to these sentiments from the audience without losing their concentration and without creating too much additional script in the process. Mandy Carlton, another long-standing Age Exchange performer in the early 1980s, commented positively on this close contact with the audience in an interview for ITV's *Help* programme in 1984:

> You can watch the recognition on their faces when you are performing, which is really very rewarding.

Some of the actors formed close relationships with people they were playing in these verbatim productions. It is, after all, a rare opportunity for an actor to be able to speak to their 'character' and ask how they feel about the representation of particular incidents and people from their lives in the play. Of course, playing a real live person who is actually watching your performance can also be an alarming experience for actors. Steve Gribbin, who performed in many Age Exchange shows, commented in the same television programme:

> It's quite a weird feeling to be presenting the stories of people we've actually talked to. It's quite a strange experience to go back to the person you originally interviewed and say, 'Was that right?' And they mostly think it was.

Summary

In this chapter, I have aimed to show how verbatim scripting has been developed in specific productions and how closely the sources of the stories have been involved in the production process. The effect on the performers of this close relationship and the way the verbatim approach to scripting impacts on their performance style have also been explored, though there is more to say on this in later chapters.

I have tried to demonstrate a range of topics which have successfully lent themselves to verbatim dramatisation and the responses of different audiences to the resulting shows. Productions included here celebrate anniversaries and seasons, and explore memories of starting work, going to war and battling for good health in poor living conditions. In the two following chapters I shall consider reminiscence theatre productions developed with and for minority ethnic elders and the social and cultural impact of such projects.

CHAPTER 4

Reflecting a Multicultural Society

Multicultural London

In the early 1980s, while working at Task Force, I had recorded the memories of a small number of minority ethnic older people for educational use with young people in schools. My impression was that they had led very different lives from their indigenous white contemporaries and that they had very significant stories to tell. Many had come to post-war Britain from the Caribbean, India, Africa and other parts of the Commonwealth to help rebuild the 'mother country', and had now reached retirement age. As the theatre company was aiming to record and reflect the past experience and current concerns of older Londoners, it was important to include minority groups in both the process and the product. The Greater London Council's Ethnic Minorities Unit and the Commission for Racial Equality agreed in 1984 to fund a new reminiscence theatre project on a multicultural theme. It would explore and dramatise the memories of elders from different backgrounds, rather than focusing on one particular ethnic group.

Presenting difference

Around that time, Peter Brook, the British theatre director, who had sought cultural exile in Paris, was doing interesting work with a performing company drawn from different nationalities and ethnicities. In preparing *The Ik*, they had spent time in the radically different culture of an African village working with the people from a tribe which was facing slow, but inevitable, extinction through starvation, making a theatrical record of their vanishing way of life. They had developed a new piece of theatre to convey the plight of that community to people in the faraway world of the west. Though criticised for its appropriation of the tribe's experience in the name of art (Bharucha 1993), the power of the production lay in the director's confident crossing of conventional theatrical boundaries, using combinations of still image, choreography, sound, music and narration in languages not spoken by western audiences.

Like many young directors of the time, I found this daring mix inspiring and liberating, pointing up as it did the unique and powerful magic the performers bring into the 'empty space' (Brook 1968). I saw in Brook's work a model for a multicultural reminiscence theatre production: actors from different ethnicities would work together to express the stories they had heard in many different languages from older people who had travelled across the world to follow a more or less unrealisable dream of getting wealthy enough to return home, and instead had settled for a very different reality in multicultural London.

A Place To Stay

A multicultural company

In Woolwich and Belvedere, conurbations to the east of Age Exchange's base in Blackheath, there were large Asian communities, speaking Punjabi or Gujerati. Two performers were recruited to play in these languages as well as English, and the choice of one man and one woman respected the need for men and women in these groups to share and record their memories separately. A Caribbean performer would represent the large local West Indian minority population in neighbouring Lewisham and a bilingual Greek Cypriot performer would represent the experience of white minority ethnic elders. In addition to the actors, other researchers with different language skills conducted and transcribed interviews with elders from their communities on the company's behalf, so we were also able to reflect the experience of Chinese, Turkish, Polish and Italian pensioners within the project.

Finding the interviewees

We made contact with organisers of clubs and day centres where minority ethnic elders met and they helped us find members willing to work with us. Some people were worried about giving interviews as they associated questioning with interrogation. In the early 1980s, there had been a tightening up of immigration laws and there was a degree of sensitivity and suspicion around the area of recorded interviews. It was very important wherever possible to have interviewers of the same ethnicity as the elders, so there would be a degree of trust and understanding.

Each actor was responsible for interviewing and recording older people from his or her own ethnic community, in mother tongues where necessary. The actors were equipped with tape recorders and an agreed outline schedule of questions. These covered life in the home country, the journey from the home country to England, how it had been for families coming to join partners in London and also how the elders were experiencing growing old in Britain. Other areas of discussion opened up, according to the interests of the interviewees, including what people missed most about their home country, how they felt about it now and their relationship with the host culture here. Each interviewer wrote up the interviews he or she conducted in the original language and also in English. We did not transcribe everything, but picked out salient extracts. Some of the interviewers could speak their mother tongues but could not write them so, in these instances, we approached professionals to transcribe the mother tongue tapes.

A publishing first

The 60 people we interviewed, mainly individually but also occasionally in groups, were recording their stories for the first time. Between them, they represented a significant body of life experience, which would be of interest to a wide readership. There had been nothing published in England which reflected the migration experience of Britain's minority ethnic elders, so the Greater London Council and the Commission for Racial Equality both agreed to support the cost of printing an edited book of the interviews in the different mother tongues of the elders and in English. The book was also the first effort there had been at a multi-lingual storybook of memories with accompanying photographs. Although most timely and long overdue, some aspects of producing the book proved very complicated. As the transcripts were indecipherable to a non-native speaker, matching the mother-tongue paragraphs up with their English equivalents during the process of editing and laying out the pages of the book was very challenging and there had to be a lot of cross-checking. However, the book became, for some years, a Bible for workers wishing to undertake reminiscence work in these relatively uncharted waters. The British passport on the cover was symbolic of the colonial past which had brought these immigrants to Britain in the first place, and their absolute right to be here (Schweitzer 1984b).

Universal themes, specific cultures

The creation of this show was a new departure point for me. Although I would be the overall director, the production would be thoroughly democratic in its process, with the actors having a high degree of autonomy in the collection, dramatisation and directing of their own interview material. Our play would address universal themes of migration, travel, settlement and ageing far from 'home' which would cut across many cultures, but of course 'home' would mean something very different for each audience and the play would need to reflect a range of countries, cultures and images.

Actors develop their own scenes

The actors were responsible for introducing the rest of the company to important ideas and information about their own culture especially reflecting the interviews they had conducted. During the devising period, the actors even cooked different kinds of food for one another so we could try to enter one another's worlds and appreciate one another's cultures. Each actor had time allocated to develop the stories he or she had heard into dramatic scenes and to directing the rest of the group in these scenes. My task was to find a holding structure for these scenes and stories and to work closely with the musical director and designer to make the end result cohere artistically.

Crossing the language divide

The show was destined to tour to many different ethnic elders' groups and we knew that many of the elders we would play to in clubs, day centres and temples would speak very little English. We could not depend too much on words to convey stories, but would need to be theatrically inventive in our production. English was the closest we would get to a common language and that would have to be the *lingua franca* of the play. However, we wanted to include some mother tongue in the production to reflect some of the diversity of language in which the original interviews had been conducted and to enable elders speaking those languages to engage fully with scenes drawn from their own culture. We developed a system whereby, if a scene required the dominant character to speak mainly in Punjabi, Gujerati or Greek, then the other characters participating in the scene would help communicate its content in English, or the meaning would be simultaneously conveyed in movement, image and song.

Songs from the elders' own words

For the first time, many of the songs were specially written for the show and reflected the different musical styles of the minorities we were representing. Jo Richler was the musical director, and she arranged the music for harmonium, traditional percussion instruments from India and the Caribbean and voices. In a few scenes she used traditional songs expressing strong emotions, especially old songs from India and from Cyprus, which the actors brought to the rehearsals. The words for the newly written songs were adapted from the transcriptions of interviews with the elders. For example there was a song about the sense of being far from home, however long one has lived in the new country:

> You arrive with a one way ticket
> You don't know how long you'll stay
> Never think of this place as home
> Because you're going home someday
>
> And the years pass like shadows
> You forget how many you say
> But it still isn't home here
> It's just a place to stay
>
> You have your friends, your family
> You have your work that's true
> But the dreams that brought you far from home
> Have all but flown from you
>
> So it's here that we find ourselves
> It's here that we'll pass away
> But it still won't be home to us
> It's just a place to stay

These words were taken from an interview with a Caribbean woman who said, 'England isn't home for me, it's just a place to stay', and it also gave us the title for the show, *A Place To Stay*. Many people spoke about how cold they were and how miserable and lonely they felt when they first arrived, and these sentiments were expressed by the cast in short pieces of music, almost like a Greek chorus commenting on the action between scenes. Music was also used to underscore scenes of strong emotion, humour and changes of mood in the play.

Working through image and action

This piece was much more imagistic than previous productions. The actors made tableaux or still images to illustrate the words and feelings of the sources. These images would then 'unfreeze' and come to life in set pieces of movement with song or instrumental music. For example, in a scene about finding a home in London, the actors moved around the stage as a group, holding their suitcases and moving to a rhythmic percussion accompaniment of bells, and knockers. On the 'freezes' one character would step out of the image to speak to the audience about his or her own experience and then the cast would move once again. It would be clear to anyone watching that the scene was a reflection of the difficulties in finding a place to stay when faced with a shortage of language and money and a great deal of racial prejudice and xenophobia.

Vocal percussion

In a scene concerned with the work the immigrants did when they first came to England, the actors moved together in rhythm, as though they were a single machine in a factory. This was to reflect the many stories we heard about how highly skilled immigrants were often obliged to take factory work and were rarely able to use their qualifications and professional experience. The repetitive images and sounds of the factory production line were made by the actors, with support from the musician on percussion instruments. The sound and action was then 'frozen' from time to time for individual speeches or short scenes taken from the stories we had collected, before the 'machine' started up again.

Speak, hear the sound, read the image

In another example of stylised action and frozen image interspersed with speech to the audience we showed the popularity of dominoes among older Caribbean men. The actors alternately slammed down their dominoes on a table, with support on percussion instruments from the musician, and then 'froze' like a still photograph of a dominoes game, while the Caribbean performer spoke in role between moves. The speech which follows was broken into smaller segments, each marked by a move by the other actors, a percussive sound and then another freeze. This stylised approach was helpful to all our audiences who did not speak the language, but who could read the imagery without difficulty, and it conveyed the physical power of the game.

> MAN: In the West Indies I would say they love dominoes. I don't know
> how I started. Nobody taught me to play the game. I just stand up and

watch and learn. Over here you don't slam the dominoes that much, because not everybody likes the noise it makes. In the West Indies, when you play you knock it loud. When you make noise, that's the sweetness of the game. When you play the game quiet it's not the same. You have to concentrate on the game, because when you play you don't like to lose. You watch your partner play, you get to know what he has. You play what he plays and he plays what you play. I tell you this is a beautiful game.

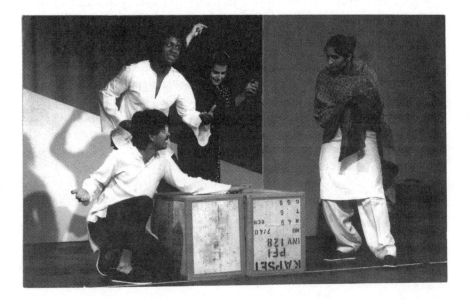

A 'freeze' from the dominoes game in A Place to Stay: *(left to right) Dhirendra, Ken Breinburg, Georgia Clarke, Ravinder Valia*

Reality behind the front doors

Interspersed between the more stylised scenes with their sustained theatrical images, there were more naturalistic scenes, set inside the family homes of the elders. These scenes used more dialogue between the characters, in contrast to those stories which were given a stylised treatment and delivered directly out to the audience. This contrast mirrored the process of the project itself, which opened doors on to the private family lives hidden behind the front doors of the elders.

Presenting racism

One scene began with the Caribbean man sitting alone on a bench in Hyde Park and remembering his childhood. He related a story about his grandmother cooking a traditional meal for all the children in his family and this was enacted by the cast playing the various roles, with sound effects made by percussion instruments of the crickets, the animals and the sea. The drama then returned to the present day, with him as an older man in the park being teased and taunted by children. We used children's rhymes and games in this scene, but they were used in a very threatening way to represent the intimidation experienced by the old people. We did this because we had discovered from the interviews that much of the racial harassment experienced by elders came from young people. The following extract shows how we moved from recorded verbatim reminiscence, taken directly from the original interview, to children's nursery rhymes and games to heighten theatrical tension.

> MAN: I love Hyde Park on a lovely summer day. I usually sit under a tree reading a book and watching people passing by. People with their children playing. This is a very pleasant sight and it reminds me of back home in Guyana when I was a child. In Guyana at five o'clock in the morning the cocks are crowing and the hens are clucking. In the yard we had pidgeon peas, okra, mangoes, star-apples, custard apples, sapodilla and papaya. Evening used to be the best time. In New Amsterdam all the houses were built on stilts and after dinner we would sit on the little porch, with the beetles chu-chu-ing in the background, children screaming, dogs barking or somebody shouting at somebody. You see I enjoy being in Hyde Park thinking about the good old days in Guyana, but sometimes I sit here and I think about the thing I dread most and that is loneliness.

The other actors playing children surround him and point fingers at him, taunting him and chanting.

> THE REST: Sticks and stones will break your bones
> But names will never hurt you.

Another actor goes into the middle of the circle, and the rest make grabbing gestures as if attempting to rob her, chanting:

> THE REST: Please put a penny in the old man's hat.
> If you haven't got a penny then a pound will do.
> I haven't got a penny or a pound for you.

A third actor is pushed into the middle as the rest threaten her:

> THE REST: We'll huff and we'll puff and we'll blow your house down.

The fourth actor is thrust into the middle while the rest attack him with pointing fingers and threatening gestures shouting:

> THE REST: Paki, paki, paki, paki, paki, paki, paki, paki
> Pakis out Pakis out Pakis out out out

Siren sounds and muggers disperse, leaving wounded man on the floor. One turns out to speak as if to a police officer, protesting total innocence.

> THUG: He fell over, Officer, I went to help him. That's why I've got blood on me bottle. (*He winks in a conspiratorial manner*) Thanks Officer.

'We'll huff and we'll puff and we'll blow your house down.' Images of racism in A Place To
Stay: *(left to right) Ken Breinburg, Ravinder Valia, Georgia Clarke and Dhirendra*

Simplicity of production

The set was an abstract design constructed out of plywood flats cut into geometric
shapes painted in single colours or monochrome with a blue fabric hanging
behind. There was a very golden sunny area of the stage with a lot of blue, representing 'home' in warm distant lands, and England was represented by the colour
grey, which reflected the first impressions of the immigrants. The actors wore
simple basic costumes in traditional styles for their country, all in white, with a few
coloured items for over-dressing. Props were limited to suitcases and tea chests.
Everything else was mimed by the actors. I think in the end it was a theatrically
economical show which was delivered by the performers in a simple but extremely
disciplined way.

Stylistic freedom

The decision to use a mixture of theatrical styles in the production was challenging,
but it was also liberating, in that we could move freely from formal to informal
playing styles where these were dramatically appropriate for the scene. The more
imagistic scenes conveyed common experiences such as constantly feeling the
cold, trying to find a job and a home, missing family and friends from home, and
coping with racial stereotyping and insults. In the more naturalistic scenes we went
inside the homes and lives of the different elders to reflect their particular

preoccupations. The cast consisted of only four members, but they had to portray 50 or so characters. Each time a character told a story, the other actors from different ethnic backgrounds played the other parts required by the tale. Although it might have been a little confusing for some members of our audience, this integrated casting approach did have the effect of universalising the experiences portrayed and creating a tapestry of interwoven stories and cultures.

Working across cultures

A Place To Stay explored the experience of migration and of growing old far from home by juxtaposing stories from different cultures and highlighting the common ground between them. The many and different audiences we played to made cross-cultural connections and links around their experience of migration and settlement as they watched the piece. I think this production had a consciousness-raising effect, lifting the profile of minority ethnic elders, perhaps the most invisible and marginalised people in our society.

Routes

Working with a single minority

From the production of *A Place To Stay* it became clear, despite its success, that there were certain difficulties around having an ethnically mixed show. Although the audiences were encouraged to make cross-cultural connections and links around their experience of migration as they watched the piece, the reality was often that different minority ethnic groups in the audience were waiting for 'their bit' to come up, and they would inevitably be more interested in sections presented in their own language and reflecting their own culture.

Because of this, I decided that it might be desirable to produce a professional reminiscence show for and about just one ethnic group, recognising of course that within each ethnicity there are many subcultures and class and language differences. In the case of elders from the Indian subcontinent, the first minority ethnic group on whom we planned to base a piece of theatre, we decided to work in just two languages, English and Punjabi, because the local Asian population was predominantly Punjabi speaking.

We cast four professional actors with Indian backgrounds. One of them did not speak any Indian languages, but his origins were Indian. He was born in Africa and came to England as a young boy when his family migrated here. The other three were Punjabi speaking, and some of the actors also spoke some Hindi and Urdu, which was helpful when we interviewed elders who did not speak Punjabi.

The themes of the show were to emerge from group sessions we would hold with the elders and from individual interviews conducted by the actors, especially those actors who spoke the mother tongue concerned. My directorial role was to bring together what the actors came up with from the interviews and their own experience, to work with them to shape the material and also to ensure the accessibility of the dramatic content to non-Indian-language-speaking audiences.

We decided to call the show *Routes*, which had a convenient double meaning when spoken: it referred to the important journeys made by our sources from one continent to another, but also to their situation of having roots in another culture, and the increasing significance of these roots for people growing old far from home.

Support and trust in the research period

This project began in 1992 with a series of reminiscence sessions organised in the local Sikh Temple through an Asian social worker, Rosie Bedi, who had trained in reminiscence with Age Exchange. Rosie was interested in developing the confidence and creativity of the elders attending a lunch club at the temple by involving them in a reminiscence project. She was convinced that it would be a highly therapeutic experience for her elders to be able to tell their stories and that it would increase their self-esteem to have these stories conveyed to a wider audience by professional actors. Her commitment to the project and her confidence in the team were essential elements, opening the door for us to an otherwise closed community and enabling the elders to put their trust in us. Since the men and women in the group met in separate spaces in the temple, we agreed to work with them in this way. The advantage of this arrangement was that both groups felt relaxed and able to speak freely.

Creating a resource with the elders

We began by asking for their co-operation as a group in making a reminiscence resource box that could be used in the future to stimulate the memories of other Asian people. We showed them some of the thematic collections of reminiscence artefacts and images we had already made to give them an idea of what we meant. For example we brought in a box full of toys and games saying: 'This is a box that we've prepared about games played by English children in the past. If we were to prepare an Indian reminiscence box on the games you played as children, what would we need to put in it?' Stimulated by the items in the box, people started talking about the equivalent games they had played in their youth. They brought in items from home and the men even made small model ploughs and cloth kites like the ones they remembered making as children. We explored many different themes in this way, such as weddings, festivals and cooking, and when the show went out on tour, the reminiscence box we had made together went with it to stimulate discussion with the audiences before and after the performance.

The actors improvise to stimulate further reminiscence

Based on some of the stories emerging from initial contact with the group, we developed some roughly improvised scenes to take back to the group in order to stimulate a deeper discussion. One very touching scene was about an Asian woman coming over to England with her children and being met at Heathrow Airport by her husband, who had already been here for some years. The actors performed this scene, showing the husband greeting her and the shyness between them on their journey home to the cold and unfamiliar house which awaited her. The elders reacted very strongly to that improvisation, the women identifying with the sadness, fear and isolation of the wife, and the men with the bitter-sweet mixture of feelings on the part of the husband: his pride in having worked hard to earn enough money to provide a home for his wife and disappointment at her initial reaction.

The elders participate through story-telling and improvisation

Many of the women in that room also had a story about how it had been for them coming to Britain, and so I asked them to go back to that time and to share some of their thoughts on their arrival here. Some of them even agreed to get up and show how it was for them, how nervous they had been of re-meeting their husbands after long separation, how cold and lonely they had felt, their fears for their children settling in this new country and their longings for home. These stories, enacted in the mother tongue by the older people, triggered further discussion in the group, with translation for the non-Punjabi-speaking members of the Age Exchange team.

Individual interviews

The actors went into the homes of some of the older people we had met through the Sikh temple and through our contact with Rosie Bedi. As their social worker, she was very heavily involved in arranging the interviews, translating where necessary and encouraging their involvement in the theatre-making process. Some of the actors had their own contacts, and interviewed additional elders through their own family networks. They even interviewed their immediate family members, a process which they said was very moving and revealing for them.

The actors participate in the devising process

Time was given during the devising period for the actors to explore through story-telling and improvisation their own relationship with the interview material. They were able to draw on their own memories of migration, adaptation and family upheaval. The rehearsal process was intensely personal, bordering on psycho-drama at times. The relevance of the actors' experience was crucial to their successful portrayal of the elders' lives, and the play benefited greatly from their sensitivity to the underlying issues.

Still images generate scenes

At the beginning of the rehearsal period, I asked the actors what photographs and images they had seen on the walls of the houses where they had been interviewing. One actor had seen an old framed photograph of the elder's father, standing very stiff and proud in his army uniform, in a carefully composed shot with his wife and children around him. As a starting point for improvisation in rehearsal, I asked him to recreate the photograph in a pose using the other actors. The military father entered the frame first and invited his wife and children to join him. The actors then broke out of the image into improvised story-telling. Several sequences in the play were devised from similar 'still' images, some based on the photos the actors had seen on people's walls, and some based on their own memories, and these 'stills' stayed in the show right through into the final production. They punctuated the action and were lit with a brighter light, followed by a moment of darkness, mirroring the frozen moments recorded in the few photos retained by the elders, and then the action of the next scene would come out of those still images.

Building a scenario

We decided quite early on in the devising process to draw on the material we had collected in the research stage to create a fictional but representative central character called Kirtar. We would follow his story from childhood to old age, with the other three actors playing his mother and father, his wife, his children and all the incidental characters. The first part of the play would be set in rural India and would draw on the childhood memories of our sources, the precarious living they gained from the land through the vicissitudes of flood and drought, the family and wedding arrangements and the danger of debt. The central section of the play would explore the time around the central character's decision to leave and his first experiences in England. The grief of a mother who does not believe in her son's fantasy of a quick return home as a rich man, but foresees instead the inevitable departure of her entire family, would be contrasted with the courage and optimism of the young man as he travels his great journey and copes with gruelling work and testing living conditions. The last part of the play would explore the arrival and settlement of the rest of the family in England, their schooling and growing up years, and the trauma for the central character in adapting to the host culture's alien views on marriage, family life and old age.

Distilling the stories

While drawing on the interviews, and reflecting the many stories we had heard, we would seek their essential elements, and represent the archetypal life journey through sound, action and image, performing it in a way which, as far as possible, would cut across all the language barriers and appeal directly to the emotions and the senses.

At moments of high drama, if something was spoken in English, the emotions underlying that speech were sung in a Punjabi song immediately afterwards, so music was used as another means of transcending language barriers.

The role of music and dance

We decided to borrow some of the idioms of the Bollywood film world, which would be recognisable to many of our audiences and would help non-Punjabi speakers to follow because of the strong gestural element and the convention of incorporating music and dance to strengthen the emotional high points of the story. For example, the tragic mother is given a set-piece song of grief with accompanying dramatic gestures when her son leaves India for England, and in another scene the four actors break into a Bangra song and dance routine associated with the plenty of harvest time. For minor characters in the play, such as the moneylender, we employed the Bollywood device of the comic stock figure using stereotypical gestures and having an accompanying musical signature tune. For wedding sequences and temple scenes, we used well-known songs in which the audience could participate. We borrowed from the temple all the necessary musical instruments, such as tabla, dholuk and chumta, instruments which many of the intended audience would recognise and remember.

An economical approach to production

For the initial production, these were the only items we had to take on tour, as there were almost no props at all (except a bedroll which doubled as a baby!) and very few changes of costume. Later productions kept to this minimalist approach, but we added a backcloth painted by a talented Indian designer, Suresh Vedak, showing a stylised image of an Indian village painted predominantly in brown and white. The inspiration for this was the village art-form of creating pictures by setting rice grains into the dung walls of the houses. We also added to our team a multi-talented Pakistani musician who played tabla and harmonium. His playing and beautiful singing greatly enriched the emotional intensity of the play, smoothed the continuity and also tapped into many more memories of the elders for whom we were performing.

The migration in sound and action

An example will illustrate how we portrayed the young protagonist saying farewell to his family, setting out on his journey, travelling by bullock cart to the nearest town, then on to the big city by train and then, over land, sea and air, to his arrival in Britain.

EXTRACT FROM *ROUTES: THE JOURNEY OF A LIFETIME*

> *Kirtar is leaving home, waving to his mother, wife and children. Wife and mother are waving back and singing a traditional song of departure.*
>
> SONG: 'Ja Way Pradesia'
>
> *The actors freeze on end of song.*
>
> KIRTAR: (*Turning to audience*) With a heavy heart I started my journey. At the main road I leapt on a tonga.
>
> *Cast make vocal sound effects representing oxen pulling cart along. Kirtar jogs in rhythm and continues addressing audience.*

Farewell song from Routes: *(left to right) Rosalene Dean and Robina Mir. Backcloth by Suresh Vedak*

KIRTAR: I told my travelling companions my plans to go to England to work. They agreed with me that it was a very good plan. Soon we were at the nearest station town.

Cast make sound effects representing station environment, including steam trains. whistles, calls, market traders, etc.

Kirtar: I bought my ticket to Delhi and boarded my train.

Train sounds continue under the following, with Kirtar looking out of imaginary window at passing landscape

Kirtar: Fields that were so familiar to me fled into the distance. I wondered what awaited me in Delhi. Soon the train was pulling into Delhi station.

The cast make sounds and actions to create the mayhem of Delhi station as Kirtar fights his way through them.

KIRTAR: I made my way to the agent. (*Kirtar keeps talking to the audience, as he mimes collecting the necessary papers*) Passport. Ticket. Voucher. With apprehension, I boarded the plane bound for London, England. India disappeared over the horizon.

Cast produce sound of plane rising in rush of air, as Kirtar twirls in circular movement as he travels across the stage, arms outstretched as the plane wings, talking to audience over his shoulder as he flies. As he arrives cast are silent.

The theatrical challenge of working bi-lingually

In another scene, based on experience of the father of another cast member, Kirtar arrives in England and cheerfully takes the only work he can get feeding the furnace in an ironworks, and sleeping in his cousin Ravi's desperately overcrowded house, alternating use of the bed around the requirements of shift work. In the extract below, the Punjabi lines have been translated for the reader. In the performance, both the Punjabi and English speeches were supported by gesture and action to help those in the audience who did not speak the language.

Kirtar learns a new way of life in Routes: *(left to right) Rez Kempton and Seva Dalival*

RAVI: O Kirtari chal day shift te teri gal ho gai ay. Main tenu kum sikha ke shift te la aaoon. (*Meaning: I have made arrangements for you to work. I'll teach you and you can start your shift.*)

Both walk across stage to factory area.

RAVI: Hello Foreman. Eh nawan bunda mein training deynda haan aetheron chukaya vich paya otheron chukia vich paya te button button hun toon kar. (*Meaning: I have brought this young man to the job as agreed and will train him.*)

Hoon hoon, shovel shovel…into furnace. Hoon hoon. Into furnace. Shovel shovel. Button button…

Ravi mimes shifting heavy material into the furnace and pressing machine buttons. He teaches Kirtar the work.

Foreman ji theek kum kar reha hai. (*Meaning: Well, Foreman, is he doing the job to your satisfaction?*)

KIRTAR: Thanks, Ravi Ji.

Ravi goes home to bed. Kirtar shovels with great energy and presses the buttons.

Button button. I can do this. Button button.

He gets slower with tiredness and goes home.

Wake up, Ravi. Work time.

RAVI: Sat sri kal Foreman Ji. Button button.

As Ravi works, Kirtar tosses in sleep.

KIRTAR: (*Tossing, turning and muttering in his sleep*) Button. Button.

RAVI: (*Waking Kirtar*) Uth kirtarey aj pay day, ae pay day!

KIRTAR: (*Working hard at furnace*) The work was hard, but when I received my pay-packet my tiredness vanished.

Kirtar stretches out his hand and receives imaginary envelope and counts notes in disbelief.

Seven pounds. I will send half home to my wife and family. That's almost a hundred rupees.

He goes home to wake Ravi.

KIRTAR: Ravi, Ravi, work. Look, seven pounds.

(*Taking two pounds away as rent*) Bachey tera khat aaya ey. Letter for you Kirtar.

Ravi hands Kirtar an imaginary letter which he reads.

KIRTAR: My dear husband, got your letter…

WIFE: (*Continues reading her letter to Kirtar*) Thank you for the money. You will be glad to know that I have got my jewellery back from the money-lender. We miss you very much. Maji and the children are well. When are you coming back? Your loving wife, Banto.

She kisses imaginary letter and blows it over to her husband. Wife sings a traditional song of waiting and missing a loved one.

SONG: Jana tha hum se door...

KIRTAR: (*Listening to her singing, then stands*) Five years were too long. I must send for my wife and children immediately. (*Writes imaginary letter*) My dear wife, I am in good health. Work is hard but going very well. I am sending money for you and the children to come and join me

Kirtar kisses letter and blows it across the world to his wife.

In this almost diagrammatic manner, the play was able to cover the years of grafting, asocial hours, cramped living, saving money and loneliness in a way which would reverberate for all immigrant viewers of the play.

The excitement of working in a bilingual context was that we could move a long way from straight narrative into a freer interpretation, distilling each story to its key elements, using movement, gesture and tone supported by narrative in one of the languages or alternating languages, but also underscored with music and rhythmical sounds conveying the atmosphere and emotion. The result had elements of opera and dance.

Increasing naturalism portraying family tensions

In the second half of the play, concerned with the family acclimatising to life in England, we included more naturalistic scenes with at least one character speaking in Punjabi and the other half of the conversation spoken in English. This had the benefit of ensuring that the meaning was clear to people who spoke only one of these languages, and also reflecting the growing reality of life for immigrant families in Britain of generations speaking different languages and finding communication difficult.

There were scenes reflecting the stories we had heard concerning the teasing and outright racism experienced by immigrant children in classrooms where there were almost no other Indian pupils and no Indian teachers to give them positive role models, and how parents often took opposing views as to how best to deal with the situation. We included in the play a more lyrical imagistic scene showing the mother taking her teenage daughter back to India to visit her grandmother and the place where she was born, in the hope that she would stay true to traditional Indian values, and the positive effects of this visit on the daughter's sense of identity.

However, many of the stories we were told had been about parents' dismay at finding the younger generation increasingly adopting the host culture and rejecting parental guidelines on dietary issues, dress, attitudes to the opposite sex and behaviour in public. So we created a contrasting scene in which the son turns his back on traditions of respect for parents by becoming increasingly rebellious until his father eventually throws him out of the house.

KIRTAR: With my boy we had a problem. I did not know what to do.

BANTO: Kithey ja rehanen. (*Meaning: Where are you going?*)

SEVA: Out.

BANTO: Kis wailey vapis aawaynga. (*Meaning: When will you be back?*)

SEVA: Don't know. Later.

BANTO:Khana kha ke ja. (*Meaning: Have something to eat first.*)

SEVA: Don't want your curry. I'll have McDonalds.

BANTO: Dekho menu ki khenda ey. (*Meaning: Look how he talks to me*)

KIRTAR: Hey, you are going out? What about the supper your mother has cooked?

SEVA: I don't want to smell of garlic.

KIRTAR: You don't want to smell of garlic? Are you ashamed?

SEVA: Yeah, I am.

KIRTAR: All right. You have no respect for us. Pack your bags and go.

SEVA: Right. (*Seva goes and packs.*)

BANTO: (*To Kirtar*) Tussi ki keh rehey ho. (*Meaning: What are you saying?*)

Banto tries to stop Seva going.

SEVA: (*Pushing her aside*) Mum…get out of my way.

KIRTAR: If you come back, I'll break your neck.

Seva storms out with his bag over his shoulder.

Hopes and disappointments

I remember one comment which was delivered by an old man in one of the reminiscence sessions where he was talking about his hopes and expectations in Britain and it was translated as:

> When you're a young man you plant a seed and you hope that, as you grow older, that seed will grow into a great tree, so that when you are old you can sit in the shade of that tree. Where is my tree?

His perception of how his children had let him down, and his sense of betrayal and disappointment of his hopes and dreams, were so dramatic that we decided to give his speech more or less verbatim in the play. It echoed the feelings of many elders that there had been all sorts of cultural and personal losses, and that they felt these acutely in old age when they were more vulnerable and when memories of their own more respectful youth were becoming very sharp. They felt the loss of their home country, how far away it was and the impossibility of returning there, and this was often compounded by the sense of loss when their own children seemed emotionally distant. With this in mind, we planned to end the play with the parents in their old age alone in their London home, the mother wishing desperately to hear from her errant son.

The elders check our progress in rehearsal

When we had agreed the shape of the play and prepared some scenes, we invited the original group of older Asians (with whom we had had continuing contact during the rehearsal period) to watch a run-through and give us some feedback. They had been looking forward to this moment very much as, by this time, they had quite a strong sense of investment in the show. They were very happy with the way the play was coming together, but they expressed reservations about the final scene. They strongly requested of us that there should be a more positive ending. They said that very often their children actually did return to the fold to some degree, sometimes having married non-Indian girls or boys and there were difficulties, but everybody had to make compromises. They did not want to put across the image of an irretrievably divided family, because they felt that they were in the process of making a great many adjustments in order to keep contact with their children and their changing way of life. We agreed to alter the ending accordingly and gave the play a more positive conclusion, but we felt that the father's sense of loss should be retained in the play, the sense that just as much had been lost as gained.

Inviting the older Asian people to the rehearsal not only gave us the benefit of hearing their response to our work in progress, but also gave us the opportunity to see if they could follow the story as told in two languages, English and Punjabi, with gesture, mime and music to support it. We were satisfied that they could and set off on a national tour of Asian day centres and temples with a good heart.

Routes on tour

We toured the show to Asian day centres, clubs, temples and community centres in London, and then we took it to other areas of England including the West Midlands, Leeds, Manchester and Liverpool, places where there was a large Asian minority.

The show was revived several times as there was so much demand for it. I was interested to see whether the show would also work in other European countries with elders from other immigrant groups, who spoke neither English nor Punjabi, so we toured the show to many venues in Belgium, the Netherlands and Germany. It was received very warmly and led to many new productions by and about minority ethnic elders in those countries. We played it in Rotterdam to elders from Surinam and the Moluccan Islands who had had a parallel sort of journey and those performances led to very animated post-show discussions. We played to Moroccans in Brussels and to Turkish audiences all over Germany. I have strong memories of the piece playing in Kassel to a predominantly Turkish audience who were deeply moved, in some cases to tears, having clearly recognised their own migration experience in the drama, without sharing a word of common language. One elderly gentleman in the audience said to me: 'I didn't understand a word, but I understood everything.'

There was an enormously empathetic reaction to *Routes* at every venue, and people who saw it still remember it vividly and the feelings associated with it. The use of comic stereotypes for minor characters, juxtaposed with the sensitive and more naturalistic portrayal of the central characters, with whom the audience identified, combined with the dual language text and the accompanying Indian music and dance, created a powerful theatrical experience which spoke directly to many audiences.

Summary

This chapter has explored reminiscence theatre based on the lives of older people from minority ethnic groups. The first example was a multicultural model in which the migration stories told by older people from many parts of the world were conveyed in English with some use of mother tongues by performers of different ethnicities. The second example looked at working with elders from the Indian subcontinent, and creating a play with plot and characters based on their stories, performed by actors with an Indian background in a Punjabi and English text. Both projects were very process-based with the actors taking responsibility for scene development based around the interviews they had conducted and their own lived experience. Both productions involved performing to many first-time venues, the vast majority of which responded extremely favourably to the production and to the creative possibilities it opened up for further reminiscence work with minority ethnic elders. These were rarely heard voices at the time, but it has been increasingly recognised that the past and present experience of these older people should be recorded and listened to, not just by younger people in their own communities, but also by the majority population.

CHAPTER 5

Dramatising Jewish
and Irish Elders' Memories

The reminiscence theatre plays *A Place To Stay* and *Routes* dealt with the remembered past of minority ethnic elders with a highly visible cultural and racial identity. In skin colour, language, religion, dress and customs, there were clear differences distinguishing these elders from the host population. It was important to capture the experience of the older generation of immigrants who came to Britain after the war, whose descendants in British towns are still just as visibly different, but whose sense of their own history may be weakened by time, lack of information, or integration into the host culture.

Valuing cultural and religious difference

In recording the memories of Irish and Jewish elders, difference was more a matter of culture and religion than any visible heritage. The motivation was rather to hold on to and value that difference in a society where integration through inter-marriage and the geographical break-up of their communities was diluting the strong sense of identity and community so valued by the older generation. The connection and similarity lies in the fact that all these minority elders, black, Asian, Irish and Jewish, felt that transmitting their experience was important and urgent in that they were among the last representatives of a particular minority group who had experienced a particular life journey and made a fundamental transition and that their experience could be of value and interest to younger generations in their communities.

In all these cases, the elders involved in the interviews felt validated by both the recording process and the theatrical playing back to a wider audience of their lives, or lives very similar to theirs. It enabled them to re-experience with others the reality of their younger days, and it increased their sense of self-worth, emphasising as it did the interest and importance in the present of their individual and shared past (Myerhoff 1980;[8] Strimling 2004[9]).

From Stepney Green to Golders Green

A vanishing community

In the early years of the twentieth century, there had been a tightly knit self-contained Jewish community living in the east end of London. I am Jewish myself, but, having grown up in Manchester, I knew little about the history of what had become known as the Jewish East End. I was particularly fascinated to learn more about what it had been like to be part of this vibrant community and wanted to record the lives of a generation of older people who grew up there. There was some urgency about this matter, even back in 1987, as this community was fast dispersing across London and its leafier suburbs, and many of those who could recall the East End in its heyday were then already in their 70s and 80s. I conducted a lot of the interviews myself with groups of Jewish elders in day centres, care homes, and also with individuals I knew through family connections and friends. I was also able to call on a network of Jewish friends to conduct further interviews with members of their synagogues and family contacts. All the interviewers had connections with those who were being interviewed, so there was a level of shared understanding and a high degree of trust.

Winning trust

Generating this sense of confidence and trust is important in any reminiscence project where people may be sharing stories of great personal significance, perhaps for the first time, but it is of particular importance with any minority group. None of the productions described here would have been possible without a great deal of preliminary work with community and faith leaders and key members of voluntary sector groups working closely with the elders. Winning the commitment of these 'door openers' by demonstrating the seriousness of one's intentions and pointing up how the project will be reciprocal, with benefits to the elders, is vital if one is to overcome the incipient distrust which is wholly understandable in minority communities.

Interviewees with confidence and panache

It is also important to recognise that approaches to reminiscence and attitudes to the telling and recording of memories will be culturally specific and must be respected. For example, the stories and songs from women and men in the Indian community were collected separately, as it would have been uncomfortable and very limiting for each group to speak or sing in the hearing of the other. In the case of the Jewish elders, some of the general 'reminiscence rules' did not seem to apply. The received wisdom on running reminiscence sessions is that eight or ten participants is about the right number and that more would be inhibiting. So when researching for the play in a north-east London synagogue, I was startled by the fact that a microphone had been set up on the stage by the acting rabbi, and 200 people were waiting in the audience. I was sure that nobody was going to stand up and speak in these circumstances, but there was an immediate queue for the microphone and people had absolutely no problem about coming up to tell their memories. There was even an element of showmanship about it: 'Do you want a sad story or a happy story?' The old people, mainly in their 80s, just relished the opportunity to tell stories, especially to such a receptive and 'tuned in' audience of contemporaries. Of course many of these people were followed up individually and in smaller groups where the exchange of stories with one another provoked much spontaneous recall, but the fact is that public oration had a role and purpose in that synagogue hall, reflecting the confidence and panache of the congregation as individuals and as a group.

Many of the Jewish elders were interviewed far from the East End of their childhood, in the relatively well-heeled areas of Golders Green and Hendon (the play was finally entitled *From Stepney Green to Golders Green*) where they had settled in adult life. Many of them were quite comfortably off in their later years, but they remained very proud of their humble origins, retaining very fond memories of the closeness and energy of that community. Indeed, there was a tendency among the elderly people to romanticise their youth in the Jewish East End, but then there were always story-tellers in the reminiscence sessions who brought the group back to the harsh realities of daily life in those days and ensured a balanced picture.

The scenario emerges

Through a series of group interviews and individual sessions conducted in people's own homes, a scenario for the forthcoming production began to emerge, following the life stages of people in their 70s and 80s who would have been children in the East End in the first three decades of the twentieth century. We would need to start with their fathers and mothers, and why they came to London in the 1880s onwards to escape the pogroms in Poland or Lithuania or Romania, often bringing little more with them on this great journey than a bedroll and small items of portable memorabilia. Some of our interviewees had had to translate in their childhood and youth for parents who spoke only Yiddish, though many of the older refugees did attend English classes provided by the community. The speakers described the crowded tenements where they had grown up, remembering how every family member, however young, had to help in the serious business of earning extra pennies to keep the household going, with stitching, pressing, rolling tobacco into cigarettes and many other 'home work' activities occurring within doors, in addition to the usual domestic tasks.

In the creation of this play we followed the general rule in reminiscence theatre making that, if many of our interviewees remembered a similar story or scene from their young days, this would certainly have to make its way into the scenario, as it would clearly reverberate with the intended audience. Fairly fond memories of school days and less rosy recollections of strict religious observance would be followed by tales of hard apprenticeships in which young lads and girls carried out punishing physical tasks for pennies. The life of the old East End markets and traders and the sporting and cultural life, including the boxing rings and the Yiddish Theatre, still flourishing in their youth, would be evoked to transport our audiences back to that vivid time. We would include many delightful tales we heard of romance and courting in the 1930s. This was the time when a lot of our interviewees got married, with elaborately catered events and Hollywood-style studio wedding photography sessions (usually undertaken by Jewish East End photographers). What better way to end the show than with a Jewish wedding?

Traumatic memories and reminiscence theatre

In many ways it seemed appropriate to end the drama in about 1938 as, very soon after that, the Jewish East End was breaking up. With the arrival of war, people were evacuated, called up into the services or munitions work, were bombed out, or just chose to move away to more salubrious areas. Our story would not cover Jewish people's stories of escaping the Holocaust or of their loss of family members during that period. There were two reasons for this decision: one was that the vast majority of the people whose recollections we recorded for this project had actually grown up in England and had limited contact with family in Nazi Germany or other occupied countries. The other reason was that our show was mainly going to captive audiences of Jewish old people in synagogue clubs, day centres and care homes and these audiences would certainly include Holocaust survivors, some of whom would have made the decision, for one reason or another, to lock away those memories for ever. It could have been very disturbing for such individuals to be presented with a dramatised version of that traumatic time. There is always an unease in rendering such atrocities in a dramatic form, and this unease has not abated, despite some remarkable pieces of theatre about the period such as Joshua Soboll's *Ghetto* (1989) and Martin Sherman's *Bent* (1979), both of which have had a great impact on general theatre-going audiences who have been in a position to make an informed choice to see these plays.

It has, of course, become more and more important to record the testimony of survivors, as those who remember are getting older all the time and have an increasing sense of urgency to set the record straight, especially in the face of pernicious historical 'doubters'. The decision to share such painful experience has to be made voluntarily, on an individual basis and with appropriate support. There is a case for creating theatre from individual stories, with the consent of the giver when he or she is still alive to give it. One such case at Age Exchange concerned a Jewish lady, Helen Aronson, whose remarkable story of surviving the Lodz Ghetto in Poland was the inspiration for a Youth Theatre play performed by non-Jewish children 13 years after the original professional production. The director, David Savill, and the young people worked closely with Helen and gained greatly in their understanding of the past and how readily its lessons can be applied to the present. Helen's family, including her grandchildren, attended the production which was a source of great pride to them, but even in these felicitous circumstances, it took a huge emotional toll on Helen who lost many nights' sleep as a result of recalling her terrible experiences and narrow escapes. The years which separated this Youth Theatre production from the show described here had encompassed the fiftieth anniversary of the end of the war, which was an occasion for much hitherto unrecorded reminiscence, and also major efforts at systematised documentation by

Steven Spielberg and others, which were not under consideration back in 1987 when we created the show *From Stepney Green to Golders Green*.

Working with Jewish performers

Three extremely experienced professional Jewish actors joined the Age Exchange Company, one of whom had participated in the preliminary interviewing. Their Jewish-ness was important for many reasons: they needed to have some insight into and connection with the memories, and they needed to be able to empathise with and respond to the memories of audience members in the post-show discussion sessions, which in the case of this show were very lengthy and lively. It was also part of the transmission process of Age Exchange implied within the company's name to have younger people learning about and representing the lives of their elders, as this sense of community continuity gives the actors themselves more personal satisfaction. An even more important reason for generally choosing performers from the same cultural background is that when actors impersonate people from a race other than their own, it can easily give offence, disturbing the sensitivities of contributors and audience members alike. In the case of the *A Place To Stay* production described earlier, actors from different ethnicities helped in the representation of one another's stories, but the lead communication with the audience for each scene was always taken by the performer from that ethnic group.

From improvisation to verbatim script

We began the rehearsal process by improvising around the interview material we had assembled. The quality of the actors' improvisations was exceptionally high and I remember being tremendously moved by what they did, feeling that I could easily script from it. But after three or four days of improvisation work, the actors themselves said that they felt the dramatic power of the original interviews was stronger than anything we could improvise from them. Unanimously, we chose to go back to the material we had recorded and to make a verbatim show. Only in this way could we capture the authenticity of tone of the Jewish elders, the colourful ways they had of telling a story, the idiosyncratic turns of phrase and the special sense of humour. For example, in the following extract, all the dialogue was given to us by the original story-teller remembering relatives crowding into the house at weekends:

> GIRL: It was card playing amongst the grownups. Solo.
>
> CARD PLAYING WOMAN: So who didn't put in the kitty yet?
>
> CARD PLAYING MAN: By my life I put in already.
>
> CARD PLAYING WOMAN: Come on, come on. I'm sitting here like a golem with the ace and the jack in my hand.
>
> CARD PLAYING MAN: Believe me, mein enemies should have such a partner. Next week, better you should go to the pictures instead.

Our show needed to portray their world using their language and vocabulary if we were to awaken in the audience that sense of a common inheritance which could inform their communication with one another in the present.

Using verbatim material taken from group discussion

At one of the group reminiscence sessions with the Waltham Forest Friendship Club, I had begun by asking: 'Tell me about some of the characters you remember in the East End.' And the older people named them all, chipping in one after another. We used this typical torrent of memories in the script at the opening of the play, the actors reproducing exactly the feeling of spontaneous recall which had occurred at the time of the recording. This enabled the audience to tune in very quickly to the period and place, recognising characters from their own past, and in the post-show discussions to enlarge on the list with their own colourful memories. After the opening music, the actors in turn spoke these lines, all taken directly from the transcribed group interview, some short interjections and others longer stories, all underlined with action and gesture by the actors, who were telling about the characters and being them at the same time.

> LINDA: In the Whitechapel area where I grew up, they were all Jewish people. Practically our whole street was full of Jews. And the characters! What about the characters?

> CHARLIE: There was Slumpy the coke man who did removals with a horse and cart. He was a short man, immensely tough and strong. Slumpy had a regular ringside seat at the Premier Land where they had the boxing. We used to see every Sunday all the big contests, Kid Lewis, Harry Mizler, Benny Caplan.

> LINDA: In our turning there was Benjamin the glazier, who carried his glass on his back.

> *Charlie staggers across stage, miming holding large sheet of glass.*

> LINDA: He was a drunk, but he never ever broke any glass putting windows in. And in the synagogue...

> *Charlie dons tallis (prayer shawl).*

> LINDA: His voice was above everybody's you know, in the chanting and the prayers.

> CHARLIE: (*Singing*) Baruch Atah Adoshem...

> Linda: He didn't drink on the Sabbath.

> *Violin lead in and Charlie does a shuffling dance while singing.*

> CHARLIE: (*Singing*) Old Solomon Levy. Tralala tralala la...

LINDA: Old Solomon Levy, you might have heard of him. He was a character who came round several streets. He had a chap with him who used
to blow on the tooter, the penny whistle. We lived on the second floor,
and we threw coins out. As a sort of prank we used to heat halfpennies
in a shovel on the fire and throw them out. And he used to hold his
hat up and his hat was full of holes where the coins used to fall
through them.

This is played out in parallel with the narration.

Celebrating Shabbat in From Stepney Green to Golders Green: *(left to right) Linda Polan,
Charles Wegner, Gillian Gallant*

Stimulating the senses

In many reminiscence sessions, discussions of food preparation and meals stimulated many memories of Jewish family life, religious observances and community
culture. Food is always an enjoyable topic in reminiscence groups, usually bringing
with it memories of family relationships, and enabling elders to place themselves
back in their childhood home environment. Incorporating such sensory memories
into the scripts, especially of shows exploring minority ethnic culture, gives audiences a ready means of tapping into their shared background and experiences,
exchanging recipes and recalling the wonderful tastes and smells emanating from
remembered kitchens past. Some productions have taken this idea to its logical
conclusion. Ekta, an Asian elders group working with their director Ajay Chhabra

some years later in 1997, actually incorporated the cooking of an Indian meal into their fantasy tale of doing well in Britain by setting up a successful Indian restaurant. The intense pleasure of seeing the play and smelling the spices as the meal was cooked in a small studio theatre will never be forgotten by those who saw the play, no matter what their ethnic background! In *From Stepney Green to Golders Green*, we limited ourselves to the words:

CHARLIE: I remember the aroma, the smell of the cucumber, the pickled cucumber.

GILLIAN: I remember walking through the Lane, Petticoat Lane, big sacks of bagels, they were hot and the smell was gorgeous.

LINDA: And Mrs Marks – she sold herrings in the Lane – she stood there with about ten or twelve barrels all around her – winter and summer she stood there. She was skinning those herrings and cutting them up.

CHARLIE: When I was about five or six years old there were steaming hot peanuts in this great big sack. You'd get a handful of peanuts and they were boiling and they were lovely.

LINDA: I still remember the fragrance and the taste of those peanuts.

GILLIAN: Particularly on Friday there were chicken stalls.

CHARLIE: And a woman would come over and pick up a chicken and feel it here and feel it there.

Charlie acts as stallholder turning to Linda who is now playing the role of the customer.

You remind me of my daughter, she goes out with fellas who feel a bit here and feel a bit there...but they never buy.

Many of the stories I had heard from Asian and Caribbean elders were about social and cultural isolation in 1950s and 1960s London, with the main dramas of their lives as immigrants to England occurring within the immediate family behind firmly closed doors. In complete contrast to this, when it came to Jewish memories, which were of course of an earlier period of 1920s and 1930s London when doors were more often open and the street was a great meeting place, people told us that families knew a great deal about their neighbours. They told us how their parents, often very poor themselves, would find discreet ways of helping neighbours in even worse straits, without in any way making them feel beholden. An extract from the play reflects this strong sense of community in the Jewish East End, experienced through many small acts of generosity. We wanted to avoid sentimentality, so chose a humorous boyhood memory given by an old man, who enjoyed retrospectively the chutzpah of his elderly neighbour. The basic story was delivered direct to the audience and inter-cut with dialogue and action, so it was both remembered in the past and happening in the present:

LINDA: Of course nothing was cheap to people who hadn't got anything. We were desperately poor.

GILLIAN: But people were generous. Everybody helped everybody else.

LINDA: (*Playing Mother*) Oh Isaac, I've cooked too much fish. Have this.

GILLIAN: They always made the excuse that they'd cooked too much or something like that.

CHARLIE: And Mrs Friedlander who lived in our road always stood outside her door on Saturday mid-day.

Linda folds her arms as Mrs Friedlander and watches Charlie as he goes on his errand.

CHARLIE: The reason was I used to go and collect the cholent (*a casserole prepared before the Sabbath and cooked in the nearest baker's oven for post-synagogue Sabbath lunch*) from the baker's shop. And Mrs Friedlander knew I was going for the cholent.

Charlie acts as young boy running past his neighbour, Mrs Friedlander.

LINDA: (*Playing Mrs Friedlander*) Are you going for the cholent?

CHARLIE: And when I used to come back I'd see Mrs Friedlander still standing there. (*Playing boy, whispering to his mother*) 'Mum, Mrs Friedlander's still outside.' So we took some out and gave it to Mrs Friedlander.

LINDA: (*As Mrs Friedlander, receiving her plate of cholent*) Oh, thank you.

CHARLIE: She'd say, as though it was unexpected.

Visual and musical memories evoked through theatre

For this play, the stage-flats were painted from images in the local history library and photographs lent to us by the contributors showing shop fronts from that period with a mixture of English and Yiddish lettering advertising their wares. The minimal props were displayed on hat stands and small tables on the acting area: yarmulkes (skull caps), tallisses (prayer shawls) and elegant pieces of millinery and flags.

Music, as always, was a very strong element of the show, and in this case many of the songs remembered from childhood were sung in Yiddish. As the characters in the play grew up, their integration into the mainstream culture was reflected in the switch to popular English and American romantic music of the 1930s, which they remembered from their courting days. To underscore the domestic and religious scenes, all the music was played on culturally appropriate musical instruments, such as violin and clarinet, with much use of the Jewish East European Klezmer style, which is now so popular again and which had emotional overtones for many of the elders.

From Stepney Green to Golders Green: *(left to right) Charles Wegner, Linda Polan and Gillian Gallant*

A sense of ownership on the part of contributors

When we performed the show for Jewish audiences their sense of identity and of having once belonged to a vibrant close-knit community came back very strongly. Many people felt that, despite increasing prosperity, they had lost a great deal in the move to other parts of London. We were representing and celebrating a very special culture and the audiences found an enormous amount of pleasure in the detailed evocation of a vanished time and place.

In the venues where we both conducted interviews and then returned to perform the show, people stood up in the audience, turned around and said to the rest of the audience, 'This is my memories. I told them all this. And I want you to know this is my story.' People had a huge sense of identification with the play and ownership of it. It gave rise to a great deal of post-show discussion and often paved the way for the setting up of ongoing reminiscence sessions and further less formal exchange of shared memories. In this way, the show not only reaffirmed the common past of the elderly Jewish audiences in synagogue clubs and residential homes, but it was also a force for social cohesion and close communication in the present. This is a vital ingredient in reminiscence theatre and, increasingly, the organisers of activities in older people's centres are aware that they are not only booking a performance, but giving an impetus to reminiscence-based activities which can increase the happiness and improve the quality of life of their clients and other staff members.

Transferability of reminiscence theatre shows to other regions

We took the production to Jewish communities all over the country, playing in synagogues, in Jewish old people's homes and day centres in major cities. There were
about 40 performances, including several in Manchester, my home town. Jewish
people of my parents' generation who saw the show there demonstrated that they
were well able to transfer all the London information to the Manchester situation,
because they had a similar very tight-knit Jewish community in North Manchester
which had then anglicised itself over the years. Here, too, relatively small communities had survived in the original areas of settlement and for them the show was as
positive an experience as it had been for the remaining Jewish East End dwellers. It
is worth noting that all the shows described to date, though emanating from interviews conducted in specific geographical areas, have readily transferred to others.
Productions about women's war work, health, employment and housing in the
London area played well in Welsh and Scottish cities as well as across England, as
older people had equivalent experience to draw on, and the memories felt very
familiar.

Across The Irish Sea

The elderly Jewish community on whose memories *From Stepney Green to Golders
Green* was based had very often lost contact or cut off ties with their families'
original homelands in central and eastern Europe, countries they had been forced
out of by anti-semitisim. Their future stability depended on laying down firm roots
in their country of adoption. If they had moved house, it would be to another part
of Britain, probably within the London area.

Continuing links with the home country

However, when we worked with the Irish elders living in London, there was a
strong feeling that Ireland was still home and that ties with that country remained
strong, with families in frequent touch and often visiting. Many people in their old
age even nursed hopes of returning to Ireland for their final years and this contin-
ual sense of cultural and geographical duality and proximity was reflected in the
title we chose for the Irish reminiscence theatre production.

The Irish people who had come to London for work, whether in the building
trade, catering, nursing or domestic service, had settled down close to relatives
who had already made the journey and were widely scattered across the capital.
Their initial social focus had often been the nearest Roman Catholic church, or in
some cases a local Irish dance club where they could meet other Irish people. They
had usually stayed loyal to these organisations as they afforded to their families
down the generations a strong continuing sense of Irish identity, focused on music,
dance, religion and shared memories of home. For our initial interviews, we therefore worked through these churches and Irish clubs, beginning with group
interviews, followed by in-depth interviews with individuals in their own homes,
conducted mainly by Maxine O'Reilly, an Irish actress who also had many of her

own contacts. The individual interviews yielded such strong material that, when the accompanying book was produced, the stories were kept in their entirety (with minimal editing for clarity and flow) rather than cut up into shorter extracts grouped around key topics as was our usual practice (Schweitzer 1989a).

Creating the scenario from current concerns as well as memories

This play was created in 1988, when Irish people were still coming to England for work, though in far smaller numbers than previously because of increasing prosperity back home, and there was a ready audience keen to both tell and hear stories of the past. Four main themes emerged from the interviews, which we represented dramatically: fond memories of childhood in Ireland; the trauma of coming to work in England during and after the war years; settling down to family life over here; and growing old away from 'home'. Unlike the Jewish reminiscence show, it seemed appropriate in this production to bring the Irish reflections up to the present and reflect the common preoccupation with land and family 'across the water'.

Childhood memories of Ireland were particularly rich, with stories of rural life, green fields, peat bogs, riding to school over many miles on a donkey and dancing at the village crossroads on a Saturday night, all far removed from the highly urban childhood their own children had experienced in London. This divide was reflected in the scenery which was a painted coloured backcloth, rather in the style of an old postcard, showing a very green landscape and a small cottage, with side-flats painted as brick walls, one containing a red postbox, to represent London life and the distance from home.

There were tales of painful decisions to leave the crowded family home in search of work and a bit more excitement, coming to London and living alone in small rooms at the tops of houses or hotels, often taking live-in jobs in domestic service or as chambermaids, as this was the only way they could find accommodation in the face of intense anti-Irish prejudice. We also heard memories of happy days out at the races and of falling in and out of love! Quite a lot of Irish people were here during the war and wanted to talk about the contribution they'd made through the armed forces, munitions, and big building projects, stories which we decided it was important to include since people felt they had not been heard in a Britain which viewed Ireland's neutrality in the war with some ambivalence, if not outright hostility.

A live story-telling tradition

Story-telling has remained a very strong live tradition in Ireland, and perhaps because of this, the quality of the narratives we recorded was exceptionally high. Some of the interviewees, especially when narrating in a group, delivered quite long monologues to honour this tradition, telling well-honed tales, or 'set pieces'. There was no question that the play would be completely verbatim in order to capture the delightful turns of phrase and to reproduce the self-deprecating style of humour, which emerged time and time again during the interviews. In the example below, 'Tom' is allowed to tell the whole story through, with minimal intervention by other characters and no superfluous dramatisation:

TOM: Of course during the war there was rationing and all that.

LANDLADY: One egg a week.

TOM: The landlady used to keep mine.

LANDLADY: It hasn't arrived.

TOM: I found her son having it one morning. I remember one morning I nearly risked my life for an egg. I had to be in work at six o'clock, which meant me getting up about five. So I always told the landlady (*addressing her here and she exits*) not to bother getting up, and I'd get my own breakfast. Well, I was frying this egg, it had been about a month since I'd had an egg, and I said, 'Well, I'm definitely going to have this one.' When you couldn't get them you thought they were marvellous, you know. I was frying this egg, and the next thing, this crash alert came on in the factories round about, which meant that there was a doodlebug approaching your area. Well, I waited until this doodlebug was directly overhead, and I said, 'Well that's very near I'd better get out of here.' So I grabbed this frying pan with the egg in it, and started to run down the garden and as I was running down the garden I tripped. It was dark, and my egg went into the grass. That doodlebug was coming down at the time and I stayed there to pick up this fried egg. It shows you how you lose all sense of proportion!

The music and language of Ireland

Because of the cultural importance of Irish music, this show called for a dedicated musician playing traditional instruments, the Uilleann pipes, the bodhran, the whistle, accordion and the fiddle. This was in addition to the usual reminiscence theatre requirement of strong singing voices, dance skills and additional instrumental skills where possible. In this case, as well as traditional songs, many of them concerning a longing for home, music was also used to underscore scenes and call to mind for the audience the many traditional tunes they remembered from childhood and were happy to join in with in their old age. In the short extract which follows, the words of Kitty are performed against Irish reels played live on whistles and pipes, with the young girl and her partner dancing and twirling, in between her breathless commentary to the audience.

TOM: Sunday night was the big night for dances in Ireland. Living in a country place, the custom there was to have open air dances at the crossroads on fine summer evenings.

Live music is played and Kitty and the other actors dance.

Songs of home in Across The Irish Sea: *(standing left to right) Janet Bamford and Nell Phoenix; (seated) Eamonn McGuire and Frazer Hoyle (backcloth by Lisa Wilson)*

KITTY: You had your Sunday dress on, and fixed your hair up, and that was great entertainment. You saw the boys and things, you know. I wasn't very successful in the dance because I was very heavy on my feet. It was like wheeling a carthorse around the floor. A couple of fellows'd ask me to dance, well, I had sort of golden hair in waves, but they soon put me down again. I suppose I tripped them up!

TOM: The men would be on one side and the women would be on the other side.

KITTY: Well, they wouldn't ask you to dance when they were sober. Only when they were a bit merry. There might be some particular lad that you put you eye on, and he'd never ask you to dance. He'd go off with somebody else!

Music fades.

Performing in Ireland

As well as touring the show to Irish communities across England, we also took the production to Northern Ireland and to the Irish Republic. There, we were playing to people who had stayed at home, but many of whom had relatives who had made the decision to leave. They found it fascinating to hear of the difficulties experienced by young Irish men and women when they first went to London. The letters they had received were often heavily censored by the young people themselves to spare their families any anxiety. In the following example, Josie has left home to take work in a mental hospital, and cannot bring herself to tell her parents what it is really like there.

Josie is alone in her attic bedroom.

JOSIE: (*To audience*) Bridie put me in the ladies ward at first for to try and get me settled in and that was in the evening. The next morning was breakfast and there was one big huge dining room for all these people, all as mad as hatters and fighting amongst themselves. Bridie told me on no account to talk about politics or religion. It was a mad house. There were no drugs of any description. No treatment at all, except the straight jacket and the padded cell. They hadn't got cups and saucers, they had bowls and those bowls were flying here, there and everywhere. I ran like hell. I got to my bedroom and cried and cried.

Music link. Josie mimes writing a letter home.

JOSIE: Dear Mam, The uniform is blue and white. Very attractive. Our stockings and shoes are made on the premises by the patients. I shall get 30 shillings a month and I will be fed and clothed so I will send money home. Hope you are well. Love, Josie.

Music link as Josie seals the letter and her sister Kitty reads it in Ireland.

KITTY: (*Reading Josie's letter*) Hope you are well. Love, Josie. (*To audience*) So Josie is well settled. That's good.

Risking sadness

In England, during the post-performance discussions, audience members told us how the play had given expression to their own longing for 'home'. We met many people who had gone back to Ireland to try to settle there in their retirement, but often this had not worked out. Here Tom speaks for many of them in words taken directly from one of the interviews:

TOM: Mary and I were going back to Ireland to settle, but somehow it just didn't work out. It's very hard to feel at home when the first question you're asked is, when are you going back? It's brought home to you that you're on holiday, you're not really going back there for keeps. I think every Irish person has that dream, a man anyway, of going back to Ireland. It was a dream with me for 10 or 12 years and that's why I took early retirement really. I was going to go back there and find a little rose-covered cottage somewhere and settle down with a fishing rod and a dog and a pint of Guinness, a nice local pub somewhere but that soon fades.

CAST: (*Song with tin whistle accompaniment*)
    Lonely I wander through scenes of my childhood
    They call back to memory the happy days of yore
    Gone are the old folk, the house stands deserted
    No light in the window, no welcome at the door.

KITTY: My husband died 12 years ago. He'd been ill for a while before that. He was a good husband. It's surprising when you sit down and relive your life. I'm 50 years here now but I still don't feel like an Englishwoman. I've given strict instructions that I'm to be buried in Ireland, and I've enough money put by to take my body over there. They may have to pay their own fares to my funeral. (*Underscoring on tin whistle here*) If I sit in my living room at home, in my rocking chair, my thoughts go to Ireland, to the ground, the soil, the air, the hills, they don't change.

Reprise of 'Lonely' song with a brief 'hold' by all the performers, followed by a switch into the reel, 'Kitty Lie Over' played and danced by all the actors, who bow to each other and to the audience.

It did seem risky to end the play on this rather solemn note, but it was a genuine reflection of the shape of the interviews and touched all the audiences profoundly. The beauty of this kind of theatre is that music can underline a pensive mood and then serve to switch and lighten the atmosphere and create a joyous conclusion. The short pause followed by the reel allowed the audience to hold on to the moment of reflection, compare it with their own feelings, and then move on to a positive ending, representing the vitality of the Irish community sustained by music and dance from 'home'.

Hearing the voices 'direct'

In the second half of the twentieth century, there was a great flowering in mainstream theatre of shows based on Irish and Jewish communities by engaged writers drawing on their own experience, including *Dancing at Lughnasa* by Brian Friel (1999), *Stones in his Pockets* by Marie Jones (2000), *The Hamlet of Stepney Green* by Bernard Kops (1991) and *Chicken Soup with Barley* by Arnold Wesker (2001). All these productions have spoken for and to many thousands of people about their own lives, since the writers' acute ear for dialogue and knowledge of that community has captured well the time, place and distinctive language. The difference between these works and reminiscence theatre around these communities is that the former are expressions of a single writer's vision of the past and his own relationship with it, whereas the latter is an amalgam of many experiences from many sources, an opportunity to hear the voices direct, albeit shaped by the writer, director or the artistic team, and to appreciate the continuing impact of the big themes of culture and identity on the lives of 'ordinary people'.

Summary

The Jewish and Irish plays featured here show how the verbatim approach to creating script is particularly well suited to capturing the distinctive speech rhythms, accent and style of a group of elders with a shared cultural background. The strong emphasis on story-telling, song and humour in both communities yielded tremendously rich material. Both plays set out to give a voice to people who often have a different experience, both past and present, of living in England, and both plays have enabled many audience members outside their communities to 'tune in' to their views and memories.

CHAPTER 6

A Sense of Place and Time

In this chapter I shall consider three different creative approaches to structuring recorded and transcribed memories into a script for a professional theatre company to perform. The first deals with material drawn from many sources around the theme of the River Thames, remembered as the central thoroughfare of people's home and working lives. The second focuses on the very small canvas of one of London's many 'villages', and even a single street within that village, working intensively with a smaller number of sources. The third approach describes the process of creating a play from the memories of a single source, covering key stages of that person's lifetime, to enable audiences of her generation to travel across their own lives in time with her.

On The River: Memories of a Working River

Death of an industry

In London in the late 1980s there was a growing sense of despondency about the state of the River Thames. The docks had ceased to function and land which had once been occupied by warehouses and wharves was being sold to developers to make way for smart housing and office blocks. The trade unions representing river and dock workers, which had once been so powerful, were in decline and represented fewer and fewer members. The trades connected with the river and the docks, such as barge building and repairing, boiler-making, warehouse work, tanning and so on, were no longer required and the vast majority of cargo was carried by road, to the detriment, many argued, of the capital's health and welfare. The grand and complex canal system had fallen into disuse except as an opportunity for leisure pursuits and, unlike our European neighbours, England had largely written off the whole concept of carrying goods by water.

The centenary of the Docker's Tanner Strike, which, in 1889, secured workers sixpence an hour, seemed to be a good opportunity to record the lives of retired river and dock workers. We approached the Transport and General Workers Union (TGWU) about funding the creation of a piece of theatre, which would depict the river in its heyday and serve as a reminder of how things had once been, when the London docks were the busiest in the world and the River Thames was a source of work and wealth to the whole nation. We decided to use the title *On The River*, as that was the general term used by the men to describe their work. The funding to Age Exchange from the TGWU was supplemented by Olympia and York Canary Wharf, the major developers of the former docklands. News International, the newspaper magnates who had moved their offices into docklands, and the London Docklands Development Corporation, the public/private organisation responsible for large areas of former dockland, also contributed to the project. All the funders were only too aware of the sense of betrayal and loss felt by the remaining traditional workers clinging on to vanishing homes and jobs in these clearance areas.

A strong desire to record a vanishing past

The circumstances surrounding the gradual closure of the docks had caused much anger, blame and disagreement and the discussions which we initiated around this theme, especially with groups of former workers, were often loaded with bitterness. However, there was a strong desire to recall and record the world of the working river and to recapture the sense of being at the heart of a thriving industry, part of a global enterprise with products being transported to and from every continent. Giving these skilled men, now retired, a chance to affirm their worth in an earlier epoch seemed to have the therapeutic effect of reinforcing their sense of identity in the present.[10] The interviewees were mainly men, and much of the interviewing happened in pubs where ex-river workers met, or in retired dockers' clubs where, again, the bar was the location. This was in total contrast with the gentler style of interview prevailing in sheltered housing lounges where the participants were mainly women and the strongest brew was tea. In fact it is generally true that women participate in reminiscence activity far more than men, so it is important to locate themes which will draw men in and encourage them to reminisce with others or to make time to record their individual lives.[11]

We also recorded many women speaking of how their fathers' and husbands' work had affected their family lives as children and adults, and this perspective was very important when we were playing to preponderantly female audiences in sheltered accommodation. Their interviews covered other themes, such as what it was like to grow up and go to school near the river, to recognise the craft and the shipping lines, to court danger in their daily play on the river bank and to seek employment in factories along the riverside and in river-related trades.

Actors conduct the research

Quite a few of the interviews were conducted by the actors, which helped them to get to grips with the language and skills of the dockers and lightermen. They found it necessary to transcribe the interviews almost immediately, while the information was fresh in their minds, as the general hubbub surrounding the recordings made them hard to hear, especially as the evenings wore on and the language became more blurred! It was important for the actors to understand about

dangerous cargos, heavy loads and exposure to extreme conditions, if their performances were going to be plausible to audiences they would play to on tour who
had lived and breathed this world. They also had to learn to distinguish between
the different trades, such as the lightermen, the dockers and the stevedores, who
did not see themselves as being all of a kind. The lightermen conveyed themselves
as the gentlemen philosophers of the trade, polished story-tellers, who had had to
go through their own very formal apprenticeship system, learning to cope with the
tides and the weather, knowing every creek and reach of the river, a bit like London
cab drivers doing 'the Knowledge' as their apprenticeship. Dockers, on the other
hand, tended to depict themselves as the rough men of the river with their own
codes of behaviour adapted to the endemic uncertainty of their lives as more casual
labourers signed up on a daily basis and lacking any sort of security. We included in
the script a typical joke by a lighterman at the expense of the docker which ran as
follows: 'Here's a docker's brain and this is a lighterman's brain. And the docker's
brain is worth ten bob and the lighterman's brain is worth five bob. And you
may want to ask, why is a docker's brain worth more? Well, because it's never
been used!'

Finding the structure in the interview material

We decided that the lightermen, dockers and stevedores (men involved in loading
and unloading ships) would have their own parts of the play to reflect their view of
themselves as separate. There would be a general chronology from childhood to
adult life of three main male characters, with the river and its changes as the linking
thread throughout, but then each actor (supported by the others) would represent a
different trade and play the lead role in scenes concerning that trade. Such an
unusual structure would not have presented itself to us, had we not listened first
and shaped the material later. It gave us the dramatic opportunity to go in some
depth into these different working worlds, while keeping the river itself as the
focus.

The older men instruct the actors

This world of the working River Thames with its own language and mores was fascinating for the actors and they were the first to encourage the older men to attend
rehearsals. Sometimes actors are a little wary of this, as they see their work as
needing to be protected from public gaze during the vulnerable rehearsal period,
but in this instance it was clear we would be laughed off the stage if we did not
show that we knew how to handle a barge, lift a bag of sugar or lower cargo into a
hold. So there were often older men in the rehearsals, who were surprised to find
themselves miming with us and suggesting additional dialogue right through to
the end. There is a certain tension which arises in a theatre company from this
arrangement, as there never seems to be enough time to learn a script, master
instrumental parts and harmonies and remember moves; and that is without the
additional strain of constructive suggestions, and sometimes scathing criticism,
from the sources. However, some of the company's most effective scenes have been

partly directed by their originators, and having them present when 'their scenes' are being worked reminds the actors that they are carrying the words and experiences of one group of people to many others and that it is important to get it right. Looking back, it is amazing to me how good-humoured everyone remained and, again, I think it is a tribute to the actors' humility and their understanding of the broader purpose of the work that they were able to cope with such an open rehearsal period and the inevitable pressures resulting.

The actors take instruction from Rod Kerr (retired docker) in rehearsal for On The River*: (left to right) Charles Wegner, Anna Palmer and Andy Andrews*

A muscular playing style

We had a cast of three men and one woman, quite the opposite to most Age Exchange shows which usually had a preponderance of female characters reflecting the balance of the older population for whom we would play. The style of playing was very muscular and physical, though variety of mood and tempo were provided musically, and the musical director wrote some original songs based on descriptions of the river from the transcripts, as well as more traditional songs connected with London, love and work. The scenery was a painted backcloth depicting the river at its busiest in the 1930s, taken from old photographs of the period, and this backcloth was lashed to a wooden bar like a mast. The only other scenery was a set of wooden tea-chests which served as tables, chairs, beds and bars, as well as the containers of cargo.

A wide appeal

On The River was performed to many groups who were closely connected with and related to the material. It evoked a very positive response because in London many older people had had something to do with the river and they felt connected with the theme through family members who had been barge repairers, tally clerks, warehouse men and so on. The show went down very well in other dockland areas too, such as Manchester, Liverpool, Cardiff and Bristol, where it played in dockers' clubs and homes for retired river workers, and where the subject matter transferred easily. Because *On The River* explored a theme of contemporary political as well as historical interest, we decided to play to wider audiences including theatres, libraries, colleges and community arts venues. For these more general audiences, the evocation in the play of the River Thames as a thriving bustling centre of trade and industry, and London's docks as the world's leading port, was in shocking contrast with the almost deserted waterway they know today.

A lasting record

The men we interviewed were the last of their line, their skills and trades no longer needed, and we felt that it was important for all Londoners that we produce a lasting record of the working river and the docks. We published our most ambitious book to date, with interviews with 74 retired workers and full plate photographs. This book has subsequently taken its place in museums across London as one of the very few documents which contains the words of 'ordinary workers' and gives an insight into their daily relations with the river and the docks (Schweitzer and Wegner 1989).

A different writing approach to the same material

The original 1989 production was revived three times in the 1990s in response to popular demand, and in 2000 I commissioned a writer, Noel Greig, to develop a new play, *In Full Flow*, based on the same research material, together with further interviews which had been conducted in 1999. His very distinctive approach to the task resulted in a completely different piece of reminiscence theatre. He took the lines of the dockers and wrought them into a kind of extended poem, with the river as a chorus figure played by the three actors in specially created masks. The stories were interspersed with newly written songs using words from the transcripts and supported by a recorded accompaniment. This altogether more abstract approach to writing a theatre script from memories showed us that very different plays can emerge from the same verbatim source material. A short extract from the two plays will show how differently Greig treats the same words:

ON THE RIVER
Musical underscoring with vocal harmonisation of 'Blow the man down' by the other actors for the first speech.

Learning to handle a barge in On The River *with Charles Wegner and Andy Andrews*

BILL: (*Rowing with Mike and sharing an oar*) Winter time, I've cried before now when me hands have been so cold, stuck to an oar you know, and I've almost cried with the pain.

MIKE: What I've done before I've gone out on the river, I've rolled newspaper round my legs and under my socks to keep them warm, and put it across the chest under me jersey.

IN FULL FLOW

BILL: Me hands
These hands
I've cried before now
With the cold
With the rowing
With me hands stuck to an oar
Almost cried with the pain

In the former example, we see two men talking naturally to the audience and each other, swapping solutions to a practical problem while together manning a huge oar. In the latter, the writer concentrates on the rhythm of the speech delivered by the actor to the audience, more in the style of a recitation. Where the original production had verisimilitude in action and dialogue, carefully prepared with the older men, this later play was put together with no direct recourse to their information, no involvement by them in rehearsal, little movement on stage and a significant concentration on the poetry of their language.

Some of the feedback from the audiences who saw the later production was that, although they appreciated the 'polish and sophistication of the show', the mask/collage style was too abstract for many in the audience.[12] They missed the strong visualisation and characterisation of Age Exchange shows they had seen before, and the natural feel of the dialogue, even though all the words were taken from verbatim transcript. The praise from staff and older people was for the performers' skill rather than the relevance of the content and the older people's ability to connect with it. However, despite the great difference in approach, the later show also succeeded in arousing memories of the working river and was a fine piece of theatre in its own right.

Interestingly, the same research material also gave rise to a very successful community play by David Savill, the then Arts and Education Officer at Age Exchange, performed by dockers and lightermen themselves, with children playing them as youngsters. Here, the script was created with the older people and the children improvising together under David's direction. The cast of around 40 people filled the stage (giving a strong sense of the energy and the strength of community on the river in the past) and successfully recreated that community spirit amongst those involved in the project. The development of reminiscence theatre to be performed by older people themselves is the subject of a later chapter, but it is important to note here that the interview material generated for one project can be used in a totally different way to generate three such different theatrical products, and that creating theatre from memories is fundamentally an artistic process shaped by the writer's and the director's aesthetic sense.

Memory Lane

A local project

In my experience, one of the most pleasurable kinds of reminiscence theatre to work on was a local piece based on memories of a particular neighbourhood. Getting to know one particular area and the people who live there very well makes researching and writing such a play more manageable and more personally rewarding than some of the wider social themes explored in these pages already. The intimacy of the village or even the street (as in the next case described) is also a way for the participants in the project to renew past social networks and to build new and sustaining relationships for the future.

Addressing universal themes

The problem for a professional company in focusing on one small village is that the eventual performances (84 in the case of the show now described) will be played to audiences who have no connection with the original place. It is therefore important that the production should address universal themes and that the story should be transferable to other communities. The characters must remind other audiences of their equivalents, and the progress of the main characters' lives must in some ways be representative as well as particular. Even the scenery, while having specific accuracy, must have a trigger effect on the memories of audiences from far afield, so they feel included, not excluded, by the production.

Memory Lane was my last new play during my 23 years as Artistic Director at Age Exchange, but it was the first time I had focused on the local area where I had been living and working for 30 years. This meant that I already knew so many of the older people and had a real feel for the area. Blackheath Village in south-east London has a less mobile population than most parts of the metropolis and has kept a lot of its eighteenth and nineteenth-century houses so that its basic layout has changed very little over the last 100 years. The large public open space of Blackheath has always been a magnet for Londoners who did not necessarily live nearby, but who came for the fair, the circus and to do their courting, and by including memories of such regular visitors, we gave the project a wider relevance.

Local enthusiasm for a local project

The Reminiscence Centre is situated in the middle of the village, and attracts many visitors to its small museum of everyday life in the 1930s, its exhibition gallery and its studio theatre. It operates as a community centre, with particular attractions for older people, so when we started researching the show, we only had to put a notice in the window inviting memories of growing up in Blackheath Village for the stories and photographs to start coming in. We received many photographs which had actually been taken in our building, as it had been the local photographic studio from the beginning of the century to 1939. The interviews, mainly with individuals, were conducted in the Reminiscence Centre and, for older and more frail contributors, in people's own homes. It was especially important that contributors should feel a sense of involvement, and ownership with this project, as it was happening on their doorstep and was going to represent their lives and local environment.

A digital archive for the stories

At this time we had just begun using a computerised archive programme called COMMA which stored in a digitised form people's photographs and memories, including spoken memories.[13] This particular software package was well suited to recording memories in a particular locale, as it featured categories and search mechanisms for schools, churches, trades, shops and open spaces as well as street names and family names. It had been piloted in many local museums and community groups and this was the first Age Exchange project for which it seemed to be ideally suited.

Olive Amos at the computer showing Jules Davison, who will play her in the show, what she looked like at 17

An interactive process

Through the COMMA approach, we could attract people who only wanted to contribute a photograph or a school report and did not feel confident that they had enough to say to warrant an interview. In the event, sitting side by side with interested people and inserting the details of their scanned and enlarged photographs gave rise to many spontaneous memories which the software enabled us to record directly onto the computer through a small non-threatening microphone. When other people came in, these short memories from contributors could be played to them, along with the relevant photographs displayed on the screen, and this triggered many more memories, making the interactive process extremely productive.

Some of these spontaneous memories recorded through the computer were transcribed along with the full interviews and became part of the eventual play-script. For the older people involved, this opportunity to see digital technology at work on their own personal material aroused great interest as well as a certain degree of mystification. For many older people, computers are a source of anxiety, and not their natural first choice as a means of recording their memories. However, there were always helpers available to show them how to enter their material, especially students who were on placement at the Reminiscence Centre, and the older people gradually overcame their fear of the process.

A lasting resource

For future generations of Blackheath children, the resulting resource, which has about 500 photos and memories, will have considerable value, especially if the transcribed interviews recorded more conventionally onto minidisc or cassette are eventually added to this archive. As we were not publishing a book on this project, we were particularly pleased that there will nevertheless be an accessible lasting outcome which could be edited as a CD-ROM at a later date.

A three-dimensional exhibition prompts memories

As an added stimulus to recollection, we created an exhibition in three dimensions, produced by professional theatre designers in the gallery space, which is visited by about 10,000 people each year. It included a large mural of the heath and its major landmarks, an array of reminiscence objects suspended from the ceiling representing the activities which people got up to on the heath, representations of local shop fronts with their names in the original styles of lettering, greatly enlarged photographs (including rarely seen images of the local bomb damage in World War II) and laminated texts taken from the transcribed memories for visitors to read over coffee. For the exhibition, we called on the local history library and the local studies collection of photographs and won the support of the Blackheath Society, which encouraged its members to participate in the project. At the centre of the display was the computer with the recorded memories and stories. By making the research process inclusive, public and physically manifest, we gave much greater depth and more lasting value to the project than would have been possible if we had limited it to the dramatic form, which is of course essentially evanescent.

Focusing on memories from one street

In the course of our interviews, we identified ten people now in their 70s and 80s who had memories of one particular street in Blackheath, called Collins Street, and they were all still living in the area. Most of them were no longer in contact with one another, but they had grown up as close neighbours who had known each other well as children. Two in particular were still very close friends. Doris Bliss at 87 and Olive Amos at 83 were both very lively minded women who told wonderful stories. With some networking, we were able to gather together their old neighbours to a meeting at the Reminiscence Centre to share photos and memories. We passed the microphone around the group and they talked one at a time remembering different stories about the same people and triggering each other's memories. It resembled a family or a school reunion with personal memories suddenly surfacing as participants caught up with one another's lives.

Group discussions between former neighbours

Three such mornings of group interviews took place, each lasting about three hours. While these sessions were in progress, by pure coincidence, people came to visit the exhibition who had either lived in Collins Street or had once had a close

The cast of Memory Lane *with the street behind them: (left to right) Jules Davison, Neil Gore, Angela Bain and in front Neil Carter (backcloth by Dora Schweitzer and Steve Wilson)*

connection with it. One particularly extraordinary incident was when a woman who had been living in Spain for 40 years, Doreen Hall, came back to Blackheath to visit and popped into the Reminiscence Centre on the day we were doing one of these group interviews. She was immensely moved seeing these people from her childhood together. She agreed to record her memories onto the computer in the afternoon with some of the other people present including Bernard Bigginton, who remembered her very well and who appeared with her on some of the early photographs we had collected. We recorded the two of them talking, and later incorporated Doreen's story verbatim into the play.

Finding the central story

Clare Summerskill was my co-writer/researcher on this project. We both realised that these recording sessions with people who had all lived as children on the same street could supply us with characters and incidents which would feel familiar to audiences anywhere. The progress through life of these story-tellers, as school children, young workers, participants in the war and 'young marrieds', could stand for many others of their generation and we could also add the best material from other people who had lived in the immediate area. We felt that the enduring friendship of Olive and Doris and their families would be at the centre of the play, and we wanted to reflect in the script the pleasurable reminiscence process they had gone through together. For this reason, the play started and finished in the present. After the opening song, the two actors addressed the audience directly:

> DORIS: We've been having a trip down Memory Lane, Olive and me, seeing how much we can remember about where we grew up.

OLIVE: We lived in the same street, see?

DORIS: Now this is going back a while. I was born in 1915.

OLIVE: And I'm a bit younger than Doris. I was born in 1919.

DORIS: Of course it was different in those days. There were no cars for a
    start. So it was safe for all the children to play in the street.

OLIVE: At one point there were 49 children just in our little turning.

DORIS: You'd have great big families in these tiny houses, lots of children,
    so you'd all be playing outside. We were like a tribe. And if someone
    came along who wasn't from our street, we'd know.

The narration quickly gave way to enactment, with Olive and Doris taking off their
coats on the line 'Of course it was different in those days' and becoming the
children they were remembering by the line 'We were like a tribe', acting out a little
childhood signal indicating membership and then staring fiercely at an imaginary
outsider, following him across the stage with their eyes. Having worked through
their lives in the play up to the end of the war, we reverted to this reminiscing mode
at the end, reminding the audience that these were real memories of real people:

DORIS: The street looks different now. It looks smaller.

OLIVE: And it's not so pretty without the trees.

DORIS: But it's still the same really.

OLIVE: And when I go down there now, I'll tell you what it does for me.
    When I go past the houses, I name all the people who lived there and
    what happened there.

Stories before structure

To write the show from the memories, Clare Summerskill and I started by telling
each other what we thought were the absolutely key stories that had to go in;
stories that we particularly enjoyed and that we thought would lend themselves to
dramatisation. After that we looked for a structure. We toyed with a day in the life
of the street, or the view from one house, but we ended up with the dramatic device
of a chronological framework covering the lives of the key characters from childhood through to the end of the war. Within that framework would be other sub-
structures including the special qualities of life on the street on weekdays and
weekends and at different seasons of the year, the progress of various courtships,
the working lives of the central characters and the impact of the war on all of them.
When constructing a play around key stories, with a chronology and sense of place
to bind them together, one sometimes finds that after recording and transcribing
the initial interviews, important pieces of information are still missing. In this
instance, our informants were all living nearby and willing to pop in and record
additional material. Several times we would phone them and ask for clarification,

extra detail, and chapter and verse about dates and times. They were just delighted to be involved in solving any problems we encountered with the script and were full of ideas for getting round them.

Input to the script from the performers

In this show, there were four experienced and versatile actors, all of whom were comfortable with the working method. They had not conducted the initial interviews, but they had a chance to meet most of the characters they were playing, to hear them on tape or to encounter them through the COMMA archive. Although the scripting was complete when the actors came on board, they were still able to input ideas and make changes, for example where they felt there was too much monologue, too little dialogue or not enough action.

Older people in rehearsal

The older people came into rehearsals now and then, especially towards the end of the rehearsal period, and they seemed pleased with what they saw. Any item they felt was inaccurate or misleading we agreed to change. Before the show was taken on tour to sheltered housing units and residential homes it was initially produced at Age Exchange's own studio theatre at the Reminiscence Centre to allow members of the local community to see the play. The main contributors attended the opening performances and we publicly acknowledged our debt to them and presented them with gifts as valued 'stars' of the project. The play was then performed across London and the south-east of England, and we need not have worried about the universality of the material. It addressed the big general themes of childhood, community, poverty, love, loss and war, although they were all channelled through one particular street.

The scenery also reflected the street: a painted backcloth of Collins Street as it had been, which remains much the same today. I remember sitting in an audience to watch the show at the other end of London and the old lady sitting next to me pointed to one of the houses painted on the backcloth and told me it was hers. This was very reassuring because it indicated that we had managed to make Blackheath's Collins Street into everyone's 'Memory Lane' and the style and atmosphere were familiar. The show provided a strong stimulus for post-performance discussions about the streets where the older audience members had grown up, their neighbours and their extended families.

A multi-faceted project

The play was not the last word on this project, as it had two further outcomes. Another project going on at the Reminiscence Centre was the making of 'Memory Boxes', or miniature display cases for life portraits of older people. Wooden boxes originally used as ammunition containers by the armed forces were being recycled with a peaceful purpose. Professional artists, trained in reminiscence, worked with individual elders over a number of sessions, involving them directly in the creative process. The elders would have the opportunity to reflect upon their past lives with the artist and to explore ways of expressing their memories and their feelings in a three-dimensional and visual form (Schweitzer and Trilling 2005).

The three key participants in *Memory Lane*, Olive, Doris and Bernard, all made Memory Boxes about their own lives. The artists spent time with them individually, deciding with them what was important to show in their box, using their own photos and memorabilia. These boxes were shown locally in the Reminiscence Centre and at international conferences. Images of them have been incorporated into a film (Schweitzer 2006) which shows the process by which the *Memory Lane* play was created from their memories.[14]

Finally, children aged nine and ten in the local primary school, which had been built in the 1950s at the end of Collins Street, studied transcripts of interviews and photographs of the older people when young. Olive, Doris and Bernard then came to the classroom to meet the children face to face and to watch the scenes the children had written themselves, giving them more information and helping with their scenes. A freelance director, Jennifer Lunn, worked with the class teacher for three months, during which time the children and older people got used to working together. They presented their work to the rest of the school and then at a big international festival to celebrate the Memory Boxes project. For those children, Collins Street, an already familiar road, was never the same again, now they knew so much about what it had been like for Olive, Doris and Bernard, who were now their friends. Jennifer Lunn commented:

> The children found the work fascinating, as all the stories were set in the immediate vicinity of their school. We also had quite a lot of photos of the street and the village in those times, so there was a real place with real connections for them to explore. Olive, Doris and Bernard were very patient with the children and very supportive. They gave the children so much detail that there was a real depth to their writing.

The Blackheath Village project was an extended and multi-faceted affair. It had a long build-up period of interviewing before the exhibition was created, and the interviews then continued, using the exhibition and the COMMA archive as an ongoing stimulus. The tour covering 84 venues reached around 5000 older people across a wide geographical area, prompting an enormous number and variety of further memories in the post-show discussions. In making their Memory Boxes, the protagonists had a chance to be creative themselves, supported by the artists, and finally they had the satisfaction of seeing that their stories had a meaning for a further generation of children now being educated in the street where they had grown up. This local project was especially significant for me as it confirmed my feeling of belonging in the area and close identification with its long-term residents. A well-known community theatre and archiving project, the Living Archive, took as its motto 'Dig where you stand' and I feel that that is good advice for anyone contemplating creating a piece of reminiscence theatre.

Once Upon A Lifetime

The third example of creating a play from recorded memories was scripting from a single source. It told just one person's life story and was called *Once Upon A Lifetime*. For this production, we still recorded interviews, used the verbatim material in the script and worked with professional actors, musicians and scenic artists to create the production and tour it widely. However, instead of interviewing lots of people and making a set of generic characters closely based on those interviews, we just interviewed one person in far greater depth and built the whole play around her life, hoping that her experience resonated with audience members of a similar background and generation.

A remarkable woman and a brilliant story-teller

Elsie House was 82 at the time interviews started in 1998. She was the cleaner of the Reminiscence Centre and she came with the building when we took it on! She never considered herself to be one of the 'older' people. She would say of the volunteers: 'They're very good, aren't they?' Or: 'It's good what they're doing.' She thought of herself as a much younger working woman, although she was older than many of them. She felt defined and affirmed by her job and took it very seriously. She was working as a cleaner for three or four local families in Blackheath, with all of whom she had a close relationship. She was also caring for the other old members of her own family, regularly taking them food and seeing that they were properly treated by social services or the staff in the residential homes where they lived. She had a really complex working life where, right up to the time she died, she was supporting other people. She was a remarkable woman and a brilliant story-teller.

Elsie found it very difficult to take the interview process seriously. My colleague Clare Summerskill, who was the writer on this project, and I often had to chase Elsie round with the microphone, snatching bits of her time between jobs, and begging her to turn the hoover off for a while. She regarded our work on the project with an amused detachment. We had included many of her stories in previous productions, and she had seen all the shows. I had always said, 'Elsie, you've got to come, lots of your stories are in it', and she'd say, 'I'll see if I've got time.' She had copies of all the books produced to go with the shows, which included her stories, and she had given copies of these to her remaining sisters and her grandchild. She was very heavily identified with the Reminiscence Centre, which she insisted on calling 'The Remission Centre' until the day she died.

When Elsie realised that a whole show was going to be about her life I think she was genuinely surprised, feeling perhaps that she had already told us her best stories and could not rise to the occasion. In fact, she now found a treasury of new stories or new glosses on old stories and was able to cover some of the more difficult periods of her life, which she had not previously shared. To give the reader a sense of her power as a story-teller, this is how Elsie described to us her mother's death and how it was used verbatim in the final script.

ELSIE: Next day there was a knock at the door and it was a policeman. He said, 'Mrs House? It's your Mother.' 'Not my Mum,' I said, 'I only saw her last night. She was all right then.' But he said she'd died. Just like that. She'd been sitting in her chair with her glasses on and the *Daily Sketch* on her lap. And my brother Bob who lived there, he was upstairs in bed. He'd been on lates and he'd asked Mum to give him a call, and he'd come downstairs and found her dead.

BOB: For heaven's sake, Mum, I asked you to call me. You know I wanted to go to the pictures…Mum!

Bob realises that Mum is dead.

MUM! MUM!

Song fragment: 'The Lord's My Shepherd' is played underneath the following speech.

ELSIE: The shock sent him. He couldn't stay in that house. He went into lodgings. He missed my Mum. And so did I. First few years I couldn't stop crying. Then I went down to the Spiritual Church to get a message, 'cos I believed in Spiritualism and she said, 'There's somebody here…the name of Elsie.' She said, 'Your Mother's here, and all the while you cry you're upsetting her.' And from that day I didn't. But I never got over her. I felt it with me Dad, and me husband later, but you feel it more with your Mum. 'Cos your Mum's you, isn't she? You're a part of your Mum and when you lose your Mum you want the world to open up and swallow you. You do. You can't believe it.

A trip to the past

I took the opportunity while working on this show to do what I'd wanted to do for a long time: to take Elsie back to the house in Elmers End where she grew up. She had said so much about it and it was still standing, so she agreed to come with me in the car to visit it. We didn't know if there would be anyone there, but we were lucky. People were at home in the house she lived in and next door and we were able to go into both. The people were really courteous and hospitable and interested in what we were doing and what Elsie had to say about their houses in the past. Elsie stood in the living room of this small house and said, 'My goodness me, there were eight mouths round this table. How did we all fit in and how did Mum manage?'

Elsie went through the house and remembered where everything had been. She looked through the window on to the garden, remembering where the outside toilet was and where the chickens had been kept. I think it made her very happy to go there and to be inside her childhood home, even though it had changed in so many ways. It was as though a little bit of Elsie had been left in the house all those years ago and she had found it again. She seemed to feel more complete as a result, and she was much brightened by the visit. As we were driving back, she talked a lot about the area and her explorations of it at different times in her life, playgrounds, school, dance halls, shops, places she worked, so lots of other memories came back as a result of that visit and she started to think more about our dramatisation process. 'Funny, isn't it? That it's all going to be in a play.' I do remember her saying after this visit, while we were in the rehearsal period, 'Is it all right? Is it going to be good?' She was very concerned that we were going to do a proper job.

Elsie with the Once Upon A Lifetime *company after the dress rehearsal: (left to right) Owaine Williamson, Claire (Elsie's grand-daughter), Elsie House, Angela Bain, Rebecca Clow, Clare Summerskill (writer) and Pam Schweitzer (director)*

The subject becomes the audience

Elsie came to a couple of rehearsals and sat in on the production process. This was quite nerve-racking for the actors, and the production team, especially as we knew it would be difficult for Elsie watching the actors struggling with lines and harmonies to imagine what the final effect would be with costumes and scenery. The backcloth was based by the designer on photographs of Elsie and her family from every part of her life, with important locations and dates incorporated. It was only at the dress rehearsal that Elsie was able to feel the full impact of what we had created from her life story. Angela Bain, the performer who played Elsie as an older woman, commented:

> Elsie came to see the dress rehearsal, and it was evident that up till then, she hadn't fully taken on board that the show was going to be her life story. When any of the actors were off-stage, we peeped through the backcloth to see her reaction. She started

by sitting back in her chair and, as the play progressed, she leaned further and further forward – she was astonished to see characters from her past come to life, saying things that she had remembered them saying 50 years ago. It was great to see her experiencing her own history.

That dress rehearsal impressed Elsie sufficiently for her to want the rest of her family to see it, and she was of course acknowledged as the star at the opening performance.

A bike ride to the sea in Once Upon A Lifetime, *with Rebecca Clow and Angela Bain (backcloth by Anny Evason)*

The life journey complete

Within two weeks of the show's opening, Elsie died. She had gone to hospital for a check-up, been told that she needed immediate treatment, but insisted on going home. She put herself to bed that night and died. This was devastating for her family of course, but also for all of us who had known her for several years. For the cast it was a terrific shock and made it difficult for them to continue, though of course they did, and were comforted by the idea that the play was a great testimony to the vibrancy of her life. Elsie's funeral tea was held at the Reminiscence Centre. She always said she would work until she died and she did.

Coping with the deaths of people with whom one has worked closely over the years is an occupational hazard in reminiscence work, especially where a project has become embedded in its community and the older people have formed long-term attachments to the workers and to one another. Over my time at Age

Exchange I have had to give many funeral addresses and spend time with the surviving members of the groups concerned, remembering and celebrating the deceased. I have discussed this with leaders of other cultural projects for older people and know that the work leads to such close connections being made that it can be like losing a family member and one often needs support oneself to cope with such repeated losses.

Personal application of universal themes

One very particular quality about the show *Once Upon A Lifetime* was that it covered all the key stages of life, even flashing back to the courting days of Elsie's grand-parents back in the nineteenth century, and travelling forward right to the end of the twentieth century and her own old age. Unlike most of the reminiscence shows produced to date, the clothes the actors wore on the set and the music they sang came up to the present day, echoing the time shifts in the life story. When audience members watched the show, even though their own story was not the same as Elsie's story, they could identify with much of it. Any audience members who had grown up in a big family, been to school, had friendships, courted, got married, had children, watched their parents grow old and die, and they themselves retire and cope with bereavement and old age, or who had even done just some of these things, were comparing and contrasting as they watched this life unfold. The play gave them pause to reflect on the progression of events in their own lives and the factors that had shaped them, and that is why the play spoke to audiences across a wide age range.

Summary

In this chapter, I have shown some of the ways in which material for very different reminiscence theatre shows can be gathered and organised, in each case depending on the context and the purpose. Underlying all is a respect for the words in which things are remembered and the honesty of the people sharing their stories and the feelings they evoke. In all these cases, the task of the theatre company has been to move from the individual experience to the representative, so that audiences are receiving the authentic specific experience, but in a way which enables them to connect with it and relate it to their own lives.

CHAPTER 7

Staging and Touring Reminiscence Theatre

Having considered the research and writing stages of creating reminiscence theatre shows, I shall now outline some of the essentials of staging and touring reminiscence theatre. Of course researching, writing and production are not always separate stages, and sometimes the writing will still be happening during the production process, through negotiation with the actors, the musical director, the set designer, the stage manager and the tour organiser, plus additional input from the older people themselves, all of whom will make crucial contributions. But it might be helpful to go through for the reader the various processes and tasks which are necessary to put a reminiscence theatre show on the road, and tour it to many very different venues.

The practical side of production

Funding issues

It is often difficult for producers to procure the funding required for a professional production in this realm of theatre. For many years, the arts funding door has mainly remained closed to reminiscence theatre. The climate is now beginning to alter a little in its favour, maybe because demographic change is exerting some influence, but reminiscence theatre has often been seen by mainstream arts officers as a hybrid form, as closely linked to social work as to the arts. As a result, the funders of reminiscence theatre have to date been an unusual mixture including voluntary organisations, charitable trusts, government departments of health, education and the environment, private industry, individual donors and certain departments within the European Commission.

Sometimes a production can be funded in stages, with a local authority supporting the research stage, a writer's grant then being secured from a charitable or arts trust, production costs coming from a mixture of donors, and touring costs partly supported from earned income. Funding for some of the performances on the tour is likely to be available from a range of different departments within local authorities, such as social services, housing, libraries, community education, arts or leisure. Other less obvious sources of financial support are trade unions, housing trusts, chains of care homes, regeneration schemes, voluntary sector groups, university conference organisers and commercial sponsorship. Involving venues in the hunt for funding often has the beneficial effect of increasing their commitment to the event and their determination to maximise its impact, some lining up related training in reminiscence for staff, students and volunteers. It is highly desirable to ensure that the cost of the performance does not fall directly on the older people themselves, except of course where the show takes place in a public space like a conventional theatre. Whenever there is a charge, people who might enjoy and benefit from the show will stay away, either because they feel they cannot spare the money or because it is too much of a gamble and they do not want to risk boredom or embarrassment.

Creating a tour schedule

After funding is secured, and usually before the actors are taken on, it is necessary to create a tour schedule for the production. One relatively easy solution would be to book theatre spaces for a week at a time and invite local older people's organisations to attend in groups. Bedside Manners Theatre Company, which worked with older people in London in the 1980s and early 1990s, did adopt this policy for a time, and found it worked quite well for them (personal communication). However, such a strategy does create financial and logistical barriers for many of the target audience, who are unable to leave the places where they live and are cared for. Consequently we decided at Age Exchange to continue taking the shows directly to the people for whom they were intended.

The creation of the tour schedule is often handled by the administrator in a small company and this person will also be responsible for the contracting and payment of the performers and other freelance personnel involved in the production. However, as organising a long tour, perhaps with some international touring involved, is a major undertaking, it is not unusual to employ a touring officer.

To be economic, a four-week rehearsal period would ideally be followed by a two- or three-month tour, since it is only during the touring weeks that the project can become income-generating. The tour organiser needs to understand the demands of a professional touring theatre contract, which are quite a minefield for the uninitiated. What can look to the inexperienced eye like a reasonable week with six or seven performances of a 60-minute play and rational travel plans can suddenly turn out to be full of problems which will cost the unwary company very dear, so the tour organiser needs to work closely with the union representative (who must be appointed from within the company by the cast in the first days of the contract) to anticipate any potential problems.

Working in non-theatre venues

The tour organiser needs to liaise with the venues as well, issuing formal contracts so that, when the actors arrive, they are expected and prepared for, with an audience informed about what is on offer. This all sounds so obvious that it barely needs stating. A reminiscence touring schedule, however, is quite unlike any other theatre tour, as one is working almost exclusively with non-theatre venues where staff are on shifts and where the person responsible for booking the show may not be on duty on the day, or may only have access to the booked space on one day a week and have little backing from those who run the venue. There is nothing more disappointing for a company than to travel miles to an unlikely venue to find only half a dozen disconsolate old people in the audience as everyone else has gone off on a trip or did not receive the information in time.

Many community theatre companies build up a regular touring circuit and go back to the same venues over many years. This also happens with reminiscence theatre tours, so that the company builds up a relationship and reputation with the people who run the venue and the users. However, if the company has a policy of preparing shows for different minority ethnic groups or specific target groups (such as people from particular housing estates, the river community or a religious community) it is likely that many stops on the tour will be first-time venues. Although this makes the organisation of a tour schedule more complicated, it is also a sign of strength and continuing development when a company opens up new links and relationships. However, it does not follow that a venue which has enjoyed one show, perhaps closely related to the users' own culture and world view, will want to book another which focuses on a very different area of remembered experience. It is important to offer venues as much information as possible about the content and style of the forthcoming show, so that they can make an informed choice and avoid disappointment.

Performances are often given in spaces which are basically unsuitable for theatre, sometimes in a vast open space or in a cramped lounge in an overheated sheltered housing block or residential home. Part of the challenge for a group of actors and the stage manager, who travels with them to set up the performances on tour, is to re-invent the space by the way they set it up and the way they perform, so that it is transformed for that brief period into something resembling a conventional theatre environment, and never feels quite the same to its regular users afterwards. When the venue and the local organisers rise to the occasion and organise a 'full house', followed by time for conversation between audience and players over celebratory refreshments, then it all feels worthwhile. This is what the tour organiser has to work towards, by effective liaison with every venue, in order not to sell the actors and the audiences short.

Designing for non-theatrical spaces

The designer has to bear in mind that what he or she creates will have to fit into many different venues, seating anything from 15 people to 500. The scenery must be very light and very mobile as it might well have to fit into lifts or be carried up flights of stairs. It must be made of durable materials which can go in and out of a van seven or eight times a week and it has to be capable of expansion with side extensions for specially big venues so that the actors can maximise the opportunities these venues provide. There has to be full discussion too between the designer, the director and the cast about how the scenery is going to impact on the play on tour. The actors will be less than happy if there is a lot of back-breaking carrying before and after every show, but the audience may not be sufficiently stimulated by a stylishly minimalist set, so the director will often have to negotiate with the designer to arrive at a light-weight flexible solution which works as a reminiscence stimulus in its own right. The main pieces of the set must not be too tall, because the ceiling height in a lot of older people's venues is very low, architects of residential homes preferring an intimate look and steering clear of reminding the old people of the dreaded high-ceilinged workhouses or the wards in hospitals of the past.

As soon as the script is ready, it is desirable to take the designer on board, and certainly well before the rehearsal period if at all possible. Normally speaking, a designer will either produce a model box or drawings to show the director and the cast what they have in mind, and this is essential when planning moves, arranging entrances and exits to fit in with the positions of musical instruments and key items of costume. Of course modifications can be made as the rehearsal period progresses, but the actors are usually more comfortable when they can imagine what they are performing in front of and approximately the size and shape of the playing area.

People might question the need for a set for a reminiscence theatre show. One obvious answer is that it will serve the purpose of camouflaging what is already there, which might not be particularly conducive to concentration and focus, and this can often be managed with a very minimal screen. However, the set can make a much more significant contribution. It can evoke whatever the theme of the play is and can act as an *aide-mémoire* in its own right, rendering an often rather barren environment much more stimulating of recall and conversation. An example here is *When The Lights Go On Again*, a play we produced about the end of the war, the reuniting of London families and the rebuilding of their bomb-damaged homes in the 1940s. The set echoed the situation depicted, in that it was built on scaffolding strewn with bunting and posters of the period, providing effective memory triggers of the time, and also giving the actors raised levels to play on, including platforms for political speeches relating to the events leading up to the 1945 General Election.

It is quite usual for the audience to be seated throughout the entire fit-up for a show, especially when they have been brought to the venue long before the event is due to begin. This might occur especially in a small venue where there is only one lounge and the older people do not want to stay in their rooms, or in a day centre where lunch is provided in the space where the show will later be performed. It is often best to make a virtue of this necessity by having intriguing and appropriate things for people to look at which will stimulate and channel their memories before the show even begins. It has been interesting to note that on the feedback forms from venues, people have stated a preference for sets with plenty of props on display, rather than more abstract designs which do not sufficiently stimulate the audience.

Philip Curtis, Clare Summerskill and Sophie Scarborough (stage manager) in conversation with the audience after the show

In all reminiscence theatre shows, the scenery has to be thematically appropriate, but also quite functional. The canvas or plywood flats, out of which the set is usually created, must often include shelves to accommodate props that are going to be used in the show and for which there is insufficient space on the floor of the acting area. The front is painted with an appropriate design and the wooden struts at the back provide places to hang costumes and mirrors, pin notes on the running order and hang small instruments.

Company and stage management

The company and stage manager (usually known as the CSM) is usually responsible for creating the scenery and properties during the rehearsal period, along the lines specified by the designer and agreed with the director, as with any other kind of theatre production. This needs careful scheduling as the director may require the CSM to attend several rehearsals to record blocking (actors' moves and positions) to note any new requirements and to plan the lighting design.

Once the show is on the road, the CSM has an absolutely crucial role in professional touring reminiscence theatre. He or she is responsible for planning journeys and getting the actors to as many as 80 venues, and looking after the production on the road, including monitoring the welfare and morale of the performers. The CSM is often the first point of contact with the venue organisers on the day of performance and sometimes this role is successfully combined with that of tour manager, which has the distinct advantage that he or she will have had plenty of communication with the venue in advance. More often, these functions are separated, and it is particularly important to ensure effective liaison between these two key members of the team.

As in any other touring theatre, the CSM is responsible for maintaining the company vehicle on the road and liaising with the administrator or tour organiser regarding insurance of musical instruments and other valuable items on the road and in the venues. He or she must organise the 'get-ins' and 'get-outs' from the touring vehicle to the performance area, consult with the actors regarding the most favourable position of the set in the space, which is often far from obvious, ensure that dressing rooms and refreshments are available and that the actors' 'half' is observed and respected. This is the sacred quiet half-hour when an actor can prepare in any way he or she likes for the performance, and the CSM has to try to ensure that this does not get eaten away by the demands of practical tasks, to the detriment of effective performance and goodwill.

It is important to have somebody 'out front' in every performance to deal with unexpected occurrences, which occasionally happen in non-theatre venues, such as organisers trying to serve refreshments during the performance, or audience members becoming extremely disruptive and damaging enjoyment of the show by everyone else, or even bits of the scenery coming adrift. These disasters are very rare, but the players feel more comfortable knowing the CSM is available to deal with them as necessary.

He or she also has the crucial role of keeping the director *au fait* with any problems arising with the show and any cuts the actors wish to make which will need to be fully discussed. Normally the CSM keeps a record or show report of every performance so that venues which present insuperable problems are not revisited and particularly welcoming venues are kept informed of any other events and activities the company may have on offer.

Theatre lighting

It might seem unnecessary and potentially dangerous to take heavy theatre lights on stands into old people's homes, but the justification for going this extra mile is that it brightens up the set and focuses the audience's attention. It helps the older people, whose vision may be diminished, to see the actors' facial expressions as well as the details of the set and the props and makes it feel like a 'proper theatre'. Ideally, reminiscence theatre should be as like the 'real thing' as it can be, with everything that 'normal theatres' use to help the play to impact on the audience. It is of course sometimes a nuisance to put lighting up for a single performance in a rather ill-suited venue, and one does have to be mindful of health and safety aspects, making sure for example that all the leads are 'gaffered down' to the floor (or carpet) so people do not trip over them, but it is manageable in most venues and makes a big difference.

Normally the CSM tours two portable lighting stands, with a maximum of three lamps on each and a small dimmer board, which he or she can operate during the show. This amount of lighting can plug into the normal power circuit without overloading the system, provided not all the lamps are on at the same time.

The designer and stage manager have to think through the lighting demands of the show with the director and use the available equipment as effectively as possible. For example, lighting cues, even in a non-theatre venue where the blackout may be less than perfect, can help to underline the mood of a particular scene or transform the way the backcloth appears when it is perhaps the setting for a song rather than a piece of narration or of naturalistic dialogue.

Sound and other effects

Reminiscence theatre performances are usually in fairly small venues which do not require microphones and most of the live music, with the exception of an electronic keyboard, is not amplified. Often the actors produce all the sound effects vocally or by using the props for percussion effects, and the audiences usually respond favourably to the humour and ingenuity of this approach. Most of the shows described in these pages have not required elaborate touring sound equipment, but it has been important on occasion to use an historic recorded broadcast, or include the voice of a famous singer, or even, on very rare occasions, to have a specially composed and arranged backing track for the actors on stage to sing with.

Back-projected slides have also been used from time to time to good effect to locate a scene in time and place, though it is often difficult to arrange sufficient blackout in all venues for this to work as well as it might in a more conventional theatre setting.

Venue layout

On the question of seating and layout, it is often a matter of awkward compromise with those running the venue. There are some places where the staff associate good times for their residents with seating them round small tables in a cabaret format or seating them on both sides of long tables laid out with refreshments. This latter arrangement is particularly disastrous for any theatrical presentation, because the tables separate the audience from the actors and give them a split focus, which halves the impact of whatever the actors are presenting. At the very least, with such a layout it is essential to take time for the chairs to be turned to the front, but better still is to prevail on the organisers to get rid of the extra tables, with the help of the company, and go for a more conventional theatre seating arrangement, with the chairs either in rows facing the front or in a U-shape, but all facing the set. It is a good policy to request this in advance in the company's contract so that there is a chance that the room will be correctly laid out for the performance. That way, when the older people come in, they feel they are entering a different space where something special will be happening.

The furniture in older people's venues is often inimical to theatre performance. High-backed chairs are hard to see round or over and are also very difficult to move. Having a raised playing area is highly desirable, but way beyond the resources of most companies and too hefty and time-consuming to set up in small venues, especially in those with low ceilings. The result is that when blocking a show (determining where everyone should be on set in every scene) the director will have the cast standing most of the time so they can be seen, or sitting on a table which can double as a bed or a chair or bench, when the script absolutely demands that the actors sit. The choreography and the staging have to be prepared with a worst-case scenario in mind, and the director and designer really need to consider these issues from the outset, building height requirements and visibility of actors and props into the concept, so that the intended audience do not miss out on any of the performance.

Costumes

The costumes are obviously related to the period of the show, or they may travel through several periods if it is a play covering a long period of time. It is often desirable for the designer to take on responsibility for costumes as well as the set and props, so that all the visual elements cohere and are complementary. Frequently there are a tremendous number of costume changes because people are playing lots of parts, so the costumes have to be very easy to get on and off quickly. Sometimes it is sensible and effective, as well as visually intriguing, to do all costume changes on set, so that the audience watch the actors change from one character to another. There might be a basic costume with added items on top, like a hat, a cape, a collar, an apron or a shawl, for different characters. Quite modest changes help the actor and the audience make the dramatic switch required and these pieces of costume can effectively be stored on hat stands or hooks which do not restrict the playing area. However, a complete change of costume makes an immediate impact on an audience, especially if there is something in the costume which speaks to them directly, such as an army, WAAF or navy uniform, a demob suit or a nurse's uniform. Having these turn-arounds conducted in their own lounge can be quite transporting for the audience, taking them back to other times and places as effectively as the lines spoken from the stage. It is always worth being absolutely accurate when costuming shows for reminiscence theatre, especially where uniforms are concerned. The wrong number of stripes, for example, can be surprisingly counter-productive, as it jars with the audience and interferes with their reception of the scene.

The performing company

Why work with professional actors?

Some might question the need to fund professional performers to play in sheltered units, homes and day centres, environments so culturally starved that any offering is likely to be appreciated, and indeed it is true that various amateur and student forms of reminiscence theatre can play a very useful role in stimulating and entertaining older people. However, I have always insisted on using an Equity union contract for all productions and paying actors the Equity rate for the job, on the basis that this is as important and demanding as any other theatre work. It requires of the actor at least as much as, if not more than, working in conventional theatre, in terms of disciplined rehearsal schedules, line-learning and music preparation, mastering choreography, audience contact time and ability to be flexible and responsive in performance.

A demanding schedule

It also exerts special rigours in terms of the large number of 'one night stands' that the actors are required to perform. There are often seven or eight shows a week, sometimes with lengthy travel between venues. There can be a shortage of set-up and preparation time, a frequent lack of proper or dressing rooms, and a lack of understanding by the venues of the professional quality of the company. The actors are required to help the stage manager in erecting the scenery, lighting and props, often in cramped conditions with the older people sitting or standing around them. The venues are not usually the most glamorous, and are unlikely to attract agents looking for the next 'star'. So for these reasons alone, the actors deserve at least the Equity rate which, after all, is far from handsome.

Setting a professional standard for reminiscence theatre

Further, by employing quality performers, many of them with enormous experience of playing in major companies, one is asserting the claim that reminiscence theatre is an art form in its own right and worthy of the best talents available. In recent years, there has been a welcome and growing tendency for drama schools and university drama departments to include it in their 'applied theatre' and community courses, recognising that students need to understand the basic principles, as they may well seek and find work in this area in a future where older people constitute an ever-increasing percentage of theatre audiences.

Working with drama students

It is pleasing when drama students arrive for a lecture or workshop on reminiscence theatre expecting it to be rather restricting and nostalgic and instead are surprised by how intriguing the process is. After exploring and dramatising their own memories in introductory workshops, students at the Central School of Speech and Drama and Greenwich University students have shown considerable enthusiasm and skill in creating original pieces of theatre, engaging with all the key stages of interviewing, transcribing, scripting, performing and reflecting on the audience's responses. Several have expressed a desire to explore the medium further because of the performance opportunities it offers.

Auditioning and assembling a cast

Are there essential qualities for a reminiscence theatre performer? Reminiscence theatre demands of the actor that he or she enters whole-heartedly into the moment, however brief, and brings it to life as though it is happening there and then. The ability to dip quickly in and out of character and situation are prerequisites for this kind of theatre. That does not mean that the characters should be caricatures or the playing style in any way superficial, but rather that the actor must find the concentration to invest the short moment, whether painful or joyous, with all the force and intensity of reality. An audience of older people responds immediately to accurate and genuine portrayals of strong feelings, and are quick to show their engagement with the players.

Actors who can 'think on their feet'

The ability of actors to think on their feet and react to the unexpected is another quality which is important in reminiscence theatre. One way of testing this in audition is to give actors a speech to read and then ask them to give back the gist of it immediately without referring to the paper, and then to respond in role to questions relating to the situation in the speech. This might sound quite demanding, but it certainly shows if an actor can engage quickly with a story, understand the implications and respond empathetically in role. A performer who can do this will cope much better on tour than one who is easily thrown or cannot engage easily with a new task or unexpected interventions.

The importance of music in reminiscence theatre

Musical skills are very important in reminiscence theatre. The actor must be able to sing and hold a harmony line, and ideally play a portable musical instrument as well. The musical director normally sits in on auditions and helps the director consider the best combination of players for the particular show. He or she hears the actors singing and playing instruments, and then arranges the music around their vocal range and skills, maximising what they can do, but not burdening them with so much that they are not going to be able to cope with all the other demands of the show.

At Age Exchange I was fortunate to have very inspiring musical directors, such as Paula Gardiner, Sandra Kerr and Peter Hayward, who between them scored most of the 30 productions, and they were able to provide the actors with arrangements which were stretching and exciting. Portable wind and string instruments give maximum flexibility in a fast-moving show, and some very imaginative effects can be produced by using the props as percussion instruments. A washboard played with thimbles, a bucket played with a scrubbing brush or spoons on enamel plates are all ingenious examples.

The actor often has to be prepared to cut into music from speech and make swift transitions, perhaps continuing a conversation with the audience while putting on an accordion, or making a very quick exit and coming back playing a flute or clarinet, maybe even wearing a different costume which is needed for the next scene, so there is a lot of very fast thinking required.

Willingness to engage with the audience

The actor in reminiscence theatre needs to be willing to engage with the audience in a kind of one-sided conversation, the subtext of which is: 'You are probably going to remember this and we hope you do', and 'Ah yes, you do remember, and it really was like that, was it?' When this dynamic is working well, the actors find they are performing to an undertow of approbation and recognition, which can be very rewarding. There will be verbal and non-verbal signals from the audience that they are connecting with the scene and entering into the emotions of the characters as fellow travellers who have known these situations and understand their dilemmas.

The physical proximity between the actors and the audience in most reminiscence theatre venues enables an intimate style of playing which leads very comfortably into the post-show discussions where the actors have to engage directly with the audience. It is a crucial element in reminiscence theatre that audience members have an opportunity to feed back to the players and to one another the memories which the play has triggered. Some actors are particularly good at sensing which parts of the play have clearly touched certain audience members and can pick up on this in discussion afterwards. Most find the direct feedback from the older people very affirming and enjoy the rare experience in theatre of having such close contact with their audience.

A dare-devil boyfriend remembered in Once Upon A Lifetime: *(left to right) Rebecca Clow,*
   Owaine Williamson and Clare Summerskill

Directing actors in reminiscence theatre

Introducing actors to the field of reminiscence work through practical experience is highly beneficial. The best way for them to understand the reminiscence process is to explore for themselves, early on in rehearsals, what it feels like to remember and to share personal memories. For example, with a group of actors performing a show called *Can We Afford The Doctor?* about health care and remedies before the introduction of the National Health Service, I led the actors through a guided fantasy, inviting them to remember a time in their childhood when they were sick, how their illness had affected them and how they had been treated. They told their stories back to one another and then, as a group, reflected on the experience of suddenly locating long-forgotten, and sometimes highly emotional, moments from their own lives and being asked to share them. Through this, they became very conscious of what they chose to edit out and what they felt comfortable to talk about.

Through personal reminiscence exercises, the actors can look afresh at their speeches in the script, remember that they result from a reminiscence process and understand how the act of remembering might have impacted on the older people interviewed. Listening to the memories of fellow cast members and suddenly finding a 'lost' memory of their own in such a reminiscence exercise also has the effect of alerting the actors to the impact their show will have on audience members who will undoubtedly happen upon memories which have been locked away in their hearts and minds and which will have very strong emotional connotations. In the post-show discussions, the resulting insight will help to sensitise the actors to the older people they are talking to and to empathise with the emotional reactions which will sometimes arise.

Playing the past in the present

The director must help the actors in rehearsal to come to a point of confidence where the way they deliver stories to the audience has the veracity and force of the original telling. The verbatim text must sound natural, lively and authentic. It must come across as though the stories are being remembered afresh, coming to life on stage and happening all over again.

Occasionally actors have difficulty in performing reminiscence scripts because they cannot see how they can be playing old people remembering being young one moment, and the next minute playing the young person whom that old person was remembering. On one occasion, an actor even asked for changes of costume during each scene to mark the passage from remembering to playing out, but the reality is far simpler than this would suggest. The convention everyone has to accept during the performance is that the actors are speaking for people who are much older than they are, but they are reflecting them at the age which is right for the characters and situations they are playing out in the particular scene. The passage from story to enactment, and from reflection to action, does not require underlining in costume, make-up or any other device. Once actors relax into this style, the problems disappear.

Making all the elements cohere

As with any kind of theatre, the director's key task is to bring together all the ideas and strategies which have been discussed with the writer, the designer, the musical director, the stage manager and the performers. How can the separate parts, the final script, the set, the props, the costume changes, the musical instrumentation and complex harmonies and the actors' carefully plotted moves, become a coherent whole? Sometimes it seems a tremendous struggle to fuse all the elements, and to overcome all the physical and logistical obstacles so that the show can flow. There is always concern about whether there is going to be enough time to get that costume change up to speed and get that instrument on and make the move from one sequence to another, all within the space of a single minute. The director (and writer where applicable) will have to be willing to make small amendments to the script to help the actors succeed in these difficult transitions. Towards the end of the rehearsal period the possibilities gradually become a reality and there is a great sense of achievement as each obstacle is surmounted. The actors too find handling the multiplicity of tasks stimulating and gradually build a sense that the show is going to work for the audiences and be fun to perform on the road. When suddenly all the elements fall into place and follow the main intellectual and emotional sweep of the play, it becomes clear that reminiscence theatre is indeed a complex art form.

Dealing with doubts

As a director specialising in reminiscence theatre, I have had to recognise that this is not the sort of work many professional actors are used to. It demands that they make compromises in terms of physical circumstances and play in venues which are not always easy to perform in or immediately receptive to their presence. There has never been quite enough money to ensure a leisurely rehearsal period for a reminiscence theatre show, but then most theatre companies feel that! However, a pool of multitalented and experienced performers who have all been in four or five reminiscence theatre shows have developed special skills in this area over the years and enjoyed getting to understand the form, its demands and its rewards. Having the opportunity to work with such actors has been tremendously exciting and fulfilling.

Sometimes, the painful process of fund-raising, and the inevitable hassles which occur with professional touring to this special sort of venue, the cancelled performances, actors' illness, transport problems and Equity issues have weighed me down. Investing all the effort required to take professional shows to places that had almost nothing by way of live entertainment and stimulus sometimes made the investment seem disproportionate, but these negative feelings almost always evaporated when I saw how the shows acted like a shot of adrenaline for the intended audiences.

Confirming faith in the method

Whenever I went on the road with the actors, I always found it to be time well spent and it invariably confirmed my faith in the method. Of course there were some disasters, where the physical circumstances were too difficult for the show to succeed or the audience was too impaired to receive it. In the vast majority of cases, however, audiences have responded very enthusiastically and seemed considerably happier after the performance than before it. As time has gone on, more and more care staff have remained throughout the performance and have had the benefit of seeing their residents' positive responses. Many have commented, both through their feedback forms and through direct communication, what a difference the performance made and how they have been able to build on its impact to promote interaction and creative reminiscence work.

Summary

This chapter has aired the many practical considerations involved in touring reminiscence theatre:

- the creation of an extensive touring schedule, probably including some quite problematic performing spaces
- the involvement of skilled professionals on the music, design and construction side
- the recruitment of an experienced and reliable Company Stage Manager to handle all practical matters
- auditioning and contracting a cast of talented actors with musical skills
- maintaining high production values
- promoting good relationships with a wide variety of audiences.

Although many of these issues will be the same in a reminiscence touring company as any other professional company, it is sometimes more difficult to succeed on all levels when one is targeting the production at venues which are unaccustomed to hosting a group of professional actors. Everyone involved needs to keep the main purpose of the shows, to stimulate and entertain older people, very much in their sights and retain a sense of humour throughout!

Part 2

Participatory and
Inter-generational Projects

Chapter 8, which opens this section, features theatre projects where audiences of older people have become active participants in the event, joining in discussion of each scene as it occurs or even taking over some of the roles themselves.

Chapter 9 explores professionally performed Reminiscence Theatre in Education projects presented in specially created environments. The actors present classes of school-children with characters and situations based on the interviews they have conducted during the research period. The children become actively involved in the drama, usually in a group role. Older people participate in the action, often also in role, and then share their experience directly with the children, who explore it through improvised drama.

Chapter 10 looks at Youth Theatre in which young people develop an original show based on their meetings with older people in which they listen to their stories or through correspondence with older people whom they then meet at the performance. These professionally supported productions sometimes also involve the older people as performers in what is essentially a joint production.

Chapter 11 looks at play-making by younger people in classrooms from the memories shared with them there by older people. The cross-curricular nature of these projects is demonstrated and there is special focus on multicultural reminiscence drama work involving old and young performing together.

CHAPTER 8

Theatrical Scenes Stimulating Audience Participation

Learning through theatre

In this chapter I shall be considering, through two case studies, the value of theatre as a stimulus for discussion and learning. The first, part of a government-funded regeneration project, will explore the adaptation of a full-scale touring reminiscence show into a very different format in which each scene is a stimulus to a facilitated reminiscence session by older people. The second, a professional theatre programme based on the experience of retirement, is aimed at older people attending courses designed to prepare them for life changes, and uses active participation by the audience as part of the learning process.

Rethinking the established format for reminiscence theatre

Most of the professional reminiscence theatre productions described so far required a cast of four or five professional actors, a touring stage manager, full costume, scenery and lighting. A full-scale production of this kind made a tremendous impact on an audience, especially if that show was coming to the elderly people in their own living space, which would be more or less transformed by the company into a little theatre for the occasion. However, accommodating such a complicated set-up in a care home or day centre did sometimes provide difficulties, and even though every venue signed a contract promising to make the necessary performance and dressing room spaces available and to clear the time slots, there were always places on a tour where these requirements had not been honoured.

Further, the plays had all been about 60 to 75 minutes long with no interval, this being considered the likely maximum length of time the target audience could sit without discomfort or loss of concentration. Bearing in mind that in many venues the older residents were brought from their rooms by staff members quite a long time before the show itself began, the whole event could last up to two hours. The post-show discussion, usually conducted informally with the performers mingling with the audience over a cup of tea, extended this time even further and this meant that memories which had been triggered by scenes early on in the performance could sometimes be difficult to retrieve without specific reminders.

After many years of touring these full-length shows, I decided to test out again the format originated by Fair Old Times in Devon back in 1980 where, instead of having a play which went straight through from start to finish, separate scenes were presented by the actors and these were punctuated by group discussion facilitated by one of the company (Langley and Kershaw 1982). Clare Summerskill, who had worked with me for many years as a performer and writer of reminiscence theatre, had recently had positive experience of such a format working well in a joint production by Forest Forge and Oxfordshire Touring Theatre Company (Shaw 1999) and she offered to test out the method with Age Exchange, adapting a show called *Just Like The Country* (Rubinstein, Andrews and Schweitzer 1991).

Just Like The Country

Homes fit for heroes

Originally, this play, written by Joyce Holliday for Age Exchange in 1990, had been performed by a cast of four, with a full-scale set and lighting rig. It was about the inter-war council housing estates built by the London County Council around the outskirts of London. As a result of trying to recruit men to serve in World War I, it had become clear that vast numbers of them were unfit for service, suffering as they were from rickets, lung complaints and other illnesses related to poor housing and inadequate diet. After the war, there was a commitment on the part of the London County Council to improve working people's living conditions and, wherever possible, to move them out of inner-city tenements into healthier environments, with special priority being given to families with sickly children. The new housing developments catered for 150,000 families and were known as Cottage Estates because the homes were modelled on traditional terraced and semi-detached cottage forms. They were built on previously undeveloped areas or farmland and, although today they may appear to be part of the great urban sprawl which is London, at the time the original residents found them to be 'just like the country'.

What was not fully anticipated was the pain involved in breaking up family and kinship networks which characterised the old East End and other inner urban areas, and the isolation felt by the women in particular from their extended families and long-standing neighbours (Young and Willmott 1989). Many of these teething difficulties were eventually outweighed by residents' pleasure at having vastly improved facilities in their homes and being part of a new community affording new relationships and many social benefits. This range of reactions and feelings elicited by the move to the new estates gave the play its tension and complexity.

Ageing pioneers

The original interviews for this project were conducted in the mid to late 1980s on all the big LCC estates around London, including Becontree, St Helier, Bellingham, Castelnau and Downham. A lot of the people who had originally made the move to these estates as 'young marrieds' were then already very elderly, and it had been important to record their memories of those pioneer days, especially as, at this time, council housing was beginning to be marginalised, or sold off under Margaret Thatcher's radical programme. We wanted to celebrate the concept of the council house and to record people's pleasure at having those facilities and receiving those amenities for the first time in their lives and the significant difference that it made to the health and welfare of their children.

Revisiting a research topic after a decade

The decision to revisit this project in the year 2000, more than ten years after the original interviews and production, was precipitated by the fact that the Downham Estate, very near to the Reminiscence Centre in south-east London, was now extremely run down and the subject of an urgent regeneration programme. Downham Pride, the organisation responsible, asked us to involve older people in a project about the estate, and to use it as a jumping-off point for wider community involvement. We decided to conduct a second round of interviews with older people on the estate. By this time, many of the original settlers had died and our interviewees were therefore people who had been children at the time of the move, and who had limited memories of the original tenement dwellings where their parents had lived. What these interviewees did recall was how well cared for the estate had been in their young days and what a thriving community it had been. Their past sense of pride in the place contrasted sharply with their feeling of despondency about its present run-down state. For some of the interviewees, participating in the project seemed like an opportunity to give the rest of the local community a wake-up call, and urge them to take better care of the estate and its residents now and in the future.

A practical rethink

Clare Summerskill edited Joyce Holliday's play into four separate scenes, to be performed by two actors, rather than the original cast of four. After each scene there was a facilitated exchange of reminiscence around the particular themes explored, led by Clare, and she was also able to support the actors musically and provide continuity between different stages of the presentation. Because there were only two actors in this adapted version of the original production, we were able to take the show to small venues which would not have been able to accommodate the full-scale original version. Furthermore, the very small cast and reduced set enabled us to mount the scenes on a little raised stage for the first time. This meant that the audience could see the players much more easily, and thus overcome the perennial problem of seeing over the usual high-backed chairs. However, because the ceiling height of these same venues was often so limited, we had to ensure that the height of the back-drop could be adjusted. The play was performed with live music and costumes and props, so it had many of the merits of the full-cast professional shows, with the added advantage of interspersed reminiscence discussions.

Inviting immediate feedback

One obvious advantage of this way of working was that the audience did not have to retain a whole play in their minds when responding during the discussion periods. The emphasis of the questions asked by the facilitator was not so much 'Which bits did you enjoy?' but rather 'Did any of you have an experience like Len and Vi in that scene? Would you like to tell us about it?' The older people were relating directly to a short episode they had just seen, and had the opportunity to respond issue by issue. The involvement of the older people in the discussions meant that the theatre company heard many new and fascinating stories relating to the themes of the play. Also, even more importantly, the older people heard a great deal about one another's experience, as a result of the stimulus provided by the scenes.

Facilitated discussion: pros and cons

The idea of introducing facilitated discussion sessions between scenes was a very useful alternative method for the company to employ and it created particularly animated interaction with the audience. There were, however, certain problems to overcome with this format, such as the quietness of some older people's speaking voices, the hearing difficulties of others and the fact that a small number of individuals could dominate the discussion. Further, the seats were arranged not in a circle, which is the conventional way of arranging seating for reminiscence discussion, but in rows, theatre style, so that the audience could focus on the performance, and this arrangement did not favour group discussion. The arrangement worked best in small venues where there was a chance that everyone could easily hear the memories of other audience members as well as the action from the stage. In larger spaces, the facilitator overcame the audibility problem by repeating in a strong voice what the elders had said, so that everyone could hear these memories clearly and add their own.

This revised form of reminiscence theatre, in which a series of scenes is interspersed with audience discussion, has proved popular with audiences in sheltered settings. It is, however, different from a piece of theatre that runs for an hour and a quarter without interruption with four or five actors sharing the full development of the stories and the musical performance, both vocal and instrumental. In the latter, the audience can lose themselves in the play, closely identifying with the characters and experiencing a range of emotions. It is a more enveloping aesthetic experience, with the possibility of being transported to another time and place and engaging fully with the developing action. Knowing that the action is going to stop in a few minutes, and that one is going to be invited to talk about what one has seen, changes the nature of the audience's relationship with the performed material.

Many Happy Retirements

Exploring Theatre of the Oppressed methods with older people

Augusto Boal has developed new formats whereby theatre is used to explore problems and issues affecting communities and individuals. The audience go further than discussing the problems raised in the performed scenes and actually have the opportunity to play out possible solutions by interacting with the 'characters' in the scenes. Boal coins the term 'spect-actor' to refer to the spectator who is thus activated (Boal 1979). Through his Theatre of the Oppressed movement, he and the many practitioners who have followed his inspiring lead have offered this idea to communities across the world as a means of empowering people to dare to envisage, and practise for, change. Actors work with a specific group or community and listen to the issues which affect them and which they would like to resolve. They present these issues back in the form of small dramas in which the situation depicted is highly recognisable and likely to provoke strong reactions. The audience members watch a scene through and then see it again, this time with an invitation to stop the action (by clapping or calling 'stop') at any point when they want to question what is happening or to intervene by taking over the role of whoever is being 'oppressed' within the situation. The other performers must respond in role to whatever is offered by the person who has intervened, but they must do this as realistically as possible, so that the suggested action is fully tested and not adopted as a fantasy 'happy ending'. The purpose is a serious one: to practise making change happen in the safety of the improvisation so that it can be more effectively undertaken in reality.

Adapting Augusto Boal's approach

Older people too have to cope with oppressive situations and, having participated in many of Augusto Boal's workshops myself, I was interested to see how reminiscence theatre could be adapted to deal with current concerns and the very recent past, as well as offering a means to reconnect with the more distant past. Some of the key life transitions faced by older people might be explored through interviews with individuals and groups, and these interviews could form the basis for theatre pieces to play to a wider audience of older people. The resulting short scenes or cameos would trigger discussion and role play with the audience. This exploration of the scenes would be facilitated by a designated member of the team, very much along the lines of Boal's 'Joker' figure who mediates between the players and the audience. Subjects such as retirement from work, giving up one's home, moving into residential care and coping with bereavement are just some of the issues older people face and which I felt could lend themselves to exploration in this way.

Basing a project on older people's recent experience

In 1986, the Pre-Retirement Association and the Institute of Community Studies agreed to work with me on a Reminiscence Theatre project exploring how people cope or do not cope with retirement. This was envisaged as a valuable addition to existing courses aimed at people who had not yet left work, but who would be doing so in the near future. In recent years, people have adapted to the idea that they will probably work in different places, retrain and relocate several times in their working lives and, whether they want it or not, will have plenty of practice in coping with change. However, in 1986 when I first experimented with this form of theatre, many people in their mid-60s were retiring from workplaces where they had spent their entire working lives. They may have occupied different positions within the workplace, perhaps benefiting from many promotions, but their energy and loyalty had all been poured into one establishment and they would usually consider themselves very lucky to have held on to jobs and earned pension entitlements as a result.

A point of transition

Major firms, aware that their employees faced a chasm at the point of retirement, were laying on courses to help them to adapt to a new situation and were specifically inviting workers to bring their spouses along with them. Although much of the input was concerned with pensions and investment, the courses also addressed issues of health, social engagement and personal adaptation. The latter was the most difficult and sensitive to explore, especially with older male workers unused to discussing emotional and psychological issues, and it was here that I felt that theatre could play a useful role.

Group and individual interviews

Interviews concerning their retirement were conducted with members of an adult education group, with members of the Pre-Retirement Association and with individuals suggested by firms and factories. How had they handled the transition and what problems had they encountered? Were they still in an adaptation period and what was sustaining them? What advice did they have for others? Themes emerging from these interviews included loss of status and identity, claustrophobia and new marital tensions at home, social isolation, financial insecurity and unresolved tensions relating to the workplace they had left (Schweitzer 1986).

Working with older actors

With two older professional actors, I wrote and rehearsed a series of short scenes based on situations described by the interviewees and we then tried them out in workshops with the two groups of retired people mentioned above. The scenes gave rise to much discussion and participants made additional suggestions, which were incorporated. The resulting show, *Many Happy Retirements*, supported by facilitated discussion around the issues raised, was offered to pre-retirement courses across the country. The take-up was immediate and the responses very positive. Course organisers welcomed this unusual way of entering the more delicate areas of discussion on pre-retirement courses. The stories were so true to life and the actors so convincing that the course participants would immediately engage with the issues and found themselves offering advice to the characters. The actors responded in role to their suggestions, playing out strategies suggested by them so they could see the consequences, and this led to further animated discussion.

Case Study 1: The man in denial

For example, in one scene, John, a man who has reluctantly left a managerial position to be replaced by a much younger person, is constantly waiting for the phone to ring. His unrealistic hope is that his old firm will realise that they cannot manage without him and will invite him back to solve problems he alone can handle. His irritation mounts as he finds that all incoming calls are for his wife, Joan, whose social networks he both envies and despises. With nowhere to channel his energy and skill, John irritates and alienates Joan by trying to re-organise the household for greater 'efficiency', getting under her feet and threatening her equilibrium.

THE AUDIENCE TO THE RESCUE

It was clear from nudges and knowing looks between husbands and wives attending the courses that some of them were anticipating, or even already experiencing, problems of their own in sharing the territory at home and adapting to one another's constant presence. However, instead of asking the couples directly how they were planning to cope with similar situations, we invited them to comment on how they thought John and Joan were handling their problems, how they could have prepared for them better, and how they could now support one another. Usually the actors handled this discussion session in role, with John asking the audience 'How was that then?' and then becoming very defensive in response to their many criticisms. By staying in his role as the rather crass and slightly high-and-mighty retired manager, he would goad the audience, and especially the women, into fiery exchanges.

Before the next scene, set two months later, the audience discussed how they thought the situation might have developed, offering predictions varying from divorce at one extreme to a second honeymoon at the other. In the second scene, after further painful confrontation with his wife, the man confronts the reality of his workless situation, his loneliness and new dependency, and the wife starts to accept some responsibility for helping him to cope. The scenes were not meant to offer solutions but to explore problems and allow the course members to figure out paths that were open to the characters to improve the situations, which were of course chosen for their typicality.

Case Study 2: Communicating about money

The cameos covered a range of social classes and kinds of household, which was necessary as the pre-retirement courses were often attended by quite a wide range of employees within a single firm. In another scene, a couple from a slightly lower socio-economic group were in unexpressed conflict because the husband would not tell his wife what pension he was receiving and how much house-keeping money would now be available to her, with the result that she has lost confidence and adopted a siege mentality:

RENE: (*Calling upstairs as she puts plates on the table*) Jack, your dinner's ready.

Jack enters and sits at table looking disconsolately at his plate.

JACK: What's this then?

RENE: Macaroni cheese.

JACK: No meat then?

RENE: We can't run to meat now you're retired.

JACK: Bloody hell.

Jack messes with his food and reads his paper.

RENE: What are you doing this afternoon?

JACK: Going down the club.

RENE: There won't be anyone there this time of day.

JACK: Eddie'll be there. He retired the same time as me.

RENE: Yes, but he's on that course now.

JACK: Well… (*He reads his paper.*)

RENE: When are you going to start painting the toilet?

JACK: There's plenty of time for that.

RENE: It needs doing soon. And we can't afford to get someone in to do it.

JACK: I'll do it when I want. I've served my time at work. I'm my own man now.

Silence.

RENE: Was there anything in the post this morning?

JACK: Not much.

RENE: Didn't your pension come?

JACK: Oh yes, that came.

RENE: (*Anxiously*) All right, is it?

JACK: Yes, it's all right.

RENE: Is it as much as you hoped it would be?

JACK: I told you. It's all right.

Silence. Jack reads the paper.

JACK: What's for pudding?

RENE: Bottled plums. It's the last lot. I don't know when I'll get some more.

JACK: I'm off down the club then.

RENE: Jack…

JACK: What?

RENE: Can you let me have some money for the paint?

JACK: Oh right.

RENE: You're sure we can afford it?

JACK: Yes.

RENE: Your pension's going to be enough then?

JACK: I told you.

RENE: How much is it then?

JACK: I told you. Enough. Goodbye, love. I'll be back at six for my tea.

MEMBERS OF THE AUDIENCE TAKE OVER A ROLE

Following Boal's method, I invited course participants to watch the scene a second time and stop it when they wanted to intervene to improve the situation for the 'oppressed' person, in this case the wife (Schweitzer 1994a). Although improvisation was a new experience for them, women on the courses were willing and eager to participate in the scene because they were irritated by the husband's complacency and wanted to shake him out of it. The actor playing the husband was therefore faced with a succession of other, more determined 'wives' from the audience, who tried a whole range of methods, from reasoning to bribery, to get him to share the information and to recognise that his behaviour was actually oppressing his wife. The actor did not make life easy for those who stepped into the action, as in reality this secretiveness about money can be a difficult syndrome to crack, especially when it is covered by frequent acts of generosity for which the wife is expected to be grateful, but despite which, or even because of which, she remains powerless. The women on the course either recognised the situation from personal experience and were keen to vent their feelings in the safe situation we had created, or they took the view that this unreconstructed man was out of the ark and needed to be brought up to date by some very straight talking. Either way, they rose eagerly to the challenge and there was humour and ingenuity in their approaches, and surprising confidence in their performances.

Case Study 3: No one is indispensable

In a further scene, Bridget, a restless wife who has recently retired from a busy accounts office, cannot bear the lack of stimulation at home and spontaneously

Many Happy Retirements *with Pamela Lyne and Godfrey Jackman*

decides to go back to visit her former colleagues at her previous place of work. When she arrives there, she finds that no one there has time for her, that new staff and work systems are in place and things have changed radically in the relatively short time since she left. Her husband, who has been contentedly retired some time, cannot understand her restlessness. The course participants were divided into two groups, each advising one of the characters how best to resolve their conflict. The actors stayed in role during these sessions, which helped the audience to relate to the problem and allowed the characters to question them about the wisdom of some of the suggestions. The two actors then met up again in character to negotiate some of the possible solutions that had been offered.

Although there was often much laughter as the audience watched the characters struggle with their situations, the underlying intention was serious. The realisation that, perhaps despite years of commitment, one's departure has not created a vacuum can be extremely painful and many on the retirement courses were anticipating this situation with some dread. 'Make sure you come back and see us' can be a very empty invitation, given the momentum of the workplace and the speed with which one loses touch with it. As the husband in this scene cynically advises: 'You don't want to believe everything they say at retirement parties.' For the course participants, watching the poignant scene in which the wife struggles with her own feelings of rejection served to legitimise their own feelings. It also gave them a way to start addressing the problem as experienced by someone else, prior to tackling it in their own lives.

Food for thought

The theatrical sketches presented on these courses gave the course participants vivid examples to refer to when they were back in their own homes and coping with similar problems, and one could see clearly from the nods of recognition and frequent nudges between couples in the audience that the scenes were hitting their mark. The sketches were revised and updated from time to time, and new ones added, but essentially the project was extremely successful in that it met an identified need and remained in demand for 20 years as a unique way of opening up discussion of the sensitive and personal aspects of retirement and adjustment to a new stage of life.

This way of working, in which dramatised scenes around significant problems affecting older people are used to stimulate in-depth discussion and involvement, can usefully be extended to cover other areas of challenge and adaptation in later life. It can bring the energy of live performance and encounters with 'real' characters to what can all too often be bland general advice given to older people by course providers about ways of coping successfully with change.

Using drama to explore advocacy with older people

An interesting example of this use of drama is a recent series of workshops facilitated by Frances Rifkin of Utopia Theatre Company and performer Raquel Aguado for an Age Concern self-advocacy project for older Asian people. The key elements are story-telling and enactment and the subject of exploration is difficulties in everyday life which the elders want to overcome. A two-hour session might begin with warm-up games and exercises, followed by story-telling by group members around an agreed topic. Problems with the National Health Service figure frequently, including dealing with incomprehensible doctors, rude receptionists and briskly indifferent nurses. The older people's stories are reflected back by the performer, who usually plays the authority figure causing the problem. Of course, it turns out that the performer has insufficient information to go on, so the older story-teller is invited up to demonstrate the unacceptable behaviour from which she suffered, something she is usually prepared to do. The facilitator then invites her to show how she responded, with the performer briefly returning to the role of authority figure. The resulting scene stimulates an animated exchange in the group about what might be the best way of dealing with this sort of problem. This advice is transformed immediately into dramatic action by the participants. The person who told the original story may try some of these actions for herself or she may be too shy or just want to watch. The group then discuss which scenarios might be feasible in reality. Following the sessions, the facilitators prepare a report for the group summarising the problems explored and the solutions proposed by the elders. This report can serve as an action plan for the participants for future self-advocacy, with copies for Age Concern staff who may be willing to support them.

Frances Rifkin (2006) commented on the process in her final report on the project to Age Concern: 'The work takes place both in the imaginative/creative and the cognitive spheres – theatre knits them seamlessly together. Confidence, group creativity and imagination, humour and understanding develop. Participants share their thoughts and experiences and play with change.'

Summary

All the examples in this chapter on stimulus through performance and subsequent discussion and active involvement are designed to lead to more confident participation by older people in society and a feeling that they can confront problems and effect change. Whether their contribution is to bring their own past experience into the discussion, as in the case of *Just Like The Country*, or to advise the characters or take over their roles, as in *Many Happy Retirements*, or to practise ways of overcoming their sense of impotence in the face of authority in the last example from Utopia Theatre's self-advocacy project, the effect is to energise, activate and build the confidence of older people and counteract society's tendency to marginalise them.

CHAPTER 9

Reminiscence Theatre
in Education Projects

Inter-generational work in focus

During the first five years of Age Exchange, 15 reminiscence theatre productions had been mounted, all using various forms of the verbatim method. However, I was worried about losing sight of the inter-generational aspects of the work involving school-children and students, which had given the company its original impetus and, indeed, its name. Gaining high-street premises in 1987, and opening the Reminiscence Centre there as a base for our work, created new opportunities and an ideal environment for bringing older and young people together to explore reminiscence arts in different forms. Theatre in Education (TIE) and educational drama were both in their heyday in the 1970s (Chapman and Schweitzer 1975) and these two closely related but separate fields had been of great interest to me for many years before I learned about the existence and value of reminiscence or reminiscence theatre (Schweitzer 1980a, 1980b, 1980c). I now wanted to explore how they could be adapted in ways which would involve older people, whether as historical witnesses or in an even more creative and participatory role.

Active involvement of children with the actors

In Theatre in Education, the actors, or actor-teachers as they are sometimes called, devise a scenario for a whole class of children, which enables them to explore and understand in a very direct way a complex situation. Playing on what every child already has, a strong curiosity about strangers, some understanding about human relationships and a love for a good story, the actors engage the child's interest in a subject, give him the detail which brings it to life, and then put him in a situation where he has to use that interest and detail to some avail – to help someone, to solve a mystery or a problem, to make decisions and choices. Sometimes the situation explored in a TIE programme is a piece of history with a contemporary relevance, and sometimes it is a more obviously topical matter, but it is invariably one which involves ethical, moral and social issues. In its most developed form, this style of work involves the actors working in role over an extended period, sometimes over a whole day, as key characters who take different and conflicting views of the situation in question. Often there is a specially created three-dimensional set or environment which the actors take into the classroom or school hall or playground to reinforce the reality of the story and enable the actors to explain more graphically how things work or what is going on in the developing situation.

A group role for the children

The actors depict for the children a complex 'as if' situation, meaning that they behave as though an imagined situation is happening in the here and now. They often help the children to enter into this 'new reality', by giving them a group role or a special position from which to consider the events as they unfold. They sometimes enlist the children's assistance, with necessary practical tasks or on exploratory quests, which help the children to understand and identify with the perspectives of the different characters in turn. Separately at first, and then together, the characters explain how they see the problem, and attempt to engage the sympathy or support of the children for their point of view. Encounters with the characters are orchestrated so that the children feel that they are the only ones who have all the information to arrive at a sensible solution. The actors confer on the children as a group 'the mantle of the expert'. This term, borrowed from educational drama, was developed by Dorothy Heathcote and Gavin Bolton in the 1970s (Bolton 1995; Wagner 2000). Listening to each of the characters in turn and witnessing their conflicts, the children try to find a way through the characters' apparently irreconcilable differences. Through their new knowledge about the situation and through their emotional involvement with the apparently real and serious problems the characters are facing, the children are able to engage with issues which might otherwise be considered beyond their presumed perceptual powers and address them in far more sophisticated ways than the classroom teacher alone could contrive.

Introducing older people into the TIE concept

I knew that the TIE approach could bring historical and contemporary issues alive for the children and had felt disappointed that, by the late 1980s, few professional companies were still able to offer these extended experiential events to single classes of children. Economic forces had limited most TIE companies' work to playing to whole year groups, or even larger numbers, with consequently less direct involvement of the children. I wanted to experiment with the form by adding in the presence of the older people to that of actors and children, to see how that enhanced the rather straightforward inter-generational work which we were already producing in the Reminiscence Centre. The older people who were volunteers in the centre, helping in the shop and the café and showing people round the exhibitions, were now regularly working with school parties visiting the centre, explaining to the children the objects and artefacts in the collection and how they had once been used. The children were always most animated when objects and stories connected with the older people's childhood were discussed and there was often an exchange of experience on a more equal footing around these topics. For this reason, it seemed sensible that our first day-long TIE programme should appeal to the children's existing knowledge, interest and understanding, and the subject of school days was an obvious choice.

Good Morning Children

I had interviewed many of the volunteers about their school days and we had held group discussions around this theme in our regular reminiscence group, which met weekly at the centre. They recalled savage teachers, stiff discipline, fierce punishments, learning by rote, playground games and much more (Schweitzer 1989b). It had emerged from these interviews and discussions that many of the older women in particular had very strong feelings about missing out on educational opportunities for purely financial reasons. A family with very limited means would often have to make a choice between sending a son or a daughter to the local high school or grammar school. The education was free, but the cost of special uniform, books, sports equipment and other extras at these schools had to be met by the families. Boys, who would clearly be the breadwinners, were given preference in many families, and girls, however bright, were often unable to take up the places they had won through examinations, even though education at these schools would have stretched them and given them more opportunities in later life. This inequality was still a live topic for the older people and they felt that children might find the issue interesting, indeed rather shocking, and would gain a new perspective on today's educational opportunities and methods.

Rehearsing with the older people

The rehearsal process involved the older people very directly, as a group of them undertook to help the performers to prepare. They became the children and told Illona Linthwaite, a highly experienced actor playing the teacher, just how she should behave as 'Miss Hood'. Illona Linthwaite commented on her experience of rehearsing in this unusual way:

> The rehearsals for this project were unique. I, as Miss Hood, was guided by the volunteers in the creation of her character. The experience was challenging and often very funny. The volunteers became the class – behaving far more wickedly than their childhood selves I'm sure – and I was instructed in the use of cane, dunce's hat, nail inspection and so on. The process was utterly organic and I was kept on my toes by this class of unruly 'children'. (Personal communication)

Creating a total environment

A schoolroom from the 1930s was created in the Reminiscence Centre with school desks, complete with ink and inkwells, slates and slate pencils, a raised desk for the teacher, teaching aids from that period around the walls, a blackboard and a large clock with a loud tick. The whole of the morning session happened in this space and the children who came in from the local primary schools were treated as

Miss Hood (Illona Linthwaite) in charge of the class in Good Morning Children

though they were a class of the past. 'Miss Hood', in appropriate dress and martinet style, took the children, all dressed in school uniform of the time, through a standard morning, with physical drill, handwriting, mental arithmetic, times-tables and geography complete with maps of the time showing the British Empire picked out in red. She projected a rigid sense of right and wrong, with due punish-ment for anyone stepping out of line. She explained that this was a special day because Elsie Dobson, one of the class, had won a place at the High School and that this was an honour for them all, and she asked the children if any of them knew why Elsie was late for school that day.

Introducing conflict and complexity

While the children were writing and the teacher's back was turned, Elsie (a very young-looking actress wearing school uniform) quietly slipped into an empty desk beside another pupil and started work. The teacher asked why she was late and why she had slipped into class in this 'sly' way. Elsie was taciturn and shrugged her shoulders. The teacher said she should feel proud of her achievement, especially as she had worked so hard for this and as her name would go up in gold letters on the school board. Elsie, looking sulky, muttered that she had changed her mind and did not want her place at the grammar school. The teacher was appalled and

Jane Cunningham (third desk back with plaits) is Elsie Dobson in Good Morning Children

demanded an explanation. Eventually Elsie's defiance gave way to misery as she admitted that there had been a great showdown at home with her father, an out-of-work docker, who had made it clear that the family could not afford it. Elsie told Miss Hood that she was very sad that she would not be able to fulfil her dream of becoming a teacher like her.

The teacher showed that she was upset too and left the classroom in Elsie's charge while she went out to discuss the situation with the headmistress. Elsie was nearly crying and the children were not sure how to react. A conversation initiated by Elsie developed between her and the children, in which she explained that her dad said she could not go as education was wasted on girls, and his word was law in her family. The children comforted her and were concerned for her. She asked for their advice and they proposed several possible courses of action, which were then considered by the class and Elsie, the latter gently rejecting any wildly unrealistic suggestions, such as running away from home, by anticipating their consequences in the real world of the time. When Miss Hood returned, she announced that the headmistress had appealed to Elsie's father, but that he had been utterly intransigent. The teacher showed that she was very upset herself, and the children understood that she had given Elsie a lot of support and only wanted the best for her. They continued to seek solutions, with Miss Hood and Elsie still 'in role', and a very small window of hope was left open at the end.

Older people participate in a drama workshop with children

In the afternoon session of the *Good Morning Children* TIE programme, the children moved to a workshop space in the Reminiscence Centre and met the older people who then worked with them in small groups of about five pupils per group. They told them stories about their own school days, and the children listened to these stories and worked out short scenes under the direction of the older people. They then played these scenes to the rest of the class, and the older people were invited to discuss with everyone their memories of the performed incidents, so that everyone heard all the stories, either directly or through the scenes and discussion of them. This method ensured that the children had a close contact with at least one of the older people and a chance to identify with that person's experience through their dramatisation of it. They also heard from those people who, like Elsie, had not been able to go to schools where they had won places, and their discussions on this matter in the afternoon sessions were obviously informed by their morning experience.

Learning by experience

Good Morning Children was a total experience as a TIE programme should be, giving the children a direct sense of what it was like to be at school 60 years ago, with much sensory, tactile and emotional stimulus. The physical experience of sitting in rows, facing the front, working in total silence except for the ticking clock, struggling with real ink, dip-in pens and blotting paper, and learning by rote in a highly disciplined manner, gave the children the opportunity to reflect on their own very different classrooms and ways of learning. Their emotional experience of wanting to help Elsie, and recognising that their efforts would probably fail, gave them a different kind of insight into the past from anything that could have been gained from a history book. The programme also helped them to reflect on their own family and school situations as compared with those faced by Elsie. They recognised the different power structures prevailing within their families nowadays, which gave them more say in their own future. They also saw the relative equality of boys and girls in today's educational provision and the link between education and the kind of work they might later be able to undertake. In the afternoon session, the older people's stories reinforced what the children had learned and gave them first-hand detailed examples of school experiences which they then encapsulated and played out in their short scenes. Illona Linthwaite commented:

> The whole experience was totally new for them and even shocking at times in the most productive way. It was a special and unforgettable time for everyone involved and a unique way of combining theatre and oral history. (Personal communication)

One of the volunteers, Lil Murrell, commented on the children's learning experience in this project:

> We were teaching them what it was like to be in school in our days and I think they were reliving our school days…I think it registers more. If, when we were at

school…instead of just learning the dates of history and the wars and all that, I think if we had actually acted out the scenes of those things that happened like the children actually living our school days, actually doing it and taking part, I think it would have stayed in our minds a lot longer. It's a lovely way of learning. It's very effective. And wasn't it fun for us to work with the children on that project! (Schweitzer 1993, p.51)

'The Intelligence of Feeling'

In their book *The Drama of History*, John Fines and Ray Verrier urged teachers to use drama to enable children to enter imaginatively into the conflicts of history through dramatic improvisation, using their own feelings and insights in order to understand the past (Fines and Verrier 1974). The importance of empathy and emotion in cognitive learning was also explored by Robert Witkin in his influential book published the same year, *The Intelligence of Feeling* (Witkin 1974). He urged teachers to use creative drama methods themselves to engage children's feelings and sensitise them to the human predicaments implicit in every learning area across the curriculum, endorsing also the special contribution TIE and other professional artists could make to classroom learning. These ideas were still very important in the 1980s, even though the introduction of the National Curriculum limited teachers' former flexibility and, initially at least, reduced their freedom to introduce their classes to imaginative cross-curricular programmes. By choosing for the next Reminiscence TIE programme the subject of World War II and its impact on London's children, we were not only marking an important anniversary, but working within the framework of the National Curriculum.

Goodnight Children Everywhere

The school days show had worked very well and the relationship between the older people and the children was intensified through this way of working on a subject close to the children's hearts, but I still felt we could discover a more creative role within the day for the older people. The new Reminiscence TIE project we undertook went some way to meet this requirement. The programme, about the evacuation of London's school-children in September 1939, was mounted exactly 50 years later when the subject was highly topical all over again. The whole project, including the creation of a three-dimensional exhibition and an accompanying publication of stories and images (Schweitzer 1990), was supported by the Inner London Education Authority. The title of the project, *Goodnight Children Everywhere*, was a signature phrase from the children's radio programme of the time, and also a well-known song recorded by Vera Lynn and others, which caught the spirit of children missing their parents and vice-versa.

'Once an evacuee, always an evacuee'

Many of the volunteers in the Reminiscence Centre had stories to tell and many more older people responded to the invitation in the local press to come and record their experiences. In addition to a series of group interviews, 80 individuals recorded their memories of being evacuated and, for almost all of these people, the project was the first opportunity they had had to do so. For many, the recall process was quite an emotional one, reviving the pain of parting from parents, often at a very young age, settling with new foster families, coping with hostility from locals and, at the end of the war, coming back to a very different London and a greatly changed home. 'Once an evacuee, always an evacuee' was a phrase several people used to show how deeply the experience had marked their lives, regardless of how welcoming their new families had been. For those who found more love in their wartime homes than with their own families, and there were quite a number of them, the return to London was sometimes more traumatic than the departure, and many people had retained close contact with their billet-families all through their lives.

The children take an emotional journey

The theatrical version of this material for children aged eight to twelve from local schools would need to take them through this emotional journey, without over-whelming them. Most children were evacuated with their schools, so the group role of an evacuee class would work well for the children in our programme. An obvious key role to be taken by one of the professional actors was that of teacher, usually the only adult known to the children on their journey to their new life. Andy Andrews, a very experienced performer who co-wrote this production with me, took on this role and steered the children through the day.

The play started in a room laid out as a 1939 classroom, but without the full paraphernalia of separate desks that we had used in the earlier theatre project. The purpose of this space was to enable the children to learn about the coming war as though they themselves were about to be caught up in its consequences. This prep-aration included hearing a very simple parable from the teacher to help them understand why Britain was now at war. He drew on the blackboard a plan of a notional school playground and marked out the areas where different groups of children with different special pastimes chose to play. He then pointed out the increase in aggressive behaviour by some of the bigger boys who were taking over more and more of the playground and bullying others into submission. The story grew to include the formation of alliances by some of the other children to protect themselves, how these allies had decided to take joint defensive action, and how the whole situation was about to get out of hand and very nasty. Turning over the blackboard, he showed a map of Europe at the outbreak of World War II, with the territories marked out in a way approximating to the playground division.

The children were then moved to a cramped improvised darkened under-ground shelter where they learned to identify air-raid warnings and all-clear signals and then, back in the 1939 classroom, practising drills for their own safety. This somewhat frightening experience was designed to help the children recog-nise the danger of staying in London and the desirability of seeking safety in the countryside.

At this point, a second actor entered the classroom, playing a parent who refused to let his child be evacuated. He shared his anxieties about the children leaving their families for the unknown and articulated the frequently expressed fatalistic attitude, 'If we're going to go, we'll all go together.' The teacher obviously put the case for the children's safety and potential danger of bombing faced particularly by London and its inhabitants, but the parent's attitude to evacuation did give the children a sense that the unknown countryside might also have its dangers.

Children arrive at the billeting centre in Goodnight Children Everywhere *with actors (left to right) Maurice Iley, Andy Andrews and Amanda Hurwitz*

The children then made their final preparations for evacuation and were marched to the exhibition space in the Reminiscence Centre. On one wall was a mural painted from a 1939 photograph of a trainload of evacuees. The children, with eyes closed, were talked through the long journey from London to the countryside, including farewells, limited provisions meant to last the whole journey running out in the first hour, uncertainty about the destination and endless delays as priority on the rails was given to moving munitions and men. At the end of their imaginary journey, the children were told that they had arrived, tired and late at their destination, the village hall in a country area, where they were awaited by the families who were going to take them into their homes. They were greeted by the third actor, the Billeting Officer, who represented all the prejudices encountered by the evacuees in the countryside, giving them a sense of being an unwelcome burden and an unwholesome mob. She lined the children up to meet the 'billet-parents'.

Older people in role

The country people were represented by the older real-life evacuees, who played out their own remembered experience of this situation. They chose their evacuees quite aggressively, which was how they remembered it: 'We need a strong boy to work on the farm. Let's feel your muscles' or 'We want two girls. Boys are just trouble.' The children were examined for nits and, if they were holding hands with their classmates, they were ruthlessly separated. For the original evacuees, leaving siblings and friends to go to separate homes on arriving at their first destination had been as traumatic as leaving parents behind in London and we wanted to evoke this for the children of today. Of course the children knew that this was a played-out scene, but this process did bring the underlying reality home to them very strongly. A group of older participants commented on what they had observed as the children played out these scenes:

> If the children act out the story themselves, I think it gives them a good idea as to what the child, say it was an evacuee, what the child must have felt at the time, being taken away from home. It gives them more of an insight into what that child's mind had felt than if they just read it. (Dorothy)

> They've actually got tears in their eyes, oh they were upset. (Margaret)

> They were choked…especially when they parted friends or split brother and sister up. (Joyce)

> They actually lived those parts, those children, especially the ones who were left behind in the billeting centre, the ones no one picked. They really felt…what it was like. (Lil)

> (Schweitzer 1993, p.54)

In the lunch break, the children met the real evacuees again, this time out of their billet-parents role, and they were shown the original letters these older people had written home to their parents when they were children, and photos taken of them in the country.

Experiencing disruption and unfairness

For the afternoon session, the class returned to the original space, now refurbished as a country classroom. All these moves to and from different parts of the building throughout the day were intended to give the children direct experience of disruption and of not knowing where they were going next. In order to enter into the feelings of children living far from home, they wrote letters home to their families as though they were far away and this focused their minds on the things they would miss most if they were to be evacuated in this way. The Billeting Officer visited them to read them a string of complaints from their country hosts concerning bed-wetting, fighting and stealing, and to instil in them the country code. This condescending and highly critical character became a target for the children's sense of unfairness, so that they were able to empathise with and express the feelings experienced by many London evacuees at the time, but which those 1939 children could never have risked voicing. In order to reassert the 1939 reality, the actor playing the teacher insisted that they temper their comments and listen politely to the Billeting Officer's criticisms.

Old and young work together

In the final session the children worked in depth with the older evacuees in groups of five or six. Each group listened to the memories of one of the older people and then worked closely with that person for maybe half an hour, dramatising their story. Because the children had to perform that older person's memories, they needed all the bits of information and detail their source could provide. They strongly identified with 'their' old person, taking responsibility for the performance of his or her story, knowing that it was true. The scenes were shared with the rest of the class, so that everyone heard all the stories, and the older people finished the afternoon by answering the children's questions in an open forum.

Creative work from experiential learning

Before the children came to the Reminiscence Centre to participate in the project, we had held workshops for the teachers, discussing how they might maximise the project in cross-curricular work. Every school received a copy of the book of stories, copies of evacuees' original letters home and photographs as a source for

Child's drawing of an evacuee after seeing Goodnight Children Everywhere

classroom work. The children's depth of understanding, both cognitive and emotional, was reflected in the high quality of follow-up work produced with teachers back in the classroom. After the project was over, this work from all the schools who had participated in the project formed a delightful display in the Reminiscence Centre for all the real evacuees and the general public to see, and this was a 'giving back' to the older people of what the children had learned on every level.

The children had learned by being and doing, as well as watching, on the basis of the old Chinese proverb: 'I hear, I forget; I see, I remember; I do, I understand.' This method of bringing history to life for children by performance and participatory re-enactment is now quite commonly found in museums, and greatly complements the traditional museum school visit with its 'spotting' tasks and tick-sheets (Kavanagh 2000). What the reminiscence-based TIE provided additionally was the presence of the older people to reinforce the personal meaning of events in recent history. The experiential adventure took place in an evocative purpose-designed three-dimensional environment through which the children could relive those events and imbue them with their own personal meaning.

Exorcising painful memories

For the older people, in addition to the opportunity to record their stories, there was a renewal of the reality of their own experience. Working with children of the age they had been when they were evacuated, and seeing their reactions, brought back sharp memories of themselves when young. They were put back in contact with the small person who was still inside them, recapturing not only the long-forgotten detailed facts of their evacuation experience, but also the long-buried emotions they had had to cope with at the time. Playing the billet-parents, some of whom had been so frightening for them when they were young, was a chance to exorcise that memory, which had left a surprising number of them with feelings of rejection, a disproportionate number of them claiming to have been the last children from their school to be chosen. Above all, having the chance to transmit their real childhood experience in an enjoyable way to today's children, and to join them in acting out their story with a small group for the rest of the class, made the older people feel purposeful, useful and creative. They enjoyed directing and, in some cases, performing their stories with the children. There was never a shortage of ex-evacuees to participate and there were nearly always at least five volunteers every day willing to join in.

A perennial theme deserving more than one production

One might think that the production of a TIE show like *Goodnight Children Everywhere*, which had 30 performances to different school classes, might exhaust the supply of 'real evacuees'. In fact, this show, which is so relevant to children's understanding of recent history, has been revived three times at Age Exchange and every time new evacuees have come forward. It is important to remember that there are always people who are sharing their stories for the first time. The older people who have the chance to record and work through their memories in this way are a tiny minority of those who could do so, and extending that opportunity more widely is a very good reason to repeat projects of this kind regularly down the years. This is particularly relevant with a topic such as the war, since media coverage of its key anniversary dates often triggers spates of memory which have not surfaced or been shared before. For children, the theme of war and its impact on families will unfortunately always be important and relevant. It is noteworthy that the 1990s revival of the *Goodnight Children Everywhere* project had special resonance for a new generation of young refugees from war-torn Somalia, many of whom were in the local schools, and whose follow-up work, both drawing and writing, reflected much of their own experience.

Hopping Mad

The involvement of the older people in role in the evacuation project convinced me that older people found it very easy to take on an acting role, provided it was in an area where they had life experience to inform their playing. The third TIE project I shall describe was around the theme of London mothers and their children hop-picking in Kent in the pre-war years. We felt sure that this would be an area of interest to today's children, and would give us a way of exploring the broader underlying themes of families coping with change, experiencing economic adversity and living through the decline of an important local industry. A visiting writer-director, Dianne Hancock, with much experience in the field, created a whole-day experiential TIE show based on the 60 interviews she and I conducted with older hop-pickers (Schweitzer and Hancock 1991).

A magical time

In the first half of the twentieth century, women in the poorer areas of London would take their children off to the hop fields of Kent for four to six weeks in early autumn, leaving behind their husbands who worked on the railways or the docks or in factories and building firms. They would go to the countryside, either by train or in old lorries piled high with everything they needed. There was basic accommodation provided, usually in corrugated iron huts or empty farm sheds, and the women made these as comfortable as they could with straw mattresses, blankets and cooking equipment. This was an opportunity for the women to earn some money to spend on themselves and their children, usually on warm clothes for the coming winter, and it was the closest they got to a holiday. Although they were expected to work hard and very long hours on the hop fields, they enjoyed the time spent with friends and relations who went to the same farms every year, sharing the cooking tasks and enjoying social time together in the evenings and at weekends. For the children, these weeks were a magical time, despite the hard work, with freedom to explore the countryside, swim in the rivers and experience a totally different environment from the one they knew in London. Many older people who had 'gone hopping' as children looked back on those days with great joy and were happy to talk about their time in Kent. In that sense, the show was much less challenging than the evacuation project, where the memories were often so much more painful.

A hand-to-mouth existence

We wanted to give the children a context for their hop-picking experience, so the actors spent over an hour with them working in groups to explore through drama how each family would have had to prepare for the trip. They learned about the economic hardship faced by so many families at the time by participating in a whole class scene with the rent man (played by one of the actors) about the consequences of failing to pay up and by acting out, in small groups, scenes about pawning valuable family objects in order to raise the money for the trip to Kent. The reality of the poverty experienced by the London hop-pickers' families in the 1930s would be reinforced later in the day by conversations with older people who had vivid childhood memories of living a hand-to-mouth existence.

The children moved physically through different spaces before arriving at the hop-fields, and again visualisation by one of the actors was the chosen way of covering what the journey would have been like for the hop-pickers. We needed to convey how very different things were in those days, when almost no one had a car and when a trip to the country would have been extremely rare. Although we did not attempt at this point in the programme to make direct contrasts with the kinds of family holidays today's children go on, the differences were clear to all.

From the original interviewees we recruited several volunteers to participate in this project. At first they met the children in role as hop-pickers from the period, and later in the day told stories for the children about their own childhood hop-picking experience, which the children then made into short dramatic scenes.

An exciting environment to stimulate the senses

The environment we created for the hop-picking show was perhaps the most ambitious attempted so far. We filled the exhibition space at the Reminiscence Centre with real hop plants reaching up to the ceiling, and there was a large hop bin in the middle of the room, so the smell of hops was quite strong. The walls were painted with a mural, which gave the room the three-dimensional feel of a whole field, and there were many authentic objects in the space and many memories and photos on the walls and straw bales to sit on. Outside, we created a cooking area with an open fire with bales around it and we also built a hopping hut from wood and corrugated iron and kitted it out with straw-filled mattresses, candles in holders, and other items which the real pickers told us they would have needed at the time. The older people loved going into the hut and talking with the children about how it was arranged in their family, so the children could imagine what it would have been like to sleep there with lots of brothers and sisters and maybe some snoring grandparents as well.

The older people inhabit the space and guide the children in role

One of the beauties of having such a rich and authentic environment was that any older person who was nervous about working with children would find the setting very reassuring. We would say to them, 'Just talk about the things in the exhibition. Answer their questions about how these things were used and what they were'. It

Children in the hop field with ex hop-pickers (Mike and Barbara Fitzgerald) and the actors in
Hopping Mad: *Carolyn Dewhurst, Dianne Hancock and Richard Ashton (design and painting*
by Lisa Wilson with Steve Wilson and Dora Schweitzer)

also helped the older people to enter into their roles, even if they had never done any performance work like this before.

For example, when the children first arrived at the door leading into the hop field, one or two of the older people were outdoors dressed as hop-pickers in the 1930s preparing their hut for the picking season. They proceeded to have quite an argument with an actress playing another hop-picker, who claimed it was her hut and always had been. Listening to these adults arguing and then grudgingly settling their differences, the children got a good sense of how families managed to rub along together with a mixture of straight talking and quick compromises. The older women had no difficulty maintaining their roles because they knew exactly how it was and could ably reproduce the dialogue and atmosphere of the time and situation. They were totally convincing, speaking with authority about what they knew about. For the children who had not met them before, they came across as 'real people' in that situation. The children knew at one level that the whole event was a drama, but the apparent reality enabled them too to behave as though the whole situation was 'happening live'. All the older people who volunteered to participate entered whole-heartedly into the situation and maintained their roles in order to advance the action and the children's understanding.

The children as workers

Before the children entered the hop field, they were addressed by the Measurer, an important authority figure played by another professional actor, as though they really were a new group of pickers. The unattractive conditions of their contract were read out to them in full and they formally accepted them, including the going rate for pickers of one shilling for six-bushel baskets full of hops. It was only when they entered the exhibition space, which felt to them like a field, and saw the hops, the bin and the basket, that they realised what a lot of work this would entail for such a small return. The older people pointed out to them that the hops were very small this year so the work would be much harder. The children and the older people, supported by the other actors, agreed together to try to renegotiate their rate with the Measurer or else go on strike. The play explored the consequences of such action, as the actor playing the Measurer spelt out how disastrous this would be for them, in that they would instantly be sacked. Eventually a compromise was reached, but most of the negotiations were conducted by the children, with the older people and the other actors always pointing up the economic realities prevailing at the time.

Bill and Eileen O'Sullivan in costume in the specially constructed hop-pickers hut share their memories with school classes in Hopping Mad

The kind of role play described above is very reminiscent of the classic Theatre in Education projects of the 1970s where the children spent some time forming an understanding of the working conditions of the time in which the action was set, then stood up for what they understood was right and found their own voice in the anger they felt, often on behalf of another. The actors worked to make the situation convincing and affecting for the children, presenting it in all its complexity and rejecting simple solutions, thus giving them a kind of rehearsal for real life.

After this session, the children stayed in the hop field with the older hop-pickers, hearing about life as it was and what the children used to get up to. During this session, the children touched and smelt the hops and learned how to pick them. They also learned a well-known hop-picking song which was what the old pickers sang to make the time pass. In their lunch break the children visited the hopping hut in small groups and carried on talking with the real hop-pickers about their memories.

Bringing the story up to date through a scripted performance

The afternoon session began with the children relaying in groups what they had learned from the hop-pickers in a series of still photos or 'freezes' which they then explained and, in some cases, developed into enacted scenes. The three professional actors brought the story up to date in a short piece of theatre covering changes in the lives of the characters they had met in the morning. The play explained what had happened to the hop-picking industry during the war years and after, including the impact of mechanisation on hop-picking and the consequent ending of an era for London's hop-pickers. This was the first time in one of the Reminiscence TIE programmes that a piece of scripted theatre was performed in an otherwise fully participatory day. It was effective at a cognitive level, giving an historically accurate portrayal of an industry in transition, but it also had an emotional impact in that the children saw how these changes affected the lives of the characters they had got to know in the morning.

Summary

In all these inter-generational Theatre in Education projects, the children from local primary schools were coming to a specially prepared environment which focused their attention on the subject in question, with specially selected and arranged memorabilia around to reinforce the action. They worked with professional actors who had thought hard to create a holding structure and a series of dramatic encounters, which would ensure a flow of information and of empathy. They worked directly with older 'witnesses' who could explain how the issues in the play had impacted on their lives. They had processed these stories from the older people into small dramas of their own. Back at their schools, they pursued a follow-up programme, the results of which were displayed for the older participants and the public to share at the Reminiscence Centre.

All these productions followed the basic TIE concept that you enable children to grapple with complex concepts through role play, empathy, identification and re-enacted reality, but in these instances there was also first-hand testimony and participation by people who had been through what they were enacting, giving it a very strong sense of reality. The mix of actors, children and their teachers, older people and an extremely rich sensory environment combined to make these plays stay a long time in the memories of all concerned.

CHAPTER 10

Reminiscence Theatre
in a Youth Theatre Context

Theatre in Education as explored in the last chapter is a particularly effective way of engaging children with the past as related by older people, but there are many less elaborate and less costly approaches to inter-generational reminiscence theatre work which can also be very effective in schools and community settings. Many towns have their own Youth Theatre or drama group meeting at weekends or after school to work on productions, but surprisingly few directors of such groups think of bringing local elders into their projects, despite the fact that they are an obvious source of stories local to the area. Involving them in the development of new productions is a way of generating new dramatic material and building community links at the same time.

Not just an acting experience

Working on a reminiscence play in a Youth Theatre group is not just an acting experience for the young people or a test of their acting ability. As well as being creative participants in the production, they need to relate to the older people, to empathise with their lived experience, and find their own dramatic idiom through which to express the material they have gathered. There is less emphasis on ego and stardom, in that the young people are channels through which the elders' experience reaches others. It is, however, important for the leader to maintain a fine balance between young and old, ensuring that the older people do not overwhelm the children with information, which might limit their creative responses to their stories.

As with the Theatre in Education projects described in the previous chapter, it is very important that the young people can relate to the topics chosen and much of the skill of the leader will lie in helping them connect with the material using their own insight and experience. Of course this will be much easier with a childhood-related topic, but this is not an absolute requirement and might be unnecessarily restricting.

Artistic licence for the young people

The process of telling a story and then seeing it played back by the young people, either straight away or after they have worked on the material for some weeks, can be very fascinating, but sometimes a little unnerving for the older people. They may be quite surprised by the interpretations the children put on their stories. Some older people may become quite insistent that every detail is played as they recall it, so it is important that the group leader spends time discreetly reminding them of the purpose of the exchange. The older people must accept the idea that exactitude is not required and that the young people's response has its own validity, especially in the context of youth theatre or drama group work, where the students have enlisted on the basis that their own creativity will be encouraged and respected (see Salas 1993).[15] As Margaret Phair, one of the older contributors to many inter-generational projects, commented:

> Don't you think that each child, as an individual, when they're asked to do a character, that they put their own personality into it? So if they're going to act the part of a Gran, they bring their own Gran into that character or one they've seen on television, and put that together with what we've said. (Schweitzer 1993, p.48)

Some examples of inter-generational Youth Theatre projects covering a range of topics and different creative approaches follow.

Good Morning Children

Good Morning Children was a Youth Theatre play produced in 1988, based on school days stories told by older people who came to the newly opened Reminiscence Centre to participate in a regular reminiscence group. Topics included corporal punishment, teachers' pets, humiliation of poor children, hiding in outdoor toilets to escape lessons, playing truant, stealing from the local sweet shop, in fact a mixture of stories with relevance to both past and present. Some of the material generated by the group was later used in the 1989 Theatre in Education production of the same name described in the previous chapter.

About 20 children, aged 10 to 14, were drawn from local schools and met in the Reminiscence Centre on Saturday mornings. In the first couple of sessions the young people heard stories from the reminiscence group about what happened inside the classroom and out. Stories of cruel punishments were of particular interest to the children, as were tales of absconding and generally getting up to mischief. The older people were especially forthcoming on these matters, which made them very popular! The young people also liked the sad stories about loneliness, bullying and poverty, including a story given by one of the older men about having to go up onto the school platform in front of all his friends to receive a pair of boots supplied by a local charity.

These stories were explored in small groups through improvisation and then played back to the whole Youth Theatre group. In addition there were whole group scenes set in the classroom, involving the teacher and the school inspector, in which the young people worked together to convey the atmosphere, spirit and typical actions of a school day in the late 1920s to early 1930s.

All the action was performed in front of a backcloth painted by the group based on an original photograph supplied by one of the older people, but with the children's own faces painted in by each one of them. The children sat in rows, as in school, but stood to speak directly to the audience. Each character introduced him or herself to the audience in a short self-written monologue, often incorporating a story told by the older people. The play then broke into small scenes, often broadly comic. These small group scenes were performed in the down-stage area in front of the formally seated class. Here is a short extract from a scene written by the participants, in which all the characters, male and female, were played by four boys:

MUM: (*Miming vigorously stirring cake mixture in a bowl and addressing the audience*) My boys don't like school.

BOY 1: (*Whining and moaning*) Mum, do we have to go today?

MUM: Yes, of course you do, so hurry up and go. (*While Mum is distracted, boys mime sticking fingers in cake mix and licking them as they run off.*)

BOY 1: I don't want to go to school today. We've got handwriting. Yuk!

BOY 2: Neither do I. We've got geography too. Why don't we go to the park instead.

BOY 1: What and not go to school? Mum'd kill us.

BOY 2: Yeah, well, she won't find out, will she?

NOSY NEIGHBOUR: 'Ere, aren't you supposed to be in school?

BOYS: We're just going. (*The boys are seen going to the park, kicking an imaginary ball around and boasting to another friend about playing truant or 'hopping the wag'.*)

NOSEY NEIGHBOUR: (*Dialling*) Is that the School Board Inspector?

SCHOOL BOARD MAN: (*Played by the same boy as the nosey neighbour who now puts on bowler hat and mimes picking up phone*) Yes, can I help you?

NOSEY NEIGHBOUR: (*Removing bowler*) I've just seen two boys going off to the park and they should be in school. Would you mind checking up on this?

SCHOOL BOARD MAN: (*Re-donning bowler*) Thank you. I'll be along in a moment. (*Puts down mimed phone and runs to catch boys and take them home to a furious Mum.*)

MUM: Oh, Officer, I'm so sorry. They're usually such good boys. I promise they won't do it again.

SCHOOL BOARD MAN: Well, this is the last warning. I'll leave them for you to deal with this time.

MUM: Thank you, Officer. (*He leaves*) Come 'ere you two. (*She beats them vigorously.*)

The children really took over the stories told by the older people, interpreting them loosely and very inventively, reflecting all the friendship and fun of their own relationships, and the bad-boy behaviour they fantasised about, as well as what they had heard from the older people. The set-piece ending was more directly taken from the older people's accounts of Empire Day when all the children dressed up and represented the different parts of the Empire and the products associated with those countries, finishing with a rousing, if rather tongue-in-cheek performance of 'Rule Britannia'.

Empire Day remembered in the Youth Theatre show, Good Morning Children. *The backcloth was painted by the members of the group*

At the performance, attended by friends and family of the children and the older people, the latter read some of their own stories from the book of school days memories published to mark the event, and so they were fully recognised as part of the creative team.

In Service

In Service, produced in 1992, was based on just two older people's contrasting stories of being put into domestic service at the age of 14, a situation quite shocking to today's children of around the same age. In this case, the two women attended several rehearsals and watched the play unfold through the children's improvisations. Laura Murphy had greatly enjoyed her time in service, been very well treated and had learned skills she could use throughout her life. Margaret Kippin on the other hand, had felt humiliated and angry about being forced to abandon her schooling and go into service because of her parents' declining fortunes and she bitterly resented the treatment she had received from her employers.

The young people, all girls in this case, divided into two groups, each working with one of the women. The fact that Margaret had such strong feelings helped them to play her story with intensity and to identify with her anger and humiliation. This was contrasted with Laura's reaction to being sent into service, where her main source of unhappiness had been living far away from her family in a strange house, but one where she was quickly welcomed and made new friends. Again, this was something the young people could understand and identify with.

It was more difficult for the children to grasp the very different class system prevailing at the time. In their improvisations they included little mutinies where they would say exactly what they thought to their boss and speak up for their own rights. It was obviously necessary for the older people to say to them, 'It simply wasn't like that in the 1930s. You didn't do that. Whatever you were thinking you couldn't afford to say it. Your mother had put you there because she couldn't afford to feed you. She wouldn't want you coming back home because you'd been dismissed.' In rehearsals, we developed the device of someone acting out the part of the 'alter ego' who spoke the words the protagonists would have liked to say but could not have risked in the actual situation, and some of these words too were taken from the information supplied by the older women.

A therapeutic effect?

The whole experience of preparing this play was in some ways akin to a psychodrama method in that the young people were re-enacting the elders' experience along lines specified by them (Moreno 1987). Margaret reflected afterwards on the process of revisiting her youth with the young people and watching them rehearsing and performing her story:

> It can be quite painful, because you've suddenly told the children something about a part of your life that you weren't very happy about and they enact it, and when we came to see the *In Service* play you know, there was a little lump there because it brought it back. (Schweitzer 1993, p.48)

She told me that she felt quite stirred up by the process, especially as those playing it back to her were roughly the age she was at the time. However, the children's work had given her the opportunity to externalise her experience, achieve some distance from it, resolve some of her residual feelings and achieve 'closure'.

From Pillar To Post: Clara's story

Working from written sources

There have been some interesting examples of Youth Theatre groups working on material supplied in writing by an older person and only meeting them face-to-face at the performance. One such example was *From Pillar To Post*, performed by the Age Exchange Youth Theatre in 1992. Clara Chesterman, an elderly lady in her 80s, who had grown up in south-east London, but was now living miles away in the West Country, had sent me a copy of her autobiography including her memories of growing up in an orphanage in the 1920s. The Youth Theatre members, an all-girls group at this time, were fascinated by the orphanage theme. I wrote to the author asking for her permission for us to work on her story and she agreed enthusiastically, sending us some photographs of herself and the various foster homes and orphanages where she had lived as a girl. Photocopied extracts from the autobiography were circulated and the girls began by drawing and painting their image of the different episodes of the story. These wonderful drawings were made into colour slides and back-projected as the scenery for the play.

Children in the orphanage in From Pillar To Post *based on Clara Chesterman's story*

The girls then improvised the situations that interested them from the book, portraying important characters such as relatives, teachers, matrons, friends and an unpleasant foster mother. It really was their own interpretation of the story, including fantasy and nightmare sequences, but we all hoped that it was true to the original in all the essentials. Here is a short extract from the play to show the relationship between Clara's own words, as supplied in her written story, and the girls' improvisation:

CLARA: It wasn't like any other day. We were dressed in strange black clothes and told to stay indoors. The curtains were closed, so the room was dark and gloomy. The grown-ups who came to the house were whispering. Two black horses with beautiful plumed heads and pulling a black carriage drew up outside. Inside was a long box covered in flowers. I was led out and put in the coach behind... I was two and a half years old at the time, too young to know that I had taken part in my mother's funeral, but that dreary day in September 1927 has never left me.

The story (still in Clara's words) was taken on by the girl playing her big sister Emily, who spoke of the terrible impact on Clara's extended family of the mother's death and the father's disappearance with someone else. The audience learned that the girls and their baby brother were sent to stay with their sick Gran and 'ran a bit wild' there. Then the script broke into dialogue derived from improvisation:

NEIGHBOUR: (*Seeing the children out in the street*) It's getting late. Who's doing tea for you little ones? Is your Gran ill?

CLARA: She can't get up today. She keeps coughing.

EMILY: We're all right, don't worry. I'm looking after Gran and the little ones.

NEIGHBOUR: But you're much too young for that.

EMILY: No, I'm not. I was seven yesterday.

CLARA: I'm hungry, Em. We haven't had anything to eat today.

EMILY: Let's go in and I'll try to find something to make some supper for us. Maybe Mrs Maisey up the road will give us a bit of their leftovers like yesterday.

NEIGHBOUR: (*To audience*) It's not right, is it? Poor little things. I've been giving them what I can but we've nothing to spare now. I think I'd better tell the welfare people.

Meeting the source

The writer travelled from Somerset to London with her family, by invitation, for the first performance of the show and was immensely touched and impressed by what the children had made of her story, giving it a completely different life of its own outside her own memory. Although in this case there was only one direct meeting with the older person, the children felt an immediate rapport with her because they had entered imaginatively into her experience and worked so closely with her written memories. It was important for them to see that she approved of what they had done, and it was positive for them to see that she had made a good life for herself after such a terrible beginning.

Für Immer (Forever)

In an interesting and somewhat similar experiment in the town of Kassel in Germany in 2005, an all-girls Youth Theatre group called *die Schlipse* (The Ties), aged 11 to 14 years, developed a play from letters written to them by a group of older people containing memories and stories about their lives. The elders were members of a community centre, which was participating in a reminiscence arts project of the European Reminiscence Network to mark the sixtieth anniversary of the end of World War II. Following a series of reminiscence sessions, the older people had all worked with visual artists to create individual Memory Boxes. These 'life portraits' were to form part of an exhibition with 56 other boxes made along similar lines in other countries (Schweitzer and Trilling 2005).[16] The whole exhibition was to be launched in the foyer and staircase areas of a very grand office block in the centre of their town before going off on a 14,000 kilometre tour of Europe.

The girls of *die Schlipse* agreed to make a piece of theatre with their director, Brigitte Sturm-Schott, to perform on the occasion of the exhibition opening in the presence of all the worthies of the town and many international visitors who were participating in the project. Knowing that the play by the young people would give the exhibition an added dimension, the older people wrote to the group about their lives, especially about the aspects they had explored in their Memory Boxes.

Over-riding the language divide

The older people's experiences, on which the play would be based, were very diverse, so there was no single theme to the piece. It was rather a set of imagistic scenes created in response to the different written stories the girls received. The group had recognised that many of those watching would not be German speakers and they had built their play around strong visual images and movement sequences which over-rode the language divide.

For example, a depiction of the devastating death toll of World War I was simply but effectively depicted by the eight young girls, wearing men's jackets to identify them as soldiers and holding rolled umbrellas to represent their guns, facing one another across a dramatic stairwell in the centre of the performance venue. The group enacted a Christmas meeting between the German and English soldiers for an exchange of greetings and songs, lit only by candles attached to their 'guns', before a retreat to their respective trenches. During the subsequent 'battle', the players folded themselves over the staircase banisters as they 'fell'. This story of the brief armistice, well known to the British through the affecting portrayal in *Oh What a Lovely War!* by Joan Littlewood, was new to the young German people and it had greatly touched them. In another scene, a child wrote to her soldier father the news about her good school results and then waited impatiently for a reply which would never come. Not all the scenes were so solemn. The girls presented a delightful story of a young girl picking mushrooms with her grandfather in the forest, learning to tell which were poisonous, by inventive use of coloured umbrellas to represent the forest and the mushrooms. Another story was a dreamy romance of a young girl whose boyfriend had gone on holiday in England, leaving her bereft and love-sick throughout the summer.

An added dimension to a European reminiscence project

The older people were interested to see what *die Schlipse* had made of the stories they had sent them, especially as they had had no direct contact with the young people until the first performance. They were delighted with the girls' inventiveness and their highly original interpretations of their stories. There was a very large audience at the opening of the exhibition, including many participants in the Memory Boxes project from other European countries, and everyone was eager to make the connections between the Memory Boxes on display and the stories in the play. Each scene was performed on a different mini-stage in the venue, with the audience moving from space to space and floor to floor, following the players, thus participating in the journey with them. The audience was immensely touched by how sensitively and imaginatively the young people had interpreted the stories they had been sent by the German elders. The simple playing of the scenes described above, and many others, was very moving for the international audience, giving added significance to the event, which celebrated peaceful co-operation between European countries in an artistic endeavour around personal memory.

The *Für Immer* production was subsequently invited to London for a European symposium on reminiscence arts, entitled *Making Memories Matter*, where the girls managed to perform in English to a totally different but equally appreciative audience. The primarily non-verbal nature of the show was what made this possible and enabled the group to communicate with an audience representing a wide age range and differing cultural backgrounds.

Blitz

Older people perform with the Youth Theatre group

In one of the Age Exchange Youth Theatre shows, *Blitz*, developed in 1991, the older people took a much more active part in the production, eventually playing in some of the scenes with the children and even performing some scenes on their own. This new development happened almost by accident and was not the intention when the rehearsals began. A change of director and other factors had led to falling numbers in the Youth Theatre group, but quite a large performing space had already been booked for the opening performance as part of a local festival and publicity had already gone out. It occurred to me that the older people might be willing to come to the rescue and appear on stage with the children.

Experiencing the improvisation method

A few months previously I had asked Charles Wegner, one of our regular professional actors, to join me in running a series of informal improvisation workshops for anyone who would like to come. Members included older volunteers, and 'Friends' of the organisation, some of whom had regularly supplied stories for theatre projects involving the professional company. These improvisation sessions were mainly focused on reminiscence themes but it was obvious that the older people enjoyed using their imaginations as well as their memories. The sessions included many basic drama exercises using standard improvisation techniques and the older people showed considerable flair for this kind of work. This core group were therefore invited to perform alongside the remaining children and make up a new joint cast and, with some anxiety, they took on the challenge.

Initially the two groups worked in parallel, with the children rehearsing stories told to them at the start of the project by the older people and adding in related stories from their own grandparents. The older people worked through improvisation to develop scenes around their own Blitz memories, which would be presented alongside the children's scenes. Each person introduced a story and enlisted the help of three or four other older people to help play it out. There was something very easy and natural about their playing as though they were walking together through their past experience. There were no bravura performances, but rather everyone just contributed truthful responses to the given situation and each person made it more real by adding their own authentic touches. There was a great deal of mutual appreciation of one another's sharpness and humour.

However, faced with the difficulty of learning lines, even though the scenes in question were taken from their own improvisations, some older people stopped enjoying themselves and felt they were failing. We quickly reverted to a purely improvised format, accepting that the scene would be slightly different every time it was played, whether in rehearsal or performance. Sometimes it was difficult for the older people to remember the order of the scenes and what had to be covered in each, so flip charts were used in rehearsal to jog memories, and each person led into their own scene with a short narration to orientate everyone else.

Performance: an alarming prospect

Appearing in a theatrical production was a very alarming prospect for the older people, even if it was ostensibly just to help out the Youth Theatre group. One of them said, 'It's one thing to make a fool of yourself in front of a few people of your own age all doing the same thing, but to play to a hundred strangers in a big space is something else.' For another participant in the project, the idea of being part of a little group of ten old ladies representing the Blitz on London was altogether too ambitious an undertaking, so she and a couple of the older people dropped out of the improvisation group and settled for reading from their own stories in the book we had published to go with the play. The rest carried on with rehearsing their stories and enjoyed introducing all the paraphernalia of the Blitz at each rehearsal, including gas masks, tin hats, suitcases, and coats and scarves from the costume store.

Joint scenes involving old and young

The joint scenes involving the children and older people were very lively and realistic. One example was a scene in the air-raid shelter where an older person, playing an air-raid warden, shepherded in a reluctant old lady with a bucket containing her goldfish, which she refused to leave behind at home, a true story remembered by one of them. It was very touching having the children and older people playing together, cowering from the raid, singing songs to keep up their spirits and emerging from the shelter to find everything changed by the bombing. This project went on to win the national Age Resource award for its effectiveness in bringing old and young together for creative exchange.

In the course of writing this chapter I talked to Eleanor Spruell, who had been a Youth Theatre member at this time, and asked her to comment on the experience of working on this and later plays with the older people. This is what she said:

> I liked feeling I was part of something that had a good atmosphere and that had adults doing things there as well as us. It made me feel that it was more than just for children. It made me talk to Granny and Grandpa more and think about them as people, other than how I knew them as grandparents. It seemed quite magic this world from years before that we talked about with the old people. I liked it that it was all true and was intrigued about the difference of their lives from ours. The excitement and horror of war seemed vivid. Getting in touch with their lives gave me more of a sense of life being an adventure, that it changes all the time and that there were things in store for me that I didn't know about yet.

Grandmother's Footsteps

The approach involving the children and older people performing together was taken further in the *Grandmother's Footsteps* show which followed *Blitz* in 1993–4. We made a virtue of the combination of the different generations in that the actual subject of the play was people's memories of, and relationships with, their grandparents. The idea was that the older people would talk to the children about their own grandparents and would represent them in the play. The children, aged about 10 to 18, would then represent the older people when they were young.

Tell us about when you were young

The older people remembered far more about their grandparents than they had originally imagined: in fact enough for a whole book of memories and photos to accompany the show (Schweitzer 1994b). They recalled particular phrases they used to say, little eccentricities, songs they taught them and how they, as children, had related to them. In the following extract, Joyce Milan recalled her grandfather, a gamekeeper on a country estate in Suffolk. She narrated the scene, while a young man of 19 played her grandfather, a boy of 13 played King Edward VII and a girl of 11 played Joyce as a child.

JOYCE: My father's father was a countryman. He had been a gamekeeper on a big estate.

GRANDPA: (*With straw in his mouth and the bottom of his trousers tied with string, welcomes Young Joyce*) Hello, little Joyce. Let's get your coat off. (*He pretends to peel it off.*) That's right. Skin a rabbit. Now we'll sit by the fire. (*They warm their hands by an imaginary fire and recite together the follow-ing verse, with Joyce joining in.*)

ALL: Warm your toties warm
The boys have gone to plough
If you want to warm your toties
Come and warm them now.

YOUNG JOYCE: Why are your trousers tied up at the bottom, Grandad?

GRANDAD: To stop the rats running up my legs. (*He demonstrates this and scares her.*) Let's go and see if the hens have laid an egg for us, shall we? (*They mime finding eggs, which Young Joyce carries very carefully. Grandad mimes bringing in a hen under each arm and standing them on the arms of his chair.*) Thank you for the nice eggs, my dears. Here's your bread and butter. (*He feeds them bread and butter and makes clucking noises.*)

YOUNG JOYCE: How did you lose your eye, Grandad?

GRANDAD: Shh…it's a secret really, but I'll tell you.

JOYCE: He told me a story about going shooting with the king of England, Edward VII, when he visited the estate. (*The rest of the cast play out the story of the shooting party.*) They had a great big picnic in a hamper and the king drank too much. (*The cast look after the king and carry him around until he is ready to shoot again. He shoots and misses, instead shooting Grandad in the eye. Grandad staggers and falls.*)

KING: Drat, I missed. Sorry about that, Gamekeeper. I'll send you a fine reward for your services.

YOUNG JOYCE: Did you ever get the reward, Grandad?

GRANDAD: No, but I will one day. I'm still waiting. (*He and Young Joyce go off companionably, singing 'To be a farmers' boy'.*)

A different world

It was intriguing for the children to have to think about the old people with whom they were performing once being young like them, but living in a very different world. We were going back 70 years and the photos of grandparents produced for the young people to look at showed them in the clothes they wore much earlier in the twentieth century. Some scenes were modelled on these photographs, espe-cially at the opening of the play, where each child introduced 'their' older person, dressed as the grandparent and standing very still:

This is Olive's grandmother. She was a dumpy lady with a big tummy and she always wore a white apron over it.

This is Bill's grandfather. He always had a pipe that he smoked in one hand and a pint of beer in the other.

This is Margaret's grandmother. She always wore gloves and a hat to go out.

This was one of the few shows where we used costume for the older people as well as the young. It was mainly simple black skirts and white blouses, but with add-on items to differentiate characters, and this was effective in emphasising the stretch of time back into the distant past which separated the older people's grandparents from today's children.

Vivid characters

The remembered grandparents were very varied and not all were very loveable, so there was little danger of sentimentalising them. Eileen O'Sullivan remembered a bullying grandfather, a complete rogue who beat his wife and used his grandchildren as cheap labour.

EILEEN: I remember my grandfather. I was terrified of him. He was always in a bad temper. (*Grandad played by a boy of 15 snarls at the audience and raises his hand to his wife, played by Laura, aged 75, and freezes.*) I think my grandma was frightened of him too.

By contrast, Margaret Kippin directed and played in her own scene concerning her very loving relationship with her grandmother.

MARGARET: My grandmother was a white-haired lady with twinkly blue eyes and apple-blossom cheeks, a very soft skin and quick in her movements. I loved her very much and I went to stay with her in the school holidays. (*Child arrives as Young Margaret and older Margaret, playing Grandma, greets her with a hug.*) Her cottage garden was beautiful and I remember the different flowers she showed me when I arrived. (*She points them out.*) Lily of the valley, roses. (*They smell the flowers and explore the garden together, Young Margaret miming picking a posy for herself.*) Let's get some water from the pump. (*In mime, they pump the water, fill a vase and arrange the flowers.*) I'm doing some baking this afternoon. Will you help me?

YOUNG MARGARET: Ooh yes, can I make my own jam tarts?

MARGARET (GRANDMA): Yes, but first go and wash your hands. (*Young Margaret mimes washing hands at pump. She and Grandma make pastry together. When Grandma goes to get jam, Young Margaret swipes at a fly and pastry drops on the floor. She looks round to check Grandma has not seen, picks it up and carries on.*) Did you wash your hands?

YOUNG MARGARET: Yes, Gran. It's a bit grey, isn't it?

MARGARET (GRANDMA): Never mind, it'll taste delicious. (*They put the pastry in the oven and sing together.*)

BOTH: (*Singing*) Where are you going to, my pretty maid?
I'm going a'milking sir, she said.

Throughout the process of making the play, the young people really enjoyed working with these stories of vivid characters from another time. The old people took great pleasure in resuming contact in their memories with those long dead grandparents, some of whom were born back in the nineteenth century, and bringing them back to life on stage.

Children and older people in Grandmother's Footsteps

Pains and pleasures of inter-generational performance

When this show was taken overseas in 1994 and performed in Germany, Austria, France and Belgium it aroused a lot of interest. Audiences in the conference halls, small theatres, day centres and schools where we performed were charmed by the old and young playing creatively together and were astonished at the wealth and variety of the stories generated by the group. Touring with a group of players aged 10 to 85 by plane, train and minibus was certainly a memorable experience! Although there were some very stressful moments, mainly caused by the radically different waking and sleeping hours kept by the two groups, the old and young grew very close and learned to appreciate each other's respective strengths. The children had no difficulty remembering lines and where they were supposed to be on stage at any one time, but often lost concentration. The older people had far greater powers of concentration and no teenage temperament, but had difficulty remembering their lines and sometimes lost their sense of orientation in the space, so they were happy to accept prods and prompts from the young people. All in all, it was a very fruitful collaboration, especially as quite a number of the children in the group were going through painful family break-ups during this period and it seemed to me that the affection of the old people was greatly valued by them. Basically each group complemented the other and together they made a very strong team.

Cheers
Developing an inter-generational play from a visual stimulus

The last example of inter-generational Youth Theatre is *Cheers*, a show based on memories of older people and performed jointly by young and old. This production marked the fiftieth anniversary of the end of hostilities in Europe in 1945 and was prepared for a European Reminiscence Network Festival called 'A Time To Remember' (Klose 1996).[17] Ten groups of older people from across Europe and beyond had brought plays made especially for the occasion, all of them performed by the older people themselves, and some with participation by younger people.[18]

Cheers was designed to animate a three-dimensional exhibition which had already been constructed by the theatre designer, Lisa Wilson, in the Reminiscence Centre. The installation included a mural depicting an end of the war street party, a bomb-site with rubble, a row of shop-fronts with rationed goods, a bomb-damaged interior with letters sent from the front displayed on the mantelpiece, and a cut-out silhouette of St Paul's Cathedral against a night sky. The young people responded strongly to the created environment, identifying with the painted children in the street party mural and playing on the bomb-site amidst the actual rubble on the floor. For the older people, the visual representation of bombed-out London at the end of the war, combined with the presence of young people, some of whom were the exact age they had been at that time, evoked strong emotions. Joan Pearce expresses her profound response to the situation thus:

> It drags out so many memories that you have suppressed. I remembered the distress I felt coming back from evacuation at the end of the war. I went away at the age of nine as an evacuee and came back at fourteen… My parents were very busy with war work and my mother suddenly had to become a mum again, for a child that had grown up. She said, 'You are big enough to see to yourself now.' And I wasn't, you see, that was the hurtful bit. I played my mother in the scene. I made her quite harsh. I began to understand the psychological reason why she couldn't accept me, why she felt awkward with me. (Schweitzer 1996, p.11)[19]

This method of starting with a professionally designed exhibition environment, and inviting old and young players to people the space with scenes from lived experience, is worth exploring further, perhaps in a museum or heritage centre context.[20] In this instance, there was room for only 40 seats and very little performing area, but the event felt special because the environment was so evocative and the historical context was so palpable. Everyone was struck by the visual impact of inter-generational performance in this particular performance space and by the way in which the children's performances were so clearly informed by the elders' direct experience (see Marziali and Topalian 1997 which contains detailed accounts of this production and other plays created by older people's theatre companies).

The last word should go to Nathan Cooper (aged 19 at the time) who played the handsome young bridegroom in *Cheers* marrying Joyce, his beautiful bride (75 years old at the time of the performance), before disappearing for five years on active service:

> I was worried about it at first, thinking I've got to get a girl my age in, to make it all right. I just thought this is going to look absolutely ridiculous. But in the end it was fine, better even. To the audience it looked like she was reliving her memories, and I was how old I would have been in her memory. That just made it work better, it was an advantage, because it added something to it, and made it quite funny. (Schweitzer 1996, p.23)

Young love and a wartime wedding played by Joyce Milan and Nathan Cooper in Cheers

Summary

In this chapter I have considered a variety of approaches to making theatre from memories with young people in Youth Theatre groups. In some, the written word in story and letters has been the inspiration, and in these cases the older people have only seen the final work in performance. In the majority of cases, it is through a series of encounters between old and young that the plays have been developed, the older people sharing their stories, attending rehearsals, advising the group and sometimes contributing readings alongside the performed scenes. At its most developed, however, the work has involved young and old performing together and this has undoubtedly been the most adventurous and fulfilling experience for all concerned. To watch the two age groups get to know, like and understand each other, work together over a period of months and develop into a creative team giving pleasure to others and satisfaction to themselves has been one of the high points for me of working in this field.

CHAPTER 11

Inter-generational
Play-making in Schools

It is relatively rare for classroom teachers to invite older people in the neighbourhood to come to the school to contribute through their lived experience to topic work, but once they have tried this approach they usually wonder why they did not think of doing so before. The older people's stories are at least as interesting to the children as the books or internet pages the class would otherwise be consulting, with the added advantage that the elders are available to answer questions and engage in creative re-enactment as consultants or participants. Although there are many ways in which older people can contribute to the curriculum through reminiscence, I shall focus here on theatre and drama in particular (Nixon 1982; Savill 2002; Schweitzer 1993).

Issues to consider

Learning across the curriculum

Although the shows described in the previous chapter were created in the context of a Youth Theatre, versions of them could just as easily have been developed by teachers with a class of school-children and older participants could then have been invited. Indeed there have been some very rich reminiscence plays developed in school time where a teacher has seen the possibilities for learning across the curriculum and where the school has had an open-door policy in relation to the local community and its older members in particular (Schweitzer 1993). (See Schweitzer 1993 for information concerning locating older people to participate in inter-generational projects.)

Preparing the older people

The older people will need some preparation for the work if they are to feel confident about it (Langford and Mayo 2001). It is highly desirable to bring them together as a group to share stories before they meet the children. This enables them to start focusing on the subject of the young people's intended play and to trigger one another's memories, bringing out the common ground between them and highlighting their very different experiences. It also provides a good opportunity to clarify with them what is expected of them, how they will work with the young people and any logistical problems concerning transport and access.

Using appropriate language

Questions of language level should be raised at an early stage. Many of the older people will have told stories to grandchildren and will know how to use simple language effectively when telling well-known stories. Applying similar language levels to relating their own experience is more difficult and takes some practice. It is a good exercise to ask some of the older people to retell the stories they have just exchanged with one another in language they think a ten-year-old would understand. The older people can also think about photographs, objects and documents they have at home which might illuminate for the children the time and circumstances they are describing.

Assuming too much knowledge

One problem which often occurs is that older people assume far too much knowledge on the part of the children they work with. Things they take for granted need spelling out. At a simple level, it might be surprising to children to know that most people did not have an inside toilet when they were growing up, or that the majority of them left school at 14. They may need to know that most women stopped working when they married and that housework and cooking took a lot longer without vacuum cleaners, washing machines and microwave ovens. The children, especially at primary school level, will probably not have heard about the General Strike, the Welfare State, the trade union movement, Winston Churchill or even Adolf Hitler. They will certainly not understand acronyms like NUM (National Union of Miners) or the RO (Relieving Office) and such things will need to be unpicked for the young people if they are to follow the story. Another consciousness-raising exercise is to ask some of the group to share a memory relevant to the subject the young people will explore and ask the others to imagine themselves as children listening. Every time the story-teller says something that might not be understood, the 'children' should raise their hands and ask for an explanation. In reality, the children will probably not do this because they will not want to interrupt, but it really helps if the older people think through in advance about what will need explaining.

Preparing the young people

The inter-generational encounter will be more fruitful if the young people have begun to think about the proposed topic in advance and delineated some areas of special interest to them. A loosely structured brain-storming in the classroom can be a better preparation than the allocation of a rigid list of questions to be asked by individual pupils. In the latter arrangement, the children often concentrate only on 'their question' and when they can ask it.

The emphasis in preparing the younger people should be on honing their listening skills by inviting them to interview one another and to see how much they have concentrated on and remembered the answers. They should also be encouraged to ask questions which require more than a one-word answer, and to practise asking open questions such as 'Can you tell us about...?' or 'Do you remember an occasion when...?' They can try asking questions which begin with the words 'when', 'why', 'how' and 'where', and their attention should be drawn to the way they sit and look when the older people are talking, so they are sending back signals that what they say is interesting. This is best demonstrated for the young people by allowing them to experience the opposite, with their partner looking away and taking no notice of what they are saying.

Middle Park

An inter-generational project based on the local area

In a recent project in south-east London, a group of older people from the Middle Park Community Centre co-operated with children aged nine and ten from the local primary school on a drama project about the 1930s housing estate where they all lived. The older people met first as a group, facilitated by Thelma Sharma and Erene Kaptani, both reminiscence theatre workers, and recorded memories of their growing-up years and their wartime experience.

At the beginning, both age groups were a little uncertain of what it would be like when they got together. The adults had generally experienced youngsters around in the community as lacking respect and not taking notice of them. They wondered if it would be hard to tell them about their lives. The children did not know whether the adults would be friendly or would take notice of them. There was also, of course, an excitement about meeting up and doing something together, but neither group really knew what to expect.

The process

Sessions opened and closed with exercises in a circle to build up a sense of mutual trust and solidarity among the participants. Each adult then worked with a group of five to six children, directing their scenes. The children took responsibility for creating the improvisations from the stories. The facilitators worked on performance skills, such as voice projection, working as a group, awareness of audience, concentration and stillness.

The first theme explored was childhood games and play so there could be an exchange of experience. Further themes were home life, the local environment and the war years. The groups worked with dialogue, still images, mime, sounds and props. Using real period props such as old money, sheets, suitcases and cigarette cards helped to consolidate the children's understanding.

The process of working together was far more enjoyable and rewarding than anyone had expected. The groups related really well and were pleased to meet up each week, appreciating the friendliness they experienced. They did feel listened to and valued.

The performance itself (in a big local hall as part of a festival of reminiscence theatre) was a challenge for all, and both groups rose to it admirably. There were a lot of nerves about performing, but the relationship they had built up meant that they supported and encouraged each other. The sense of occasion helped them to focus and brought out the best in everyone. It was good to see the pride, pleasure and relief of all as their achievement was publicly acclaimed.

The project had aimed to contribute towards the emotional, social and cognitive development of the children as well as tying in with the particular curriculum areas of literacy and history. The teacher, David Bond, commented:

> The children really enjoyed working with the adults. They were excited by the stories... The children were confident doing their parts. I was also impressed by their demeanour at the festival. While watching the other acts, the children were attentive and interested. The experience of being part of such an event was great for the children. (Schweitzer 2004b, p.47)

Thelma Sharma, the leading project worker, commented:

> I was delighted at the good relationship that was created between the generations. The project had a positive impact on how the two age groups viewed one another. Some of the attitudes the older people demonstrated in their lives, such as humour, resilience, playfulness and patience, were transmitted to the children through their stories, and doing the play made the stories memorable. I felt that it gave the children an increased sense of identity and interest in their own area and in other people's lives. (Schweitzer 2004b, p.49)

For an example of another very local-based inter-generational project see the *Memory Lane* project described in Chapter 6 concerning past life in the street where the school now stands.

Involving minority ethnic elders in classroom-based reminiscence

It is increasingly important to reflect the experience of minority ethnic elders in inter-generational theatre projects, especially in London and other urban areas, where school classes are made up of children from many cultures and backgrounds (Perlstein and Bliss 2003). Inviting minority ethnic elders to share stories about their countries of origin and their life journeys can provide children from those minorities with very positive role models. Giving weight to the elders' histories, acknowledging the existing connections they and their families still have with their countries of origin, and recognising their countries' long-standing links with Britain are all ways of imbuing the minority experience with value. (For interesting US equivalents to this work, see the work of Elders Share The Arts in New York, Larsen 2004.)

Over the last decade working on reminiscence projects at Age Exchange I felt increasingly that the involvement of minority ethnic elders was of value to all the young people and not just those from a minority ethnic background, giving to every student in the class a sense of global connectedness. Of course it is important that the elders who work with youngsters in this way are themselves confident in their own ability to share their stories effectively and this means they must be properly prepared and supported, with plenty of opportunity to share stories in a group before they meet the class. In a later chapter, I shall describe my experience of developing minority ethnic older people's drama groups and how these groups helped the elders to develop a shared sense of history and a combined strength and articulacy. At this point, however, I should like to focus on the inter-generational contribution made by these groups and how reminiscence theatre was the medium of their contribution.

We Want To Speak Of Old Times

Working with older pupils

Most of the examples of inter-generational work given so far have involved children of primary school age (up to 11 years old) but older pupils have much to gain from such collaboration, as I hope the following example will show. A Caribbean elders' circle attached to a church in Forest Hill, south-east London, had formed themselves into the Vista Reminiscence Group and were meeting to share their stories of home. I invited them to work with a group of 17- and 18-year-olds of Caribbean origin. They were students at the local sixth form college studying for an 'A' level in Performing Arts, one component of which was the creation of an original piece of theatre. They were mainly girls and the elders' group was mainly women. They were paired up for interview sessions and preliminary meetings.

Stories of home and abroad

In rehearsal, the older people worked together through improvisation to build up scenes reflecting life 'back home' with stories, songs and snippets of informal dialogue. They showed the closeness of community life, with people taking care of their elderly neighbours, and evoked the natural beauty of their childhood environment. They demonstrated the close connection with the 'Mother Country' through their very British education, reciting dates of all the kings and queens with a mixture of pride and irony and remembering Empire Day celebrations. They showed what it was like to leave home, saying farewell to their families and remembering what they had brought over with them. The young people attended some of the elders' rehearsals, learning about their young lives in the Caribbean. They then took over parts of their story, representing the elders on their journeys by sea and air and their first impressions of England. They made scenes from the older people's stories about their early days in London, working in factories and hospitals or trying to study. Then the elders took over the story again, speaking about their pride in their working lives or how they were spending their days in retirement. Each left a piece of wisdom he or she wanted to pass on to the young people and the play ended with the two generations singing and dancing together.

Despite the limited time available for the old and young groups to work together, they gained a lot personally from participating in the project. Dolly Briscoe from the Vista group said:

> It was a chance for us to tell our stories in our own way and to express ourselves through theatre for the first time. We had a chance to show that we could work amicably with the young people and we have kept in touch with some of them through the years. (Personal communication)

Bryony Ford, the students' tutor and Head of Performing Arts at Christ The King Sixth Form College, commented in her report on the project:

> Taking part in this professional level project was a really exciting opportunity for the students. They thoroughly enjoyed working with the elders in rehearsal and performance, and learned an enormous amount about devising and structuring drama, movement and music from the director. By collaborating with the elders they celebrated their own cultural heritage and deepened their understanding of the history of the Afro-Caribbean community in Lewisham. (Personal communication)

Participants in a culturally diverse Britain and Europe

The young people benefited from understanding more about what brought people of their parents' and grandparents' generation to this country, how much attitudes to living in a multicultural society have changed in recent decades and what it means to the older people to be black and British today. They also enjoyed the affection and admiration of the older people. (Personal communication)

We Want To Speak Of Old Times was performed at an international festival of theatre by and about minority ethnic elders called 'The Journey of a Lifetime' held at Age Exchange in 1998. Through the performances and workshops at this festival, young and old Caribbeans had a chance to make connections and draw parallels with people from ethnic minorities in other countries, including Turkish people from Germany and Moluccans from the Netherlands, and to share some of the key experiences of migration. Again, Bryony Ford commented:

> Taking part in the festival was a significant experience for them as performers and for myself, a most rewarding and uplifting occasion to see our students performing in such an exciting and culturally diverse event. The whole festival stays very fresh in my memory; the colleague who accompanied me still recalls it as a very powerful arts experience. For the students concerned I know it was a special journey and one which I am sure will have stayed in their memories long after they left college. (Personal communication)

The group subsequently performed for members of a Caribbean lunch club and also at a university conference on ethnic diversity and culture. A small book was made of the interviews the young people collected from the elders in the play and from more frail elders in the local Caribbean sheltered housing unit, so there was a lasting result of their collaboration (Doolittle and Schweitzer 1998).

The Place Where I Grew Up

Another example, this time with younger children aged nine and ten from Wing-field Primary School in south-east London, involved an African group called Ajoda made up of elders from Nigeria now living in London. This group had initially formed themselves to organise services for African elders through the local authority and to keep contact with one another. However, they had been fired up by the idea of making a play together with the incentive of performing in a forth-coming festival, 'The Place Where I Grew Up'. They had created a play together by working very intensively over two weeks with Peggy Pettitt, an African American colleague of mine from New York. In the group they had shared their stories of growing up in Nigeria, building whole group scenes about home life in an African village and their school days, adding beautifully harmonised songs in English and African languages, full of energy and rhythm. They also shared experience from their adult lives and worked in small groups to present these to one another: scenes about arranged marriages, culture clashes between generations and worrying about ageing parents back home. The group developed a tremendous sense of pride in the shared culture they were depicting, one in which the elders were the respected decision makers. The elders started attending the rehearsals in full African dress, all

Peggy Pettitt receives the blessing of the African village elders, as played out by the Ajoda group

bright colours and daring designs. The end result was a 40-minute play full of humour, colour, song and dance, bringing alive the Africa the elders remembered. The group wrote the following joint comments afterwards:

> Working with Peggy as a group on the play *The Place Where I Grew Up*, we all felt the scales were being removed from our eyes. It was like a tonic for us, making us feel strong and vigorous, and full of well-being as a group. As we shared memories of our school days and our other experience in common, there was a spirit of togetherness and unity of spirit which we had not found as a group before. The collective ideas which we generated during the work made the end result look like a purpose-written play. By being in touch with our shared history, members were lifted out of isolation and depression to a new sense of vitality. The play activated, motivated and stimulated us, triggering the spirit of acting which is generally found in every African heart. (Personal communication)

The Ajoda group were now keen to be involved in cultural and educational work in the local area, and to transmit their experience to younger generations, especially to African children. Their enthusiasm was an ideal starting point for a local project in a regeneration area, as one of the participating schools had a majority of pupils from Africa, quite a few of whom had arrived recently and were still somewhat disorientated. The class teacher of the Year Five class in question, who was also Nigerian, could see how the benefits for the children would extend beyond mainstream curriculum areas of English, Geography, History, Religious Studies and Citizenship into social skills, personal development, tolerance and self-esteem.

Jennifer Lunn, the director working on the project with the children and the elders, had weekly sessions with the class over ten weeks and five of these were in the presence of the elders. An unusual beginning to the project was that Jennifer introduced the group to the children first via the Memory Boxes which they had recently made as part of a Reminiscence Network project (Schweitzer and Trilling 2005). The children looked at the boxes, read the attached stories which helped to explain the contents of the boxes and then made scenes from what they understood from the information they had gathered to play back to the older people when they met face to face. The elders were delighted with this introduction to the children who had successfully engaged with their stories and shown their enthusiasm for the project. Over the weeks, the children made scenes with the elders taken from their memories of growing up in an African village, including their chores, their school day, their punishments, attitudes to their elders, customs and village festivals. They also explored the elders' memories of making the journey to England, how they had worked in their adult lives and what they missed most about Africa.

For a full account of this school project see Hatton-Yeo (2006).

Empowering children from minority backgrounds

The African elders became very close to the children and worked with them in small groups. There were moments of real transformation, as when a young girl, recently arrived from Nigeria, went from being very quiet and shy to being the protagonist of the group, thanks to the reassurance she derived from working with the elders and the importance that was suddenly placed on her cultural identity. To

Children working with African elders from Ajoda

watch her suddenly light up as they spoke to her in her native language, about where she was from and places she knew, was startling for the people watching. It was a magical project, empowering the African-origin youngsters to welcome their white classmates into their culture. Some comments from the children on participating in the project follow:

> It was good because now I know about the customs of my own country. (Natahan Adeoye)

> I found it fun to learn about another culture. (Jack Tappin)

> It was so interesting to learn about a different way of life and act it in our play. (Sunil Kozubska)

The play was presented to parents and the general public to much acclaim, with the elders in their full African costumes full of colour and style. The inclusion of songs learned by the children during the project was a vital part of the play and gave the piece an infectious energy.

Afterwards, the Ajoda group sent the following comments:

> Working with Jen and the children in performance further transformed and stabilised us as a group. Children were able to understand our stories through our actions and working with us increased their levels of awareness, tolerance and understanding. They were able to consider the great changes the elders have gone through in their life journeys from the innocence of their disciplined school days in Africa to their present-day experience as elders in Britain. The play made the group plan and work

together as a team, giving us a foundation for future projects. The collective ideas and
ideals pursued in the overall project are things we want to maintain in our future work.
The project helped Ajoda as an organisation be mindful of the needs of its members
and other groups, both old and young. (Personal communiation)

Summary

I hope the examples I have included of classroom-based theatre work around
elders' reminiscences have demonstrated that this approach furthers many areas of
the curriculum in ways which are pleasurable and educational for both generations.
The older people involved in these projects have been motivated by a desire to set
down or to present in some way their experience as first-generation immigrants
and to share their experience with younger people to enhance their sense of
cultural identity and their feeling of global inter-connectedness. The African elders
had told the children 'It takes a whole village to raise a child' and had made it clear
to them that the village elders have a crucial role in this process. Giving their time,
their stories and their love, they can imbue the village children with a sense of
security, a feeling of belonging and an understanding of their community's history.
The power of this idea was communicated to the children through their direct
experience of working with the elders from Ajoda.

By marginalising older people and limiting their interaction with the young in
our 'advanced' western society today, we are missing out on their potential. Fortu-
nately, there is now a growing understanding that inter-generational work,
whether in school time or in community-based leisure and cultural projects, has an
important part to play in building a healthier and more cohesive society
(Hatton-Yeo 2006). Theatre projects such as those described in this chapter involving young and old provide a particularly productive way of bringing the generations together for creative co-operation and mutual appreciation.

Part 3

Older People Dramatising and Performing their Memories

The final section explores direct involvement by groups of older people in creating and performing reminiscence theatre and drama.

Chapter 12 locates the work in an international context and identifies it as part of a new way of thinking about empowering older people to represent themselves. It shows how a particular group of older people, the Good Companions, moved from being rather reluctant improvisers in a one-off experiment, to being a fully-fledged performing group who travelled across Europe performing the many shows developed in their 12-year existence. It also explores the role of the director in these projects and the older people's assertions concerning the value to them as individuals of their group identity and shared activity.

Chapter 13 looks at reminiscence theatre work between older people from minority ethnic backgrounds with young people from their own communities and also with classes of school-children.

The final chapter, Chapter 14, demonstrates the use of spontaneous dramatic enactments and group improvisations in creative reminiscence projects in residential homes and day centres. It shows how these small-scale dramas which emerge from conversation around remembered objects and situations can enliven life for the participants and promote friendship and communication between them. This chapter goes on to explore the use of drama as a valuable means of recapturing memories in the present to support people with dementia and their family members. It explores the particular appropriateness of improvised drama as a means of communication in which people with dementia can participate actively and successfully and explores how long-term relationships within families coping with dementia can be supported through such activities.

CHAPTER 12

Older People Enacting
their Own Memories

Older people speaking for themselves

In the late 1980s and early 1990s there was a new mood pervading older people's issues and a growing recognition that they could speak for themselves, rather than only having a voice through professional caring agencies. Major demographic change in western societies, with longer life spans, better health and higher expectations concerning quality of life, led to a gradual change in public perception of old age. Older people's organisations spoke less of providing, and more of enabling and empowering. The European Year of Older People in 1993 was a recognition of this changing landscape as well as a catalyst for further change. It enabled sizeable amounts of money to be channelled into programmes supporting large and small, national and international initiatives in which the older people were the protagonists.

Senior Theatre USA-style

In America this sea change had begun much earlier in the late 1950s, with associations like the AARP (American Association for Retired Persons) who aimed to promote independence for older people and 'to serve, not to be served', and more radical groups like the Gray Panthers who spoke out on weighty political matters from the early 1970s. In the arts, parallel to this movement, there was a rapid development of Senior Theatre groups, usually made up of retired educators or long-term amateur players, wishing to perform their own material or their own versions of established works, rather than wait for type-cast character roles in younger people's productions.[21]

In 1991, I had my first exposure to such a group when I attended an international Senior Theatre event in Cologne, Germany. I had been invited to show a new Christmas production based on wartime memories by our professional company, and to explain our way of developing a verbatim script from older people's stories. This fascinated delegates from Germany, France and the USA for whom such an approach was a new experience. There were performing groups made up of older people and I was startled by the range and quality of work on show.

Grandparents Living Theatre from Columbus, Ohio, presented their *Wonderful* show, the main song of which proclaimed, 'Once I was young but now I'm wonderful.'[22] A retired professional actress was the narrator of a dramatised journey through the decades enacted by the other company members, many of them experienced amateur performers. It was based largely on their own stories developed through improvisation and skilfully combined in a musical show by Joy Reilly, the director. The play was performed by a 20-strong group of talented all-singing, all-dancing elders and the production was very professional. The older players had memorised everything to perfection and were clearly having a wonderful time performing (Basting 1998). The three older people from the Reminiscence Centre with whom I had travelled to Germany really enjoyed watching it, but did not feel any connection with that kind of work. Lil Murrell, who had taken part in intergenerational projects and occasional improvisation workshops at Age Exchange, said, 'Ooh, I hope you're not going to ask us to do anything like that!' I knew I would be wasting my time trying to introduce that style of show to elders in London who had not acted in front of an audience before, and who were not even sure they wanted to get involved in anything theatrical.

Senior Theatre German-style

Just as striking as the *Wonderful* show, and a great deal more transferable to the London situation, was the *Jahrhundert Revue* by Ingrid Berzau and Dieter Scholz of the Freies Werkstatt Theater, our Cologne hosts. A group of 20 older German people presented scenes from their lives, from earliest memories, including the Kaiser visiting the town, through school days and first kisses, to the war and the rebuilding of Germany which followed it, and right up to the present day. The older people had worked with their two experienced and dedicated directors over a two-year period to make this impressive piece of theatre, entirely from their own stories. The ensemble work of the group was very precise, with simple but effective choreography and a wide range of theatrical styles, ranging from straightforward narration to satirical dialogue, whole group tableaux and individual dances. I was particularly impressed with the way the performers, some of them in their late 70s and 80s, emerged as strong individuals with their own stories to tell, as well as working effectively as a chorus in the whole group scenes. Even without a knowledge of German (a brief summary of the scenes was supplied in English) one grasped the essence of each scene and felt in touch with the very particular angle on Germany's troubled history which the group had collectively created.

A British model?

Inspired by what I had seen, and aware of the changing perception of ageing, I felt that it was time the older people in London had the opportunity to be centre-stage themselves, rather than supporting the work of younger professional actors. I invited Ingrid Berzau and Dieter Scholz to come to London and work with the group of older people who had recently been doing some improvisation workshops for the first time and performing short scenes with the Age Exchange Youth Theatre (see Chapter 10). The German directors agreed to spend two weeks working with the group in London, helping them to build a new show from scratch. They offered the extra incentive that, if the initiative had a successful outcome, they would invite the group to Cologne for the premiere.

The older people in the USA and German productions had been attracted to them by a love of theatre and a desire to perform (Basting 1998). At the Reminiscence Centre we had a very different set-up, where the main supporters and volunteers who participated in all the projects had not come with a view to performing, but rather as volunteers, greeting and sharing their stories with visitors of all ages and with members of the professional theatre company. They had often been invited into rehearsals, to show how a dance was danced or to teach a song or verify a performance of one of their own stories, so they were quite comfortable being in the role of consultants and advisers. Some of them had even taken on roles and participated in inter-generational projects (see Chapters 9 and 10), but they did not think of themselves as performers. Clearly we would need to work together to develop our own style of theatre, probably with less panache than the American style and a little less tightly orchestrated than the German style, but incorporating a touch of British irony and understatement. Perhaps we would set ourselves a more limited objective whereby the members of the group would help one another to act out their own stories around a theme which we would choose together, and perform them with linking songs to an audience of invited friends and relations.

I Remember When...

Ingrid and Dieter had always rehearsed once a week with their older people and they had very gradually, over a long gestation period, built up a show, so it was a great challenge for them to put a play together in just two weeks, and to do so in a second language. However, that was all the time they could spare and I only had limited resources to pay for their time, so we decided to attempt this through a series of story-telling and improvisation workshops.

An international collaboration

In the weeks before the workshop, I collected many stories from the older people about their young days, about going to the fair on Blackheath, about starting their working lives and about going out to enjoy themselves at the cinema or 'on the town'. I sent transcripts of these stories to the directors in Germany, so they could start planning the workshops. I invited anyone who wanted to come along to the workshops to do so, on the understanding that the work would be quite intensive and they would be expected to come every day. There was initially little response and people virtually had to be cajoled into coming on the basis that it would be embarrassing for our guest directors if there was no one there for them to work with. I promised the older people that if they did not enjoy it, they need not come back after the first morning session. A group of 12 older people assembled, ten of them women. Most were in their late 60s and 70s and two were over 80. None of them had performed in anything since their school days, except for one, Joyce, who had done a bit of amateur dramatics and loved the theatre, but had never expected to be performing again.

Using physical memory

Perhaps because Ingrid and Dieter were struggling with the language and constantly had to ask them for help, the older people did not find their professionalism intimidating and they started to feel more confident. They were asked to do all sorts of physical exercises and non-verbal improvisations, which freed them up and made everyone laugh. I gained a lot as a director by watching them stage the stories very exactly, rather like choreographers, focusing on physical memory by trying to put the older people back in touch with how their younger bodies moved and felt (Boal 1992). They developed scenes based on the reminiscences collected, choosing stories with plenty of movement and action, and I saw that the group were more willing each day to be pushed to produce something of quality. Ingrid and Dieter scripted the best material at night, and every day the older actors received new sections of script so they could see the results of their work from the previous day and sense that they were making progress. Some sections of the script were in delightful 'foreign' English, which caused much good-natured hilarity. Stage directions were also written into the script by Ingrid and Dieter thus: 'Everybody takes away silently his chair. Kathleen takes away the chair of Joyce too' or 'Everyone looks in their trousers in an individual way and finds a penny and decides to go to the Ghost Train'. Nobody dropped out of the sessions and, in two weeks, the first version of the play came together. The directors left behind a draft script entitled *I Remember When...* for me to continue developing until we made our debut visit back to Cologne.

Spatial orientation

Interestingly, spatial orientation was sometimes more of a problem for the older players than remembering the words of the script. Scenes involving moving from one position to another on stage needed endless rehearsal, especially if these involved rearranging chairs. The most helpful device here was music played on the piano by one of the group with the cast singing along, since this allowed people time to remember where they were supposed to be and regroup for the next scene. When we later started to perform the play in other spaces, I discovered that it was necessary to go through all the moves in the play before the show, so that everybody could re-orient themselves in relation to the new space, the audience and one another. They relied heavily on those supporting musical prompts, so most stage movement was accompanied by songs of the period, chosen by the older people themselves and thematically connected to the action. The songs were the glue that held the stories together, and although the arrangements were much less sophisticated than in the professional shows, the older people sang well together.

The Good Companions step out

For a couple of months after the two-week workshop, I worked with the group once or twice a week, helping develop their confidence, stage presence and powers of projection. Getting ready for the German premiere of the show entailed a tremendous amount of practical work and psychological preparation. Some of the group did not have passports, had never flown before and were very nervous indeed. Husbands had to be left and freezers stacked with labelled meals for every day we would be away. People would have to share rooms, which was also quite a challenge for those who had lived alone for many years. However, there was a lot of excitement in the air and the group became very close as they rehearsed and planned together. We thought for a long time about a name for the performing group and then someone remembered a wonderful novel from the 1930s by J.B. Priestley, *The Good Companions*, all about a touring theatre company. We adopted that name and it seemed very appropriate because the members really were good companions to one another, in fact rather better than the ones in the novel. Their capacity to function as a group was sorely tested very early on, when one of the group died on our very first journey. Harry was an apparently very fit 86-year-old and an experienced traveller, but on a hot day at Gatwick Airport, he had a massive stroke from which he never recovered. The shock to all of us was terrible and we were not sure whether to continue the journey, but it was felt that he would not have wanted us to cancel it on his behalf and we were expected to perform in Cologne. Harry's family were tremendously supportive and we all attended his funeral on our return. His son, who was a professional actor, joked about how he hoped he would be as lucky as his father and be in work as an actor to his dying day.

We had to re-rehearse up to the last minute when we got to Germany, re-allocating Harry's lines and adjusting all the moves. The play was extremely well received in Cologne and later travelled to Belgium, Ireland, Norway and Denmark, often linking up with the European tour of our professional company, as well as performing in many parts of the UK. We kept it going for a whole year as there was quite an appetite for the group's work and there had not been anything quite like it before. There was a lot of international exchange in 1993 as part of the European Year of Older People, so other groups came to the Reminiscence Centre and saw the Good Companions at work and left with plans to replicate the idea in their own countries.

Growing confidence, growing skills

The more they performed, the more confident the older people became, encouraged by applause and positive feedback from contemporaries and much younger audience members. Perhaps because the devising and rehearsing process were very stimulating, mentally and physically, it was noticeable that people's communication and memory skills improved, and this at a time in their lives when they might expect a decrease in memory function. After the performances, the group could not wait to get out to the audience and hear what people had taken from the show.

They were very good at listening to other people's stories or chatting about themselves and answering questions informally. Quite often in foreign countries we held formal discussions after the performances so that everybody's contribution could be translated, and in this way there was a pleasurable exchange of stories crossing the usual language divide.

I Remember When... was initially seen as a one-off project and many of the group felt, 'We've given all our memories now. We won't find anything else to say.' In fact there were to be ten further projects by the group during the next 12 years, covering many topics from going on trips to the seaside in the pre-war days to more ambitious productions such as *Our Century And Us*, which encompassed the whole lifetime of the players. Some of the shows were developed in partnership with young people from the Youth Theatre, as described in a previous chapter, but by now the lead often came from the older people's group, with the children's scenes slotted in and sometimes separately rehearsed. This proved to be a very rich seam, which absorbed much of my creative energy for more than a decade, exploring the art of the possible, which became just as stimulating as working with professional actors.

Physical work and vocal warm-ups with the group

Every rehearsal started with physical and vocal warm-ups, and this helped to relax the older people, to focus their energy and to encourage sensitivity and acute listening. The physical warm-ups were simple limbering exercises, loosening, warming and stretching different parts of the body. This was also a time when group members could complain about bits of their bodies which were troublesome and the group would give those areas some special attention with sympathy, humour and physical contact. For example, if one person had a back-ache, the whole group would stand in a circle facing sideways and massage one another's backs, then turn around and repeat the exercise with the person on their other side. In the vocal warm-ups, there were breathing exercises, humming and singing together, copying rhythms, sounds and actions. All these exercises were designed to help people concentrate and work together effectively as a group.

Use of Playback Theatre methods

Some exercises from Playback Theatre were incorporated into rehearsals because I felt there were many useful cross-overs between this form of improvised theatre, which is based on stories told by players and audience, and reminiscence theatre (Fox 1986; Salas 1993). Each member would 'check in' with a story about what had happened to them during the week or how they were feeling at this moment and the rest of the group 'played back' to them their version of what they had said. For example, a member told of a letter she had received saying her grand-daughter would be getting married at Christmas in Australia, and she was not sure whether she would feel able to go. Each member of the group posed in a way which represented her dilemma (flying with arms outstretched, looking at her own wedding ring, crouching in fear, etc.) so that together they made a joint image for her to look at and reflect on. The older people enjoyed participating in the Playback exercises, which also served to alert the group as to how individuals were feeling, physically and psychologically, and to 'tune in' to one another. These exercises also demonstrated for them that it was possible to make a scene out of anything and that elaborate scripts were not required to communicate effectively through movement, image and sound (see Schweitzer 2002a for a complete script and a detailed breakdown of the rehearsal process).

In the next pages, I shall cover some of the working methods explored with the group to arrive at two Good Companions productions: *Work In Progress* and *Our Century And Us.*

Work In Progress

This play was based on the group's memories of leaving school, in most cases at 14 years of age, and starting their working lives. At the outset, I asked members of the group what had been their ambitions for their working lives, and was roundly told: 'In those days we didn't really have ambitions. You didn't have many opportunities.' However, when we included childhood fantasies they had of themselves as grown-ups, they came up with plenty of ambitions, like being an engine driver, a nurse, a film star, and some more down-to-earth predictions of being a mother and a housewife, and we included these in the final show. When the group members were voicing these ambitions, they actually seemed to become young again, as though the child inside them was speaking. This was not through any exaggerated 'child acting' behaviour on their part; it was rather that, through remembering and discussing together their childhood fantasies about the future, they had got back in touch with their young selves and brought them into the present moment. So when Barbara, aged 78, cradled a baby and said, 'I played with my dolls and put them to bed, I wanted to be a mother', one saw her simultaneously as a little girl and as an old lady who was now a mother, a grandmother and a great-grandmother. And when Joyce said, 'I wanted to be a school teacher so I could smack all the children's bottoms', she was fully 'in the moment' and also laughing a little at her child and adult selves.

Remembered fantasies becoming realities

We started to discuss how far they had managed to fulfil their fantasies in other aspects of their lives, even if not in their working careers, and the results were quite surprising. Ralph, the would-be engine driver, has filled his garage with a complete train set with locomotives, sheds, signals and track. Joan had not become a nurse but has worked for many years as a volunteer at the Red Cross. Kitty, who wanted to 'be a singer and dancer and go on the stage', had sung with the band of the biscuit factory where she worked before her marriage and was now the leading dancer and singer of the Good Companions. Hilda, who had watched her father shift scenery back-stage at Stratford East Theatre in London, and had always wanted to be a film star and 'go in the pictures', now also felt very fulfilled performing with the Good Companions, telling us: 'My daughters always say, "My mum's on the stage.'" Olive, who had dreamed of being a pianist, and who had not touched a keyboard for 30 years when she joined the group, was now rediscovering a surprising amount of her youthful facility and delighting thousands of people through her performances as accompanist to the Good Companions. In one way or another, most of the group seemed to have accommodated their childhood wishes, and were intrigued by suddenly seeing connections between very different parts of their lives.

School reports

During the rehearsals we moved forward towards the time they would leave school and start work. I remember asking the group if they could say something about how they thought they were perceived by their teachers and what their teachers' hopes had been for them. To respond to these questions, the group members had to step back from themselves and recall those sometimes quite perceptive general comments made by their class teachers at the bottom of their school reports. Some of the comments were recreated memories, but some were actual school reports kept all through their lives. These included lines they could not have made up themselves, such as: 'Anne is a very reliable girl who always finishes what she has begun' or 'Lilly is a very studious girl, but she must learn to stop talking in class.' Again, even when they did not quite agree with the comments, group members were often struck by the light they shed on their characters. Some were rather painfully true, such as Olive's 'teacher' speech: 'I'm worried about Olive, she's such a good pianist and she should be going into it professionally, but I understand that there are financial problems in the family and now she's going off to work in Woolworths and I think that's a pity', but others were comical as they had patently turned out to be so wrong, as when Joyce, now a strapping 75-year-old with a cogent opinion on everything, said as 'teacher': 'I'm worried about Joyce, she seems such a quiet, thin little thing. I don't think she'll come to anything much.'

The group created a school photograph tableau representing them at school-leaving age, which came to life as individuals spoke the feelings they had at the time: 'I can't wait to get away, I never liked it here anyway' or 'I wish I didn't have to leave. I'd like to go on studying but my parents can't afford it' or 'I want to get out so I can earn a bit of money of my own' and the boarding school girl who said, 'I'm going to miss all my friends, but I can't wait to meet some boys!'

The working world

People then worked in pairs, showing each other the journey they had taken to work, by pacing it out on the floor with their partner, mentioning the neighbours they would have waved to, the early morning buses and workmen's trains they caught to save on fares. Working in pairs in this way is often helpful, as one person's memories can revive another's, and physically walking through the journey helps the body to remember the various steps and stages entailed. This scene was eventually included in the play and performed with a song (a lively rhythmic number from the 1930s entitled 'Sing As You Go') as the whole group made their separate and simultaneous journeys. This device of several people performing simultaneously but separately can be problematic for an audience, who may not know where to focus their attention. However, when it is used to make a point, as it was here to convey the kind of complex journeys these then young people had to make to their workplaces along busy thoroughfares in rush hour, it can be very effective.

A song for every occasion

It appeared that the actual jobs they had were mostly terribly boring and repetitive, the only pleasure being the company of others of their own age and the briefest of lunch-time breaks. The latter was conveyed by three of the women acting out a shared memory of walking by the River Thames at lunch-time and gazing at the big liners. As they dreamed of sailing away to distant sunny parts of the world, the whole cast sang a short chorus of 'Red Sails in the Sunset', waving at the imaginary ships going by. As so often in these shows, a snatch of song holds a moment, underlines its mood and enables the action then to move on. Our German partners have been amazed by the wealth of songs known to the group on every possible theme, and even if individuals had forgotten some of the words, the group could always come up with the complete version by pooling their resources.

Much of the humour in the play came from the ridiculous things they often had to do at work. Joyce was filing letters in a dark office round the corner from home with one old man with a dreadful cough, before she escaped to a number plate factory 'up town' where she had fun with the other girls and boys. Penny was learning to ride a bike to do deliveries for the dairy and Hilda helped drive her father's horse and cart to his regular market stall where she sold kettles while he went off to the pub. Eileen, who desperately wanted to be a florist, had to settle for work in an envelope factory, but folded all her envelopes inside out because she was left-handed, and Barbara frantically counted bank notes in the Bank of England vaults hoping to find a forgery and get the reward. Lil packed dog biscuits and Olive reluctantly sold ice creams and then toy animals in Woolworths to horrible children who made her life hell. All these little stories were new to me and had not been covered in previous discussions in the group. Acting them out brought the group to life as young workers and helped us see other aspects of their personalities.

For most of them, these jobs were only for a brief period of their lives in the 1930s and 1940s because they had then got married and had stopped working. You were not expected or even allowed to continue to work when you married, unless it was wartime. One of the group, Joan, remembered that the annual summer outing from the glass factory where she worked took place just before her marriage. This gave us our cue for the play's ending: a charabanc trip to the seaside and a farewell to one period of her life and the friends she had worked with.

Working spontaneously

There is a particular pleasure when creating a play, if the structure of the piece emerges organically from the story-telling and improvisation. Often a whole scene can be developed from a spontaneous recalling which has not previously been shared in more structured reminiscence sessions, or in the pieces of writing group members sometimes prepared at home between sessions. Someone will say, 'That has just reminded me of something that happened…', and the group will immediately proceed to act out what that person has just remembered. Or someone will produce a phrase in an improvisation which reminds the person who told the story of additional elements which could be added. For example, one day Joyce and Olive were playing out a scene set up by Hilda, based on her memory of her father, who liked his drink and was always surly until he'd been given a shilling by Hilda's mum for a visit to the Lion, his local pub down the road. Joyce, in role as Mum, said to Olive, as Dad, who had just dumped himself in the only armchair with the evening paper: 'You're only rattling that paper for a row.' Hilda suddenly remembered how her dad, when he was in these moods, would shout at all the old gossips who used to congregate in their second-hand clothes shop and send them packing. This quickly turned into a comic scene with a part for everyone, with Hilda giving the other performers parts to play based on characters from her own memories. Afterwards, Hilda commented: 'I think my mum and dad are watching me wherever they are…it's a funny feeling, a nice feeling…Joyce is so like my mum and she talks like her too. My mum'd laugh if she could see us now' (Armitage 1996).

Consciousness-raising through interviews about the process

The making of this play was the basis for a BBC Radio Four programme entitled 'Calling To Mind', in which the older people were asked about their feelings and reactions to creating theatre from their own experience in this way. This had the effect of raising the consciousness of the group, as they had to reflect on their own creative dramatic improvisation process, which few people of their generation were exploring, but which they had already begun to take for granted. Their ambivalence about performing was captured by Olive, one of the strongest performers in the group, who started by saying she had not wanted to act, 'I felt a right prat doing it at first!', but quickly went on to admit: 'It's brought me alive in the last two years. I've become much more mentally alert. You've got to, to keep up with it.' She did concede that 'Joyce and I usually have a slug of Scotch before the show, just to get the old adrenaline going!'. Joan confessed that every time she did a performance she was in such a state of nervous panic she got ill, but she never missed a show and many positive things had come out of it for her. For instance, she had found a lovely singing voice she did not know she had: 'My husband's never heard me sing and if he did he wouldn't like it, so I never sing at home.' Penny, a relatively new member of the group, spoke about the change in her outlook since joining, from being very dependent on her son, very sorry for herself and often depressed: 'Before I just wanted attention. My son can't get over the change in me. He says,

"You're like the old Pen…like you were when Dad was alive." This is a reason for living. When we go on I say to myself, "I'm going to do my best and give it all I've got'" (Armitage 1996).

'Ordinary people' doing extraordinary things

From the outset, I had been impressed with how the Good Companions impacted on their audiences. The fact that they were not professional actors, that they were 'ordinary' older people, had quite an electrifying effect, whether they were playing for other older people like themselves, to professionals from the caring professions or to academics at conferences.

They did not have the physical skills and powers of projection of professional actors, but they gave very natural, rather understated performances. They came across as people who had lived ordinary lives but who were now doing an extraordinary thing by performing these lives. There was something about their integrity on stage and the fact that what they were showing had genuinely happened to them, which audiences of all ages found startling and often very moving. I have seen conference delegates with tears in their eyes give standing ovations to the group at the end of a show. Watching these older people (some of them quite frail) performing had given younger audience members a real jolt, perhaps also reminding them of grandparents they wished they had got round to interviewing while there was still time. They particularly admired the older people for standing up and telling how it was for them, and then afterwards chatting confidently with the audience about their memories or about their work with the Good Companions.

Perhaps because the group were not too polished, the older people watching them perform often felt that they too could have a go at doing this. Staff and professional carers in sheltered housing where we played were always very delighted with what the group did. Often our performances provided a jumping-off point for staff for creative work with their own older people. Sue Heiser, a social services manager and dementia expert, commented: 'I remember the Good Companions performing in a care home in Chelsea, with residents with advanced dementia totally engaged and alert – often to the surprise of the staff' (Heiser et al. 2005, p.12). Sally Knocker, a dementia care specialist trainer who watched a Good Companions show with a group of care staff from a wide range of cultural backgrounds, was struck by its educational value for these workers. She recalls one of the Nigerian workers saying that he wished he had seen this show as part of his induction because it had given him enriched insight and understanding of the lives of the predominantly British older residents with whom he was working. He now felt he had more possibilities for conversation as well as an increased desire to find out more, because of his genuine engagement with the content of the show.[23]

Our Century And Us

Following our German mentors, I decided that the forthcoming millennium celebrations gave us the perfect moment to try an English version of *Jahrhundert Revue* called *Our Century And Us*. Within one play, our older people's theatre group would travel from the group's earliest memories up to the present day. The prospect of this ambitious undertaking was very alarming for some of the group, so we approached it tangentially through a series of exercises and improvisations focusing on sensory and emotional memory. A good start was for each person to announce triumphantly their names (first, middle and maiden names) and their date of birth, the oldest being born in 1920 and the youngest in 1933. The players then recalled their earliest memories and played them out to one another. Joyce remembered standing up in the huge bed in her grandmother's house as a two-year-old and playing with the brass balls of the bedstead, unscrewing them and hearing them drop with a satisfying thud and roll across the wooden floor. In her sensory memory she had stored, and could recall, the smell of the brass on her fingers. Margaret remembered the shame of being sick down the new white coat that she'd been given as a tiny child. Ralph remembered going outside the door with his daddy and being shown the Zeppelin airship in the sky, and Kitty remembered sitting on her dad's knee when he came home from work and sometimes having a bit from his supper plate. The first memories were of feeling, smelling, touching, tasting, holding and seeing, and between them the group tapped into all the senses in their memories.

Up and down the decades

Because the people in the group had lived so long (about 750 years between them!) they were constantly saying 'You can't do all of our life stories, it's just too much', which of course was true. I devised an exercise with them designed to open up some possible avenues for exploration in which we would consider times in their lives they would and would not like to revisit. Chairs were arranged across the playing area to represent different ages, from 0–10 years, 10–20 years, and so on right to their present decade. I asked them to go and sit in a period they associated with maximum happiness, when they had felt very positive about themselves and the people around them and their living circumstances. The group scattered up and down the decades and people individually explained why they had chosen that time: 'I was having my children at this time and I was so pleased to be settled' or 'I loved being a child, I had a very happy childhood' or 'This was a good time for me because we moved into our own home for the first time and stopped living with my parents' or 'This was a time I met my intended partner.' Of course these memories did not coincide exactly with the decades, and I was asking them to bundle years and memories together, but it was an interesting exercise in which group members expressed themselves very freely.

Respecting privacy

I then asked them to go to a decade which they would not like to go back to, and sit on one of the chairs representing when they were in their 20s, 30s or whenever they had found life particularly testing. I knew that some of them had had personal tragedies in their lives which they would not wish to speak about in the group, so I gave them an option of just being in that time and not saying anything about it, an option which one or two people exercised, especially concerning the death of their mothers or their children. It was important to respect people's privacy and not pressurise them into revealing more than they wished, but the Good Companions really had got to know one another very well and there was a high level of trust within the group. This exercise threw up memories of divorce and bereavement as well as loneliness as young marrieds and times of financial privation and war. Some of the sadder and often more personal material in the play grew out of this exercise and made the final piece much more affecting than if it had been limited to happy memories. It afforded us a more balanced perception of how things had gone well at some times but not at other times and how resilient the group members had been through the ups and downs of their long lives.

Everyone marries Ralph in Our Century And Us

We followed through the main events in the lives of the group, such as school days, courting days, marriage, babies, working life, retirement and old age. There was only one man in the group at this point so all ten women had to use him as their bridegroom, which he greatly enjoyed. This was actually a much more dramatically effective way of covering all the wartime weddings in particular, rushed affairs that they were! We were making a virtue of necessity here, as we had often attempted unsuccessfully to recruit men to the group. Perhaps this highly interactive, inter-personal activity appealed less to men, or perhaps the preponderance of women in this particular group was a little daunting. When it came to the parenting scene, everyone enacted their own experience as young mums and dads simultaneously, playing with imaginary babies at home or in the park. It was absolutely fascinating to watch how each person slipped easily back into the kind of parent they had been, to the accompaniment of a nursery rhyme medley on the piano.

Women's liberation?

An interesting devising session portrayed the impact of washing machines and vacuum cleaners on the lives of women in the 1950s and 1960s. Although this might sound like a side-issue, the women felt it was important to show how machines had revolutionised their approach to house-keeping and liberated them to return to work once their children were off their hands. However, they did not want to overstate this change, as most of them who had gone out to work had ended up racing back at lunch-time to get children's or husband's lunches and again after work to cook their teas. It was important in this play to avoid too much narration and to use more economic dramatic images and devices to convey the meanings. We attempted to cover this 'half- liberation' in a series of short choreographed pieces. First the women stood in a line, each one passing the heavy washing from one tub to another (as in the twin tub machines they first had), and then everyone stood with arms folded and watched, heads rotating, mesmerised, as their washing did itself behind a round glass door, all this to a lively piano accompaniment. The scene proceeded with the women doing their chores and pausing to dream about things they would like to buy if they could earn some money of their own. Ralph, still playing everyone's husband, responded 'typically' and this led to a great flurry of mimed action as follows:

RALPH: I don't mind you getting a little job. But you must have the children's meal on the table when they come home for dinner. And my tea ready for me when I come home from work.

ALL: All right.

Women take off aprons in mime and travel to work to the tune of 'Music While You Work'. Everyone arrives and starts miming their jobs: serving people in shops/pubs, waitressing, office work, work with children, etc. When the verse ends everyone looks at watches.

ALL: Better get home and do the children's dinner.

'Housewives Choice' music. Everyone rushes home, mimes putting on aprons, making lunch for children, feeding them in a hurry and packing them off back to school. Look at watches. Take off aprons. Dash back to work with 'Music While You Work' music and start work again until the verse ends.

ALL: Better get home and get the tea ready.

'Housewives Choice' while the women do lightning speed shopping on the way home, get aprons on, cook and finally slap plates on table for Ralph who arrives and takes his coat off, standing centre-stage as music ends.

RALPH: I've had a very busy day. Is my tea ready?

Everyone groans. They take off aprons in mime and turn their backs on Ralph.

RALPH: (*To audience*) I don't know. Women!

Working with strong images

Although some scenes in this production involved naturalistic dialogue or narration directly to the audience, we also wanted to look for visual ways to express the
action through mime, movement, group choreography, sounds and song. This was
important for another reason, which was that we would premiere the show at an
international festival in Cologne and we wanted to make a play that was not wholly
reliant on spoken language. In the scene described above, even an audience
speaking no English would be able to follow the story of the women who rushed
from home to work and back home again, like circus artists keeping all the plates
spinning. Another example of choosing a strong visual image in preference to a
speech was when the group were exploring through improvisation their experience of retirement. The image chosen was a ticking clock, partly because there was
suddenly a lot of time for them to fill, partly because many of them experienced
loneliness and silence at that point and also because they had had the feeling that
their time was running out. We conveyed this by the group forming a circle, slowly
rotating to a ticking sound made by one performer, and as each person arrived
centre-stage, they gave a few words to summarise how they had felt or what they
had done at the time:

JOYCE: When you retire, time hangs heavy on your hands. You wonder what
to do with all those long hours. (*Pause for four ticks, then all start moving
clockwise.*) I was frightened of being lonely and bored. So I took on
lots of voluntary work. Too much.

BARBARA: I felt I had no spine, I lost confidence. I had to be very brave to
join Age Exchange and meet new people.

ANNE: I had to retire to look after my mum. She was very sick and for her
last nine years I had to do everything for her. I got very cut off.

KITTY: When I retired I felt free. I had the house to myself and could do
what I liked. I went shopping every day. I loved it.

OLIVE: I was terrified of retirement. I felt I was losing my identity and
cracking up. And I thought my brain would pack up, so I joined lots of
classes: recorder, speedwriting, crochet, anything to keep my brain
working.

HILDA: My husband got on my nerves. He was indoors all the time. I had to
get out of the house so I took a part-time job.

EILEEN: For the first time, my husband and I had time together. We spent
hours walking round London and enjoying each other's company.

Joan Pearce and Margaret Phair in pensive mood in Our Century And Us

Bereavement, a sensitive topic

Everyone knew that bereavement would be one of the most difficult issues to deal with but, as most of the group were widows, it was obviously a very important milestone in their lives. There was some disagreement in the group as to whether we should tackle it at all, some thinking it would be upsetting for older people watching a scene on this theme, and others thinking we should not be frightened of exploring it. Because of these differing views, I kept postponing the decision.

Then one day, I arrived at the rehearsal and found the older people in quite a grumpy mood. It was very hot and they said they were tired and they didn't want to do anything, so I said: 'I feel just like that too. Let's all just go to sleep.' And everybody laughed and they sat in their chairs with their eyes closed. I then said: 'While you're sitting there, I'm wondering what are the things that keep you awake? And are there certain dreams that you keep on having?' They were not asked to reply, but after a few more minutes of quiet, I asked them to turn to another person in the group, tell them what they had been thinking about and try to convey some of this in action to the rest of the group. Eileen and Olive, both of whom had been widowed relatively recently, worked together and shared the content of their dreams, but were unclear how to convey them theatrically. They had expressed the feeling that their husbands were still there in their dreams and sometimes comforted them, but that they had also felt lonely and left behind in their widowhood, feeling for a while as though they were only half a person.

We considered how best to play out these feelings. I experimented by placing the two women back to back and then asking them to walk slowly away from each other, turning to look over their shoulders once and then walking on. The others in the group found this a very affecting image and so we decided to do it as a whole group, each back-to-back pair separating and turning round for a last look. Everyone felt this would work, but we needed a song to go with it which was not overtly about death and dying, which could have made the scene too maudlin. In the end, we came up with a beautiful Kurt Weill song called 'From May to December' about maximising time together as autumn approaches.

As a way into the scene, Lil was willing to tell the story very simply about how she went to the doctor and discovered that her husband had only a couple of months to live. Hilda played the doctor and the whole scene was only five lines long:

LIL: My husband became very ill and I went to see the doctor about him.

DOCTOR: Sit down, Mrs Murrell.

LIL: What are you trying to tell me? How long has he got? Six months?

Doctor shakes head and holds Lil's hand.

LIL: Three months? (*Doctor shakes his head.*) Oh no…

Lil pulls away from the Doctor and sobs silently.

Piano introduction and then everyone sings very softly as they pair up back to back and slowly walk away from each other, turning once.

ALL: (*Singing*) Oh, it's a long, long time from May to December…

The song goes on to express the sense of urgency about time running out and the wish to make the most of the 'few precious days' remaining. Some of the Good Companions were slightly uncomfortable with this sequence, saying: 'Is it fair to make people upset? Is it fair to remind people of these painful things?' But when they actually performed the show, this was one of the scenes many audience members wanted to talk to them about.

The same anxiety was felt about showing a scene depicting divorce and its impact on the life of one of the group. In this instance, the woman concerned, Joyce, was very courageous and felt able to play out the scene referring to her subsequent loneliness and depression. She talked about the immediate change she experienced when all the doors and windows on her council estate, which had up to then been such a friendly place, were slammed in her face and no one had time for her any more. This rejection was conveyed by the whole cast who at first mimed opening imaginary windows and calling out friendly invitations, then slamming these same windows shut and shaking their heads at Joyce in a disapproving manner. Because her husband had run off with the next-door neighbour, she was somehow considered blameworthy and even dangerous, since she was now viewed as a predatory single woman. Again this was a scene which people wanted to discuss with the cast after the show (Bornat 2001). Joyce received many tearful thanks from audience members for showing her experience in this way and she heard much in confidence from them about what they too had gone through.

Life as a continuum

Working on the production *Our Century And Us* was the most powerful experience of the many I had with the Good Companions. I was very taken up at the time with the idea of reminiscence as a means of stock-taking and life review. The theory expressed in a seminal article by Robert Butler (Butler 1963), and very much endorsed by later writers on reminiscence, is that as you get older it is both natural and psychologically necessary to look back over your life and see how the different stages cohere, to view where you are now in the light of what has happened in previous years and see it as a kind of continuum (Gibson 2006). I had been working a great deal with people with dementia (see Chapter 14) and I had become convinced that bringing into consciousness the relationship between the past and the present was a very healthy activity and helped people to see the present, however difficult, as part of a bigger picture. Betty Bowden, one of the family carers in the reminiscence group I was running for people with dementia, said:

> It has been a wonderful opportunity to remember our lives as a whole, and not to dwell only on those bits, like the present, which are often difficult to get through. Both in the group, and in the quiet moments at home between sessions, it has helped me to take stock of my long life, my 84 years, and consider them well spent and full of happy moments and fulfilment. (Personal communication)

Locating elements of self that were present in very early days and are still actually there in the present is a way of maintaining a sense of identity and degree of self-acceptance. The approach of the millennium, with all its century reviews and retrospectives, was influencing everyone to engage in reminiscence and the *Our Century And Us* show was a perfect vehicle to capture and reflect this mood.

Reflections

Thinking back over 12 years of working with the Good Companions, I recall that the group members would always start by saying they did not have enough good stories, that people would not be interested in what they had to say or how they were going to say it, and they were very nervous about whether they would be able to remember everything. Joyce Milan, one of the group, said in an interview conducted in 1995 'I'm always a bit apprehensive at the beginning of a project. Each time I've said "I can't see this coming together", and it's always turned out to be better than the one before' (Schweitzer 1996, p.4).[24] Yet, despite their doubts, every new show was warmly greeted by loyal audiences and they won new friends wherever they performed (Basting 2001). Considering that over those 12 years they had been ageing, and moving into a period when memorising is progressively more difficult, I think I was asking a lot of them, but they always rose to the occasion.

Watching the coronation of Elizabeth II on television, a new experience in 1953

The Good Companions see the Mauritania coming up the Thames

Perhaps the increase in self-confidence they derived from performance and consequent acclaim actually deferred normal memory deterioration. It was noticeable that new members had a lot less confidence, whereas the long-serving Good Companions became more and more competent, and knew that if they sat up at night going over the lines that some of them at least would stay in. If anyone did forget completely what they were supposed to be doing or saying, it was not seen as a major failure either by myself or their fellow actors. I would just call out a cue to the older person and they would quickly get back on track. When this happened, it was quite a useful reminder to an audience that what the performers were doing was difficult and demanding, like when a circus artist wobbles and nearly falls off and this alerts the audience to how very difficult it is to walk a tightrope at all.

It would have been much more difficult if they had been asked to do a scripted play by somebody else. The fact that they were telling their own stories gave them more control. They always had the memory of the original event to fall back on, even if the memory for the exact words in the script failed. No two performances were ever identical, but the essence was consistent, and most people in the group felt a responsibility to their fellow actors to give them their required cue; a high degree of trust thus developed between them. Their name, the Good Companions, was very significant and they all valued the friendships they had made at a time in life when that is notoriously difficult to achieve. Joyce Milan, a founder member, said:

> It's like a family really, I think we all feel that. There's a bond of friendship. I think people are quite envious of us because we all have such a great time. I am close to my family, but they don't need you that much when they are all grown up and going their separate ways so there's a big lump goes out of your life, especially when you've always done a lot for them. All I can say is that if you ever took this out of my life there would be very little left. (Schweitzer 1996, p.4)

Joyce's daughter, Joy Nettleton, wrote to me after her mother died and commented:

> As a member of the Good Companions, Mum realised her love of acting and dancing as well as giving her the opportunity to travel abroad within the security and companionship of this well-bonded group. Mum threw herself whole-heartedly into her involvement with Age Exchange, renewing her self-esteem and providing the stimulation she craved to give her life more depth and purpose.

This form of work enabled the older people to create moving pieces of theatre seen by thousands of people in this country and abroad, increased their self-confidence and, in many cases, altered the way they were perceived by their own families. Barbara McKenzie's grand-daughter Natalie wrote:

> It's been nearly two years since Granny joined the Good Companions and I don't think anyone could have predicted the changes that we've seen in her life. It was as if the routine of her life had fallen away and left a stronger and wiser woman with an unfamiliar child-like curiosity to experience every facet of life to its fullest. My grandfather would have been so proud of her. What strikes you most about the Good Companions, is that it's a youthful spirit of living which finds its joy in the ability to share with others this incredible gift of restoring and nurturing memories. (Age Exchange Annual Report 1995–6, p.3)

For me, this work with the Good Companions has been a high point and for many years I have been sustained by the warmth and companionship of this truly remarkable group.

Summary

In this chapter, I have traced the development of a group of older volunteers with an interest in reminiscence into a theatre company with a 12-year record and ten original shows under their belts, all based on their own lives. I have tried to reflect the importance of this work in the lives of the older performers as they explored different aspects of their past together and found new ways to express their individual and joint experience. The chapter also gives some indication of the impact their performances had on others, both old and young.

The chapter outlines the six crucial elements involved in reminiscence theatre as devised and performed by older people:

1. It is a group activity demanding of the participants that they work closely together in an open manner with a considerable degree of trust.

2. It involves the sharing of experience around an agreed theme, to provide the raw material from which the group and the director will create the eventual product.

3. It involves putting each person's experience 'on the floor', allowing it to become the general property of the group while it is worked upon in many different ways.

4. The individual stories and experiences must be welded together into a coherent whole through the creative process, usually with the help of a director, so that together they make a new artistic statement with its own internal logic.

5. The artistic creation is communicated and impacts on its audience in a variety of ways, changing, even if only a little, the way the individuals in that audience and the audience as a whole perceive the world.

6. The response of the different audiences to the work shown has an impact on the players in terms of their sense of themselves in their communities and their social roles.

CHAPTER 13

Minority Ethnic Elders Make Theatre from their Lives

My experience of working with the older people's theatre company, the Good Companions, prompted me to plan further similar work, but with a multi-ethnic dimension (Schweitzer 2002b). I had already worked some years earlier with a group of Caribbean elders on an inter-generational project *We Want To Speak Of Old Times* (described in Chapter 11) and some of the cast of that project had stayed together, working on a further production, *Market Day*, with a Caribbean choreographer, Leon Robinson, which Age Exchange had presented at the Senior Theatre World Festival in Cologne, Germany, and at the London International Festival in 2000. I felt it would be interesting to bring together the members of this group, now calling themselves 'The Islanders', and the Good Companions to make a combined show. Peggy Pettitt,[25] an African-American colleague who had worked for several years with the New York group Elders Share The Arts,[26] had set up a group of older African-American story-tellers called the Pearls Of Wisdom, so I invited her to England to co-direct this new project with me. Because of her limited time and a tight budget, we decided to try to put a show together in a week. In fact we announced it to potential participants as a workshop week, as we were not sure it was feasible to prepare anything in such a short time, which could be shown with confidence to an audience, and we did not want to put undue pressure on the participants.

The Birds and the Bees

Finding the common ground

It was quite challenging for black and white elders to work together so intensively, and we were therefore delighted when 11 women, five white and six black, turned up on the first day. Several people said they were 'just there for the morning', that they 'couldn't stay' and were 'not available for the rest of the week'. They were generally hedging their bets. However, as it turned out, we had such a good time together that no one left the group during the week. We had decided that it would be good in this all-women's group to focus on sexual love, a topic which was not often spoken about by older people and which would be enriched by the mixture of backgrounds and ethnicities in our cast, but also where there might be a lot of common ground. We would revisit stages in their development as young women, including where and how they had discovered 'the facts of life'.

Re-engaging with childhood experience

We began with practical exercises to get people mixing and physically relaxed and then we shared stories about their growing-up days and about the people and places they had loved. We revisited childhood games and the two groups learned each other's songs and rhymes. This was a means of re-engaging with their very different childhoods and of getting into the atmosphere of excitement and specu-lation they experienced as children when they were discussing 'where babies come from'. Some had many brothers and sisters but were very hazy about their origins, with ideas varying from 'the doctor brings them in his bag' to 'the hospital sells them to the mothers'! This led to the development of a sequence in which a series of games and rhymes were interspersed with short scenes of children guessing and whispering, and where the only one who really knew the answer was absolutely disbelieved by the rest!

Tackling taboo subjects

The next day we explored questions of puberty and menstruation which had rarely been mentioned in previous reminiscence work and were certainly only possible in an all-women's group. Some of the stories were about ignorance, fear and denial, as so few of them had been prepared by their mothers for the transition. The women were able to revisit their sometimes painful youthful experiences with humour and mutual acceptance. A warm trusting atmosphere developed in the group as members helped one another to act out their stories. For example, Norma Walker from Jamaica remembered how shocked she was as a girl by her growing bosoms and how she bound them in bandages hoping her mother would not discover this unwelcome development. With the help of the rest of the group she played out the remembered scene where these bandages started to unravel in the school play-ground and her friends taunted her, so she had to bribe them to secrecy by sharing her dumpling dinner with them.

We also played out some of their horror when their first periods arrived, with one English woman saying that she thought she would bleed to death and a Carib-bean woman running to the old village wise woman to ask her help as she did not dare speak to her own mother.

Editing for comfort

People edited their own stories, revealing as much as they felt was comfortable to share and discuss, and there were extraordinary contrasts and a great deal of laughter in the sessions. Hyacinth Thomas, a woman who had been brought up on the Caribbean island of Antigua, said: 'I knew everything from the word go. I watched the animals and I understood.' At the other extreme were Joyce Milan and Barbara McKenzie, who grew up in south-east London. Joyce told how her mother always pulled Joyce's beret down over her ears so she would not hear when conversation turned on somebody being 'in a certain condition'. Barbara said: 'Sex was unmentionable in my family. Nobody mentioned it. I didn't know anything about my body or anyone else's.' Mostly the white women knew very little about sex, and some apparently only found out on their wedding nights.

Telling, but not playing

In fact people told many confidential stories in the group, covering a range of experiences including illicit relationships and unwanted pregnancies, but they did not want these staged. Group members decided what they felt comfortable to share and what they were willing to dramatise, and these were not always the same. Sometimes a woman would be willing to tell her story on stage, but did not want it played out or physically enacted by the others. One such narrative concerned a typical misunderstanding experienced by a Jamaican woman. Her grandmother had warned her never to kiss a boy, but had been too embarrassed to mention any other forbidden activities. She had been delighted to find that the periods which had been such a nuisance had stopped, and proudly informed her grandmother of this and how she no longer needed monthly help with washing her clothes. The grandmother, horrified, put two and two together, but the young girl was mystified, as she said: 'We did everything else, but I was really careful. I never once kissed the boy!' The woman concerned told the story with tremendous humour, playing both characters herself, and differentiating brilliantly between her naïve self and her outraged grandmother.

Romance and lack of it

On Day Three, stories of romantic love were easy to tell, and delightful to watch, with the women swapping race and gender quite happily. In one scene, Hyacinth, playing herself as a girl in Antigua, met her boyfriend near the well where she fetched the water. A small white woman, Margaret Phair, playing the boyfriend, put 'his' arm around the black woman's waist as she hoisted the water jar on to her head, and winked at the rest of the group expressing 'his' admiration.

One or two people were willing to talk about their wedding nights and I need hardly say that we used narration here, rather than enactment! Joan, a white woman who was new to the group, but who had considerable performing experience, was particularly open and she told the whole story of her wedding night and how shocking it was to her when she suddenly realised that she had to 'really do it now'. Her story was funny and painful at the same time and there was a frisson in the group at her courage in speaking of these things.

The Birds and the Bees: *(left to right) Hilda Kennedy, Hyacinth Thomas, Avis Lewison and Joyce Milan*

Telling the truth

An interesting incident occurred when a Caribbean woman told us that her wedding night had been in the Hilton Hotel and had involved scenes of wild abandon. Knowing the woman quite well, something struck me as out of character in her story, so I questioned her about it afterwards when we were alone. She said she had invented the story because she thought it would be more interesting than the reality. She was genuinely surprised when I said that her real experience was what mattered and that we needed all the stories to be true. We could of course dramatise a fantasy, but then we would have to explain somehow that that was what it was, because our 'contract' with our audience and one another was to tell them the truth. I realised that I had taken this agreement for granted, but of course it should be reiterated with each new group one works with through reminiscence. If there is any chance of misunderstanding, the absolute authenticity of the stories should also be explained to the eventual audience.

The play finished with stories of childbirth experience, including Norma's Jamaican experience of being rough-handled in the bush by a lay person who specialised in producing babies the hard way, and Hilda's horrifying and hilarious story about her London hospital experience:

> NORMA: I can remember those country women, those bush ladies and when you're going to have a baby they were fierce. They just grab you and shout 'Push. Open…get more oil. (*Norma and Hilda play the midwives, grabbing the screaming Avis, holding her and forcing castor oil down her throat*

telling her to push until the baby comes and they cheerfully announce) It's a boy!'

HILDA: After I had my baby, the nurse went and fetched the sister and she looked up me and said, 'Well, I've never seen one like that before!' And to this day I don't know what I've got that no one else has got! There was a doctor who sewed me up. It was unusual to have stitches in those days. My mum said, 'Stitches!? Never heard of such a thing.' But there he was puffing away on his pipe and stitching me up, like he was doing embroidery. Then he went out, and after a few minutes he came back and said, 'Has anyone seen my pipe?'

A play in a week: our process

Each rehearsal day was divided into warm-up sessions, always related to the theme for the day, story-telling in the group and then putting the stories on the floor. Every evening Peggy and I would write up what we had done, including the dramatisations the women had given us in improvisation, so people had a sense of progress and development. On the fourth day we had a complete script which we rehearsed scene by scene and we agreed that, rough and ready as it was, it would be fun to perform it on our last day together and see what others thought of the results of our intensive work.

We topped and tailed the play with the whole group chanting quietly, almost whispering the Cole Porter song:

They say that birds do it, bees do it
Even educated fleas do it
Let's do it, let's fall in love!

Audience reactions

An audience of friends and relations and members of the Reminiscence Centre came to see the show and the general reaction was one of surprise and delight. There was a very small minority who felt that there was a lack of propriety in exploring these subjects and they found the play slightly embarrassing. The humour and panache of the black and white women and the special relationship they had formed by working together on such personal material was warmly appreciated by the majority. After the first performance the players all gave each other a big hug and I felt that was evidence of the extent of their mutual co-operation, toleration, understanding and empathy. Peggy commented: 'This has not been work; it has been an inspiration. It has been a situation for learning and growing and reaching out with a group of women who were open and loving and very generous.'

Previously when Caribbean elders had come to the Reminiscence Centre they had worked in a closed group and there had been very little overlap with the white elders and on this occasion there had been a great deal of communication and a high level of co-operative work. I think some of the success of the project lay in the way Peggy and I modelled a black and white director working harmoniously and trustingly together.

The performance was filmed and has been shown in many countries since the event, with most viewers finding both the stories and the way the women performed them quite irresistible in their humour, courage and honesty.

Mapping Memories

Places to meet and share

Over the last 20 years, local authorities, faith groups and voluntary organisations have gradually been setting up new meeting places in sheltered housing lounges, clubs, day centres, temples or mosques where elders from specific minorities can have lunch, informal conversation, and religious and cultural activities. Many of the users of these centres did not imagine when they first came to Britain that they would be spending their old age here, but they are now having to adapt to circumstances and settle for ending their days far from 'home'. It is an important source of comfort and reinforces a sense of identity for them to be with people from a similar background who speak the same language and share a common culture and many memories.

Recording life stories with minority ethnic elders

In 2002 I received some Lottery funding to run a project recording the lives of minority ethnic elders within the London Borough of Greenwich. The project was jointly undertaken with the borough's Council for Racial Equality and its Arts and Culture office. A training course for community artists, group leaders and volunteers who would conduct the life story interviews and participate in other creative aspects of the project was held at the Reminiscence Centre. Like all experiential reminiscence training, this course involved the participants undertaking personal reminiscence work about their own lives, so they would be alert to the need for sensitivity and the inevitability of touching on painful subjects.

Introductory sessions were held in all the relevant meeting places, led by Meena Khatwa, the project leader, supported by Satya Devi Paul, the highly effective officer with responsibility for minority ethnic elders, who gave every encouragement to the groups to participate. Elders offered to give one-to-one life story interviews for inclusion in a book, *Mapping Memories*, to be produced at the end of the project (Schweitzer 2004a). Some of the interviews were conducted through translators but quite a number of those who volunteered were happy to speak in English.

A time to reflect

Elders from China and Vietnam, from Africa, the Caribbean, India and Somalia participated in these interviews. For many, it was the first time they had had a chance to look back over their lives with an interested and sympathetic listener. They built strong personal ties with the interviewers through this process. The recordings were transcribed and edited and thoroughly checked by the contributors. The older people were all photographed in their own homes and in their meeting places by Rado Klose, a local professional photographer who worked closely with the group leaders. Rado accompanied the elders on shopping trips and social visits and photographed them participating in all aspects of the project.[27]

From interview to creative involvement

It was part of the brief we had prepared for ourselves to try to involve the interviewees and other members of their groups in some creative reminiscence activity, so the freelance project workers, who received reminiscence training throughout the project, were contracted to work with the groups over a ten-week period. During this time, they were to develop several artistic products reflecting the interests, skills and enthusiasms of the older people. Elders meeting at a Caribbean day centre took part in a sewing project making a colourful tablecloth depicting the fruits and vegetables of their home islands. Chinese elders worked on a craft and construction project resulting in a boat made of silk and bamboo covered with Chinese writing and images. A Caribbean club created an installation around their memories of 'Sunday Best' in Jamaica. Indian women worked with a choreographer to create a dance piece around memories of home, and men from the Sikh temple worked with a theatre director on a piece about their working lives. Theatre projects based on memories of home were prepared by an African elders' group, a Caribbean over 50s club and Chinese elders from a sheltered housing unit. (See Chapter 11 for a description of the theatre work of the African elders, including an inter-generational production.) All the groups were filmed as they worked on these creative projects and the resulting edited films, in CD-ROM format, have been included in the book of the project, *Mapping Memories* (Schweitzer 2004a).[28]

A time and place to share

It is always helpful to have an event to work towards with this sort of many-branched project, such as a festival or community day where the work of all groups can be shared. This provides an opportunity for people to enjoy hearing about lives very different from their own and they can pick up additional ideas about how to give creative expression to their own life experience. In this instance, everyone was working towards a joint festival called 'The Place Where I Grew Up' at which the book of the life stories of the group would be launched, and groups would spend three days together sharing food and music from participating cultures as well as their own productions.[29] It is my experience that the energy generated by preparing for and participating in events of this kind has a very positive effect on participating groups, creating a sense of cohesion, of celebration and of pride. All the groups taking part in the event increased in confidence and most have since gone on to prepare new creative projects independently, including work with younger members of the community. (See Chapter 11 for a description of the theatre work involving African and Chinese elders with school-children.)

Isolation through language

Establishing contact with a local sheltered housing unit for about 15 Chinese elders was particularly satisfying, since they are one of the less visible minorities in London. The manager, Helen Kon, is bilingual, which is necessary, as most of the elderly, somewhat frail members of her unit speak no English and need help in dealings with doctors, social services and other officials. Some of them have tried living in mainstream sheltered housing units but have felt very isolated. They are all very happy to be in this special unit where there is a shared approach to life and a common language and culture. They grow Chinese herbs in their garden, play Mah Jong, have Tai Chi dance sessions and enjoy many celebration meals together, where all the older people, many of whom worked in the restaurant trade in London, share out the cooking tasks. Helen Kon was very enthusiastic about the group attempting to make a play for the forthcoming festival. She agreed to co-operate very fully, translating for every session, but also narrating in the final performance and ensuring that her older people felt comfortable and confident in what they were doing.

The value of difference

The stories from this group of elders were very different and, although the process of working through translation took more time, the information was always worth waiting for. In an early meeting, the group members explained their names, which all had very specific meanings, often pertaining to the circumstances of their birth. They were then invited to talk about their childhood homes, concentrating on the sounds they remembered which were associated with that time. Some came from a busy urban environment and others from a rural background.

A sound collage

The rest of the group were then invited to work together to make a series of sound collages, one for each speaker. One by one, people added new sounds, either suggested by something the speaker had mentioned or coming from their own imagination. The story-teller then listened with eyes closed to the combination of sounds, which rose and fell in volume as I conducted them. Other memories arose, and were added to the story so the picture of the childhood home was filled out as a result of the sound stimulus. One woman in her 80s, Mrs Liu, accessed an entire portrait of her childhood home through this exercise. She talked about her father who owned a silk farm with pits full of silk worms. The silk worms were fed on mulberry leaves and she wanted the crunching sound of two million silk worms crunching mulberry leaves in her sound-scape. She remembered that they used to take all the detritus from the pits and feed it to the fish in her father's ponds. It would land in the fish pond with a great plop and then she would hear the fish breaking the surface of the water with a soft sound to gulp this food. She remembered this as a whole sequence and it was played back by the group as a sound-scape. She then remembered the sound of her father's footsteps which she wanted added into the sound collage. Apparently he would carry her on his shoulders as he walked on their own land and also in the countryside round about, and this was a very strong and physical childhood memory for her. This lady later worked with a visual artist and used these memories to create a three-dimensional Memory Box featuring the silk farm where she grew up. (Her Memory Box is featured in Schweitzer and Trilling 2005.) This shows how different art forms can complement one another in reminiscence work, and how the older people can find rewards in exploring their own memories through different media.[30]

Accessing in-depth recall through enactment

The example of creating a group sound collage, which could later be built into a scene in the eventual play, is just one of many ways in which new memories from the past were accessed. Through many such drama-based explorations, the theatre worker can take the story-teller further and further into his or her memories, thus encouraging spontaneous, animated and detailed story-telling. This can be a highly dynamic and interactive process involving the whole group, in which little electric shocks of memory are generated, causing surprises and sudden accesses of energy, as the older people locate bits of the past which have not surfaced for decades. So we can almost suggest that one makes memories from theatre as well as making theatre from memories!

Theatrical images generate spontaneous recall

This is a completely different process from the more chronological interview conducted for historical purposes in the 'holy hush' of the interview room, where the interviewer is an intensely interested but largely silent observer, recording the interviewee's oral account from earliest memory to the present. The theatre worker thinks in a much more imagistic, and a much less linear, way, and has an absolute requirement for detail, a 'need to know exactly how it was'. This approach is more in line with the way memory often functions, with extracts from the past cropping up in response to a stimulus, a particular sound or image, word or action or the related experience of others. It involves a mutual operation, the giving of memory and the creation of something relating to that memory by the recipients.

Crossing the language divide through theatre

Sharon Morgan, a 'Mapping Memories' project worker who had much experience of Playback Theatre, worked with the Chinese elders over several weeks, exploring their memories through different theatrical games and exercises around their reminiscences. The group enjoyed playing childhood games in one session, and the extraordinary sight of a lady nearly 90 years old playing a version of five-stones and not missing a catch was startling in the final version of the play. In another session Sharon used image work in which, as they heard a story told by one member of the group, the rest would form a 'group sculpture' whereby they would hold a pose reflecting what they had heard. Whole group scenes were developed based on stories of family life, including helping with the ploughing, weaving in the family home, going to market, fishing and spinning. These were expressed in gracious and careful mime with songs sung by the elders or on soundtrack to accompany them. The whole group participated in a presentation of a Chinese wedding and the play ended with an evocation of the Chinese New Year. Sharon helped the group to find visual and musical ways of expressing the stories in ways which could be understood by a non-Chinese audience. A young Chinese music student, Esther Liu, supported Sharon, helping with translation and creating a music soundtrack and background visuals which showed where all the elders came from.

Sharon found the work very demanding as she was not always able to understand discussions and occasional disagreements within the group and not everything could be translated for her. However, she forged a close relationship with the group, with Helen Kon's help, and we felt that the advantages of her being from a different culture in this situation outweighed the disadvantages. Because everything needed to be explained to Sharon, nothing could be taken for granted, which meant that the elders had to be very clear in explaining their remembered rituals and practices. Many of them had lived turbulent lives dictated by political upheavals, and I personally found it helpful to refer to the Internet and an atlas when trying to get to grips with their stories of travel and war. The elders realised that what they had to tell was special and interesting to Sharon and me and also to their eventual audience.

The Chinese elders perform a tea ceremony

Energy through performance

Seeing these frail elderly Chinese people, beautifully dressed for the performance, on stage presenting their lives in a series of striking dramatic images created during their extended rehearsal period was immensely moving and very pleasurable. The English translation and the continuity between the scenes was provided by Helen Kon, for whom this was an absolutely new experience. She felt that it had been immensely valuable for the group and that she too had learned a new way of working with the elders. Some family members were present to see the play, but all the other 200 members of the audience for their first performance were participants and guests at the 'Place Where I Grew Up' Festival from countries across the world. It must have been a tremendous challenge for this normally separate group to join in such a large and culturally diverse event and tell their stories. For these Chinese elders, whose voices and opinions are rarely sought or heard in any public forum, this was a rare and empowering experience.

The dramatisation of their lives gave them the possibility to represent themselves not just as old people, but as children, as young men and women and as adults. The extreme sense of disjuncture, so much a feature in the lives of elderly immigrants from Asia, was partially overcome as working on the scenes of the play knitted their lives together retrospectively into a whole. Both during the devising/rehearsal period and when performing, an energy was generated by the group from which all individuals benefited as their sense of self was being enhanced and strengthened.

'Flow in creativity'

Leonie Hohenthal-Antin from Finland, who has researched older people's theatre, comments that making and performing plays about their own lives 'gives older people permission to exist differently on the stage than in everyday life' (Hohenthal-Antin 2001). She quotes Mihaly Csikszentmihalyi, the architect of the notion of flow in creativity, who claims that creative expressive work is a way of

> being completely involved in an activity for its own sake. The ego falls away. Time flies. Every action, movement, and thought follows inevitably from the previous one, like playing jazz. Your whole being is involved, and you're using your skills to the utmost. (Csikszentmihalyi 1996)

From her observation of the Finnish elders involved in the Kutkutus Theatre group, Leonie concludes that 'Theatre making as a collective and public form of art offers its makers life full of flow, which the actors of Kutkutus describe with passion and pleasure'.

Avoiding assumptions and stereotyping

As a director or facilitator working with minority ethnic elders, one has to counteract any tendency to restrict creative approaches by any form of stereotyping. The first time I worked with a group of elderly Chinese people was about 12 months before the work described above, on a project with the National Maritime Museum on the theme of life journeys.[31] It really confounded my assumptions and expectations that the Chinese elders meeting at the Indo-Chinese Community Centre in Deptford were absolutely open to working through drama. The memory of one woman leading us all in the butterfly dance she performed as a child when all her hopes were focused on being a dancer, and the rest of the group singing along with her, stays with me now, even though the happy scene was tinged with sadness as all her ambitions had been thwarted by war and the family's consequent flight.

I was sure the elders in this group would not want to talk about their escape from horrendously difficult political situations in their home countries but, to my astonishment, they were very willing to talk about those experiences and even to act them out. Working with translators and another trained project worker, Erene Kaptani, I had split the group and asked them to prepare scenes on the subject of journeys. One scene to emerge concerned a Chinese woman, rowing a boat across the river to safety, with all her papers tucked into her clothing. She was escaping Vietnam, where the ethnic Chinese were being discriminated against, and travelling via mainland China to Hong Kong. This was a very painful story of leaving behind everything she had ever known and of making a very traumatic journey. I would not have asked this woman to play out her story, for fear that it would be too distressing, but she had volunteered to do so in the small group and was quite willing to elaborate on the story when it was replayed to the whole group.

Archetypal images

On another occasion, we set up a row of chairs which represented the flight of stairs which they would walk down from the plane and asked them to re-create what it was like to arrive in England after the epic journeys they had made by land, water and air. What was the first thing they saw? What did they bring with them from the home country? In many cases, this turned out to be little or nothing: very often just what they stood up in. They went on to 'play out' their extraordinary experiences of being new arrivals in this country, of living in temporary camps and unsuitable houses and of struggling to be reunited with their family members. One woman told how she and her husband were moved from her camp to a flat in a small market town called Beverley in Yorkshire where there was one Chinese restaurant, but no other Chinese people, and that two weeks later she gave birth to her baby. Her husband, an accountant back home, was working in the local canning factory, the only work he could find. And when I said to this woman: 'Show me how it was for you in those days', she rolled a shawl into an imaginary baby and cradled it in her arms. She was rocking the baby, parting imaginary net curtains and looking out of the window to see if her husband was returning, and gently singing to the baby. Two other women in the group quite spontaneously came and stood behind her and sang a song about missing home and loved ones. In that song and the image of the mother cradling her baby, the three of them created an archetypal image of the woman alone in a foreign land with no support except for her memories. The rest of the group applauded them and the atmosphere was very emotional. I asked them to play the scene again because I found it so beautiful and the women were happy for the whole sequence, shot on video, to be included in a short film demonstrating this approach to reminiscence work.[32]

Dramatic exploration of the past had enriched the present

Towards the end of my ten weeks with this group, I asked them to work with large pieces of paper representing in drawings and captions those aspects of their lives today that were most important and fulfilling for them. Some people drew their gardens where they grew Chinese herbs, some drew their children and grandchildren, some the club for Chinese elders which provided a focus for all their activities, and some a television screen and microphone, because they really enjoyed singing Chinese songs karaoke style. People shared their drawings with the rest of the group and with me and co-facilitators through translators. At the end of the last session, the elders, dressed in special clothes, served us a wonderful banquet of food they had made themselves to celebrate what we had done together and we sang Chinese and English songs to mark the occasion. Our principal medium of exploration had been dramatic improvisation and it was this, I am sure, which had brought us so close together across the huge divides of language and culture.

Summary

In London, a city where more languages are spoken, and more minorities are represented, than anywhere else in the world, finding ways of expressing the experience of the growing population of ethnic elders through story, music, movement and costumes is a crucial aspect of reminiscence theatre work. The underlying themes of childhood home remembered, journeying, adventure and opportunity, homesickness, loss, adaptation, changes in language and culture, and longing for 'home' in old age are universal, but the experience of them is personal and specific. In this chapter, I have sought to show that empowering people who do not normally have a public voice to air these themes in their own way and helping them to communicate effectively through theatre with their intended audiences is important work. Personal, artistic and group confidence grow and the participants speak of an increased sense of identity and belonging and an enhanced quality of life.

CHAPTER 14

Use of Drama in Outreach Work and in Dementia Care

The Reminiscence Project in care homes, day centres and hospitals

The professional reminiscence theatre productions, with their live music, costumes, scenery and lighting, made a tremendous impact in the older people's venues where they toured, but there were some audiences, especially in care homes, for whom the plays were too complex, too concentrated, too sustained. Handling the raunchy badinage from lively and engaged elderly audience members was not a problem for the actors, especially for those who came from a stand-up comedy background, but where the interruptions were signals of distress, such as older people wanting to leave or not knowing where they were, or even at times wandering on to the set, it was worrying for the actors and for the staff. A more flexible format for reminiscence, geared more specifically to meet individual needs, was obviously desirable. So within about two or three years of setting up the theatre company, I piloted a parallel series of outreach reminiscence projects to complement the work of the professional theatre company and called it the Reminiscence Project. A new colleague, Caroline Osborn, who came from a social work and visual arts background, soon took over responsibility for this work, which attracted separate funding from the Department of Health and various charitable trusts.

Improvisation as a stimulus

A key form of relating to the older people in these groups would be improvisation, which would stimulate memories in similar ways to the professional shows, but on a very much smaller scale, more spontaneous and informal. By creating moments of interaction using character and situation, supported by appropriate reminiscence objects as props where possible, we would aim to open dialogue with individuals and small groups of older people. The older people would be encouraged to join in short enactments playing remembered roles, such as mother, daughter, pupil, waitress, husband or factory worker, in whatever situation was being presented. Their additional memories and impromptu comments in the enactments would then be fed back to the whole group, so that the smallest contributions would be maximised, added to the whole, and valued as part of a communal reminiscence event.

Tailor-made reminiscence sessions

The idea of the Reminiscence Project was that we would tailor-make the reminiscence interventions to the needs of the participants who would be a small group, maybe eight or ten people, often with physical or mental frailties. We recruited 20 project workers with backgrounds in drama, music and visual arts and offered them an intensive week of reminiscence training with ongoing support and supervision. They were then given freelance work as session leaders, working in pairs over eight or ten sessions with groups in residential and nursing homes, day centres and long-stay wards of hospitals. The project workers made preliminary visits to find out from the staff about the individuals who would be in the group, their interests and their backgrounds, and then developed sessions around themes likely to stimulate their memories.

In-service training and support for care staff

Previous experiments involving care staff in reminiscence had shown that job satisfaction and sensitivity of care increased when the worker had more personal knowledge of the client's past and an opportunity to work on a more equal basis with the client in a relaxed and sociable context (Gibson 2004; Kemp 1999). So part of the plan was that care staff would attend these workshops and be actively involved in the planning and running of the sessions. It was hoped that, in this way, they could become sufficiently familiar with the reminiscence approach to continue the work after we left. The contract we drew up with the care homes involved them in committing two members of staff to attend all sessions. This also had the effect of increasing the ratio of support staff to older people, so there could be more one-to-one attention and time for those less able to assemble their memories quickly. Of course this did not always work out, as rotas and schedules do not always run to plan in these settings, but the majority of venue managers welcomed the chance for an enjoyable and manageable form of in-service training for their staff, and many of these staff continued the work very competently as a result. By conducting the projects in the care homes where the staff worked, they saw how they could adapt the basic ideas to fit the needs and the capacities of people in their care and would be less tempted to say, 'It's a really nice idea but it wouldn't work with my group.'

Using reminiscence objects as physical prompts

Raiding junk shops, markets and our own attics and cellars, Caroline and I gradually built up a supply of miscellaneous objects connected with everyday life between the 1920s and 1940s. Handling items from the past, such as a candle in a holder, a dip-in pen, a pair of 'bloomers' or a fur stole, stimulated memories and enabled participants to show what they remembered about how these items were used or worn. The objects were arranged thematically in small suitcases around subjects such as school days, washday, courting, marriage, the seaside and so on.[33]

The session workers on the Reminiscence Project took these cases with them to the venues, using the objects to jog memories, to help the conversation along and to provide a focus for group activities. For example, the project workers might set up a session around the theme of washday, and have the old equipment such as washboards, mangles, clothes-pegs, washing lines and old irons available for the older people to handle, so that they could focus on that subject. The workers would encourage the older people to use the equipment, actually using water and the original strong-smelling soap which they would be likely to remember from childhood. These actions would sometimes alarm staff, who were worried about 'making a mess', but they were effective in evoking, through sensory stimulation, physical sensation and action, related memories of younger days, and from these memories new stories and scenes would arise.

Sometimes, the project workers would play out the stories remembered by the older people, who would be seated around the action. They would invite the older people to suggest dialogue or action, and sometimes the older people would briefly take on roles themselves in response to the invitation, 'Show us how it was.' Making small scenes from the older people's stories and involving them in the enactments often worked really well, raising the adrenaline level in the group each time there was a little 'performance' and giving the participants 'star status' for a few moments, and a round of applause to confirm that. What evolved was a mixture of role playing, improvisation and story-telling (Quinn 1989).

Group evocation of past experience

Two sessions illustrate the approach used. One was a session on going out in the summertime and we had set the scene with a rug laid out in the middle of the floor on which were objects connected with going out on a day trip with a picnic. The introductory exercise was a prompted visualisation. We said to the whole group: 'Wouldn't it be nice if we could go out today? Let's go on a picnic in our imaginations. Where could we go?' And people called out suggestions of familiar destinations from the park to the seaside. This led to more questions, 'Are we going by bus, or charabanc, by train or on a bike?', to which everyone responded with their own remembered transport and we accepted them all with: 'What good ideas! This is going to be a good outing.' The next question was 'Shall we take a picnic? What shall we take?' We then passed round an old-fashioned straw basket and asked everyone to mime putting something in which they would like or which they remembered from a real picnic in the past. People put in things like tobacco for Dad or a drink of lemonade crystals in a glass bottle with one of those rubber tops with a metal clasp, sweeties of various kinds and sandwiches. Gradually the picnic was coming to life for us as a group creation, with everyone recapturing a little of the excitement of the real outings remembered.

Inclusion of isolated people in reminiscence group work

I recall worrying if Alice, one of the women in the group, would cope with this. We had been given to understand that she had a very unhappy childhood and a diffi- cult life to follow. She seemed completely out of touch with what we were doing in the group, anxious and distracted, muttering to herself through much of the session. When the picnic basket came to her, she mimed putting something in and said quietly in a quick-fire monotone, 'Ham sandwiches. And the ham was off', before passing the basket on. This gave us a real jolt, as we realised that this woman had not only been following the session, but that she had been able to feel a part of it and that our activities with the basket had triggered memories of an incident from long, long ago. Towards the close of the session, during which we explored many people's memories of such trips through conversation and small improvised scenes, we suggested, 'Now we'd better pack up and go home. Shall we sing on the way?' and then everybody sang together songs they had sung on return journeys from day trips in the past, and Alice joined in. We had no reason to doubt that Alice was remembering a real picnic from the past where the ham was off, even though, when the session ended, she ran in small steps to the television and turned it on to silence the more persecutory voices in her head which were oppressing her so. For the moment of her interjection she was a group member and we all learned some- thing about her. The staff were amazed and it helped them to see her as an individ- ual in her own right with her own history and submerged memories, which could be awakened if the stimulus was right.

Re-enacting past skills and competences

In another instance in the same home, the subject of the session was starting work and we arranged the session along the lines of 'What's My Line?'. Everyone talked in pairs about his or her first job, preparing something to show the rest of the group and everyone had to guess what work it was. There were older people in the group who could not speak any more, certainly not intelligibly, and I was paired up with one of them. In his working life, Charlie had been a parquet floor layer, starting as an apprentice and ending up as a supervisor. It took a long time to work this out from what he said, but his movement was quite good and he showed the actions better than he could describe them. I took on the role of an absolutely new appren- tice to get him to show me how to lay a herring-bone patterned parquet floor and, using simple mime, he showed me what to do. What was interesting was that Charlie took on the role of 'the person who knew' and, for a man who has lost most things, to have that little moment when he was the expert, and I was the rather hopeless apprentice who needed to be told how to do the job right, was very helpful for his morale, his sense of self, and his sense of worth. Everyone took turns miming their jobs for the rest of the group. Of course parquet floor laying was really difficult to guess and Charlie and I had to work hard at 'our job' to help people fathom out what it was. It was also enormously good fun and, during the sharing of the mimes and the guessing game involving the whole group, everyone in the room learned something about one another.

Dramatic improvisation as a natural means of exploring memory

Although improvisation might seem to be a very alien activity for older people in a care home to engage in, the fact was that it proved to be a very helpful means of bringing the past to life in the present. It provided a very natural and easy way of finding and expressing memories, with the added benefit of social interaction and engagement in what can be rather lonely environments. Some of the project workers who were not from a drama or theatre background initially felt more comfortable asking the older people to tell memories or to explore them visually through drawing and painting, rather than to re-enact them. However, there was no doubt that some of the most animated sessions emerged from the imaginative playing out of 'as if' situations. By entering into remembered situations and performing them as though they were happening again now, the older people could retrieve knowledge, competence and confidence long submerged. During those short enactments, and some were only of about three lines in duration, the older people shone and became the centre of attention. It was their moment and they relished the applause their efforts produced. Because these moments were unusual and special, they were also memorable, and could be referred back to in the subsequent session to encourage a positive mood and a feeling that equally interesting things could happen 'today'. The increase of energy which moments of drama provided was palpable and supported the developing notion in the 1980s that old people's homes could be places of fun and laughter and worthwhile activity (Osborn, Schweitzer and Schweitzer 1987).

The Reminiscence Project has been an important initiative in an area where stimulus is needed to improve communication and life quality for some of our most neglected citizens. *The Reminiscence Handbook* (Osborn 1993), in which Caroline collected the most successful ideas emerging from this project, has been reprinted and translated into other languages, and has inspired many professional health and social workers and activities co-ordinators to stimulate the frail older people in their care through reminiscence.[34] Several other practitioners have been developing inspirational projects in parallel, contributing to a sea-change in opinion as to what older people in residential care can participate in and respond to when they have the opportunity, encouragement and support (Killick and Allan 2001; Kitwood 1997; Knocker 2004; Perrin 2005; Sim 2003).

Remembering Yesterday, Caring Today: an international project for families coping with dementia

Setting up reminiscence groups in sheltered settings where the older people are a captive audience is relatively easy (Woods and McKiernan 1995). Creating such groups in the community is more complicated, especially where the intended members are families coping with dementia. However, there has been growing awareness of the unmet needs of family carers, who can feel very beleaguered within their own homes, often experiencing depression resulting from their social isolation. There has also been a growing body of experience suggesting that reminiscence can be a successful way of maximising the intact memory of people with dementia (Bender, Bauckham and Norris 1999; Gibson 2004; Woods *et al.* 2005). In 1997, at an international conference entitled 'Widening Horizons in Dementia Care' organised by Age Exchange for the European Reminiscence Network, experts in reminiscence and in dementia from five continents shared their experience in both fields (Schweitzer 1998).[35] Speakers and delegates agreed that it was time to test out the value of reminiscence as an intervention which might help both people with dementia and their carers.

A European project in ten countries

Ten partners in the European Reminiscence Network formulated a collaborative action research project entitled *Remembering Yesterday, Caring Today*, with the aim of helping families to maintain communication and social engagement, to support their relationships and improve their quality of life. With funding from the European Commission's Health Promotion Unit, the Network partners piloted the project in 16 cities across Europe between 1997 and 1999.[36] All the groups they set up went through the same processes and the same structured sessions around agreed themes with the families involved, though of course there were inevitably variations from country to country and different emphases, depending on the skills and interests of the project workers. This common approach helped in evaluating the project (Bruce and Gibson 1999a, 1999b).

Composition of the groups

One of the most important elements of the project was to offer the ten families in each of the pilot projects a friendly meeting place where they could have an enjoyable time together with others in a similar situation. Our intention was to provide as much assistance as we could for the person with dementia to function effectively in the group and to maximise their intact social and memory skills, especially their long-term memory. Over the 18 weeks of the project, we would try to build a reminiscence community led by trained project workers with arts and reminiscence skills and supported by local older volunteers. The latter had a very important social role to play, because they normalised the situation, making the meetings feel more like the get-togethers of friends. They could relate to the life experience of the people with dementia, drawing them out by showing recognition of what they were remembering so they felt encouraged to share their intact memories. The volunteers were also helpful when starting any activity, as their confident participation set a positive tone and encouraged the family members to risk joining in.

Thematic exploration of memories

The reminiscence sessions were organised thematically and followed key stages of life, usually starting with the older people's memories of early days and family life and moving forward chronologically through their school days memories, the jobs they had, the boys and girls they courted, their marriages and the birth of their children. It was important to have relevant reminiscence objects and documents laid out at the start of a session to stimulate informal conversation while waiting for the whole group to assemble. Groups in each country participating in the project assembled their own collections of reminiscence artefacts from junk shops, markets and their own friends and relations. The Belgian partners even went so far as to rent and furnish a flat in Brussels for the duration of the project, so that families could maximise their involvement both during and between sessions.

Structuring the sessions

Each session was broken down into a series of exercises and activities, beginning with simple warm-ups related to the theme, to get people working together as a group, gently waking their bodies up with light physical exercise and creating an informal, almost party-like atmosphere. These exercises would be followed by work in small groups, often using the objects assembled around the theme of the session. Four or five people, maybe two couples and a volunteer or project worker, would explore through discussion, or drawing and writing, their memories on an agreed topic, with time being given particularly to the people with dementia to assemble what they wanted to say or show. The small groups then fed back to the rest some of the most interesting stories to emerge, featuring especially any contributions offered by the people with dementia. These stories would then be developed further in the small groups, or through whole group activities incorporating singing, dancing, cooking and eating and the creation of improvised scenes using the objects. The session would usually conclude with a song, and a summary by the project workers to remind people of all the things they had done together that afternoon, ending with the announcement of the next session's theme, so that the families could begin to focus on it and find relevant memorabilia to bring in.

Enactment as a key element

All this may sound a long way away from making theatre from memories but in fact drama came to play a very significant part in the resulting project and in our understanding of how memories can be stimulated. Through the drama exercises and improvisations tried in the project, we began to understand how the memories of people with dementia could be activated through re-playing scenes from their past as though they were happening in the present and that successful participation in these enactments built up people's confidence and sense of belonging to the group. We also saw that carers who re-experienced earlier parts of their lives which had disappeared under the clouds of present caring were more ready to remember that their partner or parent had once been for them funny, competent, clever and beautiful, and that deep down they were still the same people now. Working together to retrieve and re-enact happy moments from their past served to reinforce the central relationships and helped to create new ones with other families who shared a lot of common ground. The feeling of warmth, closeness and freedom in the groups was certainly due in part to the fact that drama was a significant medium of exploration and, certainly in the London branch of the project, this was central to each reminiscence session.

Improvising seaside memories in Remembering Yesterday, Caring Today

Some examples from the London project illustrate the many different ways in which drama in particular was used to stimulate and energise the groups (Bruce, Hodgson and Schweitzer 1999).

Stimulating physical memory

For a session on childhood games we laid out plenty of old-fashioned toys and board games for people to handle as they arrived, usually the authentic article, but sometimes modern equivalents. When everyone was assembled, we formed a circle so everyone could be seen. The opening exercises involved everyone taking it in turns to mime the actions of a game they had enjoyed playing as a child and everyone copied their actions. This led into rhymes and singing games, some of them with actions, such as 'Oranges and Lemons' and 'The farmer's in his den', which we played as a whole group, or with a small number of active participants and others watching, singing along and clapping.

People then chose an object that interested them and took it back to a smaller group, usually including a mixture of people with dementia, carers and a volunteer. In the quieter atmosphere of these small groups they shared childhood memories and played with the objects. I remember with pleasure the looks of disbelief on the faces of a group of visitors when they came into a roomful of very old people playing hopscotch, conkers, marbles and skipping, all totally engaged and some of them showing great skill and confidence.

The same response to handling the objects and hearing the old rhymes was noted in the Amsterdam branch of the project. A family carer noted:

> We were looking at childhood toys in our group and someone showed us a spinning top. Suddenly my wife began singing a song about tops which I had never heard her sing. She remembered it as she held the top in her hands. She could then remember some other things she did as a child. I thought, 'How is this possible?' Something returned to her and it was good for both of us, as we had a bit of contact through this. (Bruce *et al.* 1999, p.78)

The stories and actions which surfaced in small group discussion and action were then fed back to the whole group, so that many more memories were prompted. Some of the older people with dementia were able to perform unexpected physical feats in the course of these feedback sessions, relaying their stories through improvisation and actions. For example Rose, a very elderly woman who was really quite fragile, terrified her husband when she started skipping with a rope and would not stop until she had done 24 skips, presumably some magic target recalled from a long ago time, for which she received tumultuous applause from the whole group. This was just one of many examples of people engaging physically long after their carer or partner had believed any such response was possible. It was as though, through the acting out of the memory, the older person's body had woken up and found some of its youthful vigour, or even as though the body had its own independent memory.

In another session on school sports days, there was more startling evidence of the capacity of the people with dementia to surprise their carers and everyone else with their daring physical acts. One of the volunteers, knowing the subject for the afternoon was sports day, had hard-boiled some eggs so we could have an egg and spoon race, which everybody joined in with great enthusiasm. I remember running a three-legged race partnered by Eric, an old man with dementia who could barely walk, and he was belting along the room to his wife's astonishment, and was very pleased to be the winner. How did he find this energy when he arrived at the group with crutches hobbling painfully to his chair? He was always very warm and smiley with me after that and I think he had retained some memory of a pleasurable joint action crowned with success.

Remembered skills and competence

There was something about performing past actions as though they were really happening in the present which gave people a different kind of energy. The freedom to pretend in this way conveyed to the families a sense that they were in a special place where anything could happen. The people with dementia surprised themselves and their carers by relocating deep-rooted skills and having the confidence to show them off to others.

Physical re-enactment was particularly helpful in exploring people's memories of their working lives. We often found that having the tools of the trade to hand helped people to remember former strength and skill. For example Jim, a former docker who now remembered very little, could speak with confidence

Handling the tools of the trade in Remembering Yesterday, Caring Today

about his work when he held the docker's hook in his hand, felt the weight of it and demonstrated its use to the whole group. It was not always necessary to have the object if the improvisation could conjure it up in the imagination. I remember Fred, a former railwayman, and Ralph, a volunteer who was very keen on railways, playing out a story from Fred's days as an apprentice. Ralph played the boy, and Fred taught him how to fry an egg on his shovel in the furnace. When the boy placed the egg on his shovel, Fred released a great whoosh of steam which shot the egg out through the chimney. All of us watching could 'see' the egg, the shovel as well as the shock on the boy's face, and the scene came to life much more vividly than a mere telling of the story could ever have done. The same afternoon, Alec, a retired ophthalmologist with moderate dementia, played out a typical appointment with a client from his working days, supported by a volunteer as client and a project worker as his assistant. Obviously he did not have any relevant equipment with him, but as he pretended to try out various lenses and to set the client at ease, we all saw him as he had been, a quiet competent expert in his own field. Some of that feeling of competence stayed with him all afternoon, especially as it gave people something more to chat with him about informally and that made him feel more valued in the group.

Acting out shared memories with the whole group

In a session on school days, we set up a schoolroom by rearranging the chairs as though they were rows of desks facing the front, with a blackboard and other memory triggers around the room. One of the project workers played a fierce teacher and treated the group as though they were a class of pupils, which helped to reinforce the remembered situation. The whole group recited their times tables, guessed the spelling of difficult words and cheerfully stood up and sang hymns together. It was noticeable how the people with dementia could succeed in reciting by rote and singing by heart things learned so many years ago, and there was pleasure for all in chanting the remembered lines together. They entered willingly into the whole fiction, so it was not long before paper pellets were flying round the 'classroom' and ribald schoolboy comments surfaced. We would cut in and out of the enactment, with pauses for reminiscences from individuals in the group whose memories had suddenly been stimulated. People enjoyed hearing stories of naughtiness and punishment, but they enjoyed even more acting them out. The teacher would usually pick on carers, volunteers or fellow workers, rather than a person with dementia, to do a difficult spelling or mental arithmetic test, and everyone enjoyed watching them struggle, with much whispered help.

We went on to remember prize day and asked who had got a prize at school. People put their hands up and told about prizes for good handwriting, sportsmanship, French or good attendance. We re-enacted receiving these prizes by inviting prize-winners individually to come to the front, shake hands, and be congratulated. They received a book (in two cases, the original prize book which had been awarded some 70 years ago and brought in specially for the school days session) and then a round of applause. Somebody had brought a school report in, carefully preserved over a lifetime, and the 'pupil', now a very elderly lady with dementia, sat there blushing, as though hearing it for the first time, as the 'teacher' read this highly complimentary report out loud. The enactments were obviously 'pretend' but they were also real, because the old people had really won those prizes, or had these reports, and it was good for them and their carers to remember past moments of success and pride.

Some readers might be concerned that this method could infantilise the group, but there was no evidence that the participants felt patronised, and plenty that they enjoyed re-enacting scenes from a distant period of their lives. I always felt in these whole group improvisations where we were all enjoying the 'play acting' together that there was no 'them and us' division, no condescension, no power differential concerning the people with dementia. There was always a certain irony and detachment in the way we played out these scenes, as though we were almost audibly saying, 'We know this is not really happening, but pretending it is helps us to remember more and it is often quite funny too.' Carers, volunteers, project workers and particularly the people with dementia often made witty and apposite interjections and scenes took on a life of their own. Because the schoolroom was a memory common to all the group members, and because children in a class have a fellow feeling when faced with the authority figure of the teacher, this session also served to build group solidarity while allowing for some spontaneous star turns.

Small group scenes

Going to the cinema featured large in the memories of our families, whether it was the small local 'fleapits' where they had watched Saturday morning film shows as children or the glamorous big picture houses where much of their courting had been conducted. A session on cinema was always popular and we used small group and whole group improvisation to explore it. We asked people to work in small groups, including people with dementia, carers and volunteers, to make short scenes about their cinema memories and to be prepared to play them back to everyone afterwards. There was a great buzz of activity as groups all over the room shared stories and planned scenes. I remember one scene played back by two volunteers in their mid-70s, and one lady of 100 years old, May, who rarely spoke, but did enjoy attending the sessions with her daughter, Pat, aged 75. The two volunteers played children and May played their mum. 'Come on, Mum,' one of them said, 'can we have that money to go down the pictures?' And this old lady said, in a husky voice that seemed to come from somewhere deep inside her, 'No, you've had your pocket money for this week.' One of the volunteers persisted: 'Oh, Mum, go on! You said we could go.' And May, pretending to fish around in her pocket, said, completely in character as the mother, 'All right. Here's a penny. But don't tell your father.' With the 'spotlight' on her and everyone watching, May had suddenly produced an appropriate response, probably recalled from her own mothering days, and it was dramatising the situation which had enabled her to re-engage with her younger self. She was certainly amply rewarded because everyone clapped and congratulated her and it could be seen that she felt absolutely great about it. Her daughter had been part of a different scene with two other volunteers, where she had been playing a child participating in a talent contest at the local cinema, and she had produced a 'take-off' of Shirley Temple singing 'Good Ship Lollipop' as her turn. She was surprised and delighted that her mother had had such a pleasurable time, completely independent of her, preparing and performing this scene.

Everyone is a performer

In the larger group improvisation which followed, everyone formed a queue waiting to go into the cinema, while Ted, one of the volunteers, played the commissionaire, greatly aided by an all-purpose peaked cap as costume. Everyone in the queue sang a song connected with ABC cinemas which many remembered from their youth. They then pretended to buy their tickets or trick their ways into the cinema and make their way to their seats, which were laid out in rows for the purpose. As Olive, the pianist, played different types of cinema music in turn ('spooky', Chaplin-esque, 'thriller' and 'weepy') the whole group pretended to be the audience watching these very different kinds of films. On 'God save the King', everyone stood up, and some pretended to grope around for shoes they had taken off for the movie, and then to shuffle out sideways so they could get out before the great rush at the end of the national anthem. All the actions of the group, made up of volunteers, carers and people with dementia, were spontaneous and reactive, but entirely appropriate, demonstrating shared memories, common experience, as well as considerable humour and creativity. There is something very compelling about having a whole roomful of people playing out a representative cinema trip or a classroom scene or whatever the theme is for the session, and the 'as if' situation can be sustained for quite a lot longer than in a short scene played by some to others who are spectators. This whole group improvisation is an approach which gives people who are slow to formulate ideas and words plenty of time to participate and it does not put pressure on anyone to do anything they do not want to. There is no audience and everyone is a performer.

A failure-free environment

Joining in an improvisation enables people with dementia to demonstrate that they can still react appropriately in remembered and imaginary situations, even if they feel that they sometimes 'let their carers down' in real situations. By creating a failure-free environment in the whole group improvisation, we ensured a far higher level of enjoyment and participation than mere discussion would have yielded. You might also say that we were capitalising on the lack of inhibition which often accompanies dementia, seeing it as an opportunity and not a threat. I do not think we ever exploited it, as the spirit of trust in the group made it a safe environment for everyone to participate in their own way and on equal terms, without judgement. Anyone coming into the room during one of these whole group improvisation sessions would have been unable to say who were the people with dementia, who were the carers and who were the volunteers. The near-anarchy which occasionally broke out was always contained by firm leadership by the project workers. The more physical and rowdy sessions usually concluded in a more reflective mood, looking back in relative tranquillity at whatever outrageous things we had all found ourselves getting up to in the last couple of hours.

Loving memories

Courting days and wedding memories were particularly important to the project, as they gave couples, whose current relationships were often under serious strain, opportunities to revisit some of their happiest times together. A whole range of drama ideas could feed into one session here, each serving a different function. For example a simple pair exercise was used to help focus on remembered physical appearance and dress and hair styles. People took it in turns to be their partner's mirror and reflect exactly what they were doing as they prepared to go out to a dance hall or a party. Women applied make-up, rolled or waved their hair and checked their seams, while men shaved and struggled with their ties. People with dementia were well able to retain their concentration, both copying and leading in this non-verbal mirroring exercise, and some pairs chose to show their work to the whole group. It was good for carers to see their relative in real contact with someone else and to remember that they could still relate socially when the task was made manageable.

The next stage was for pairs to try to remember what they wore to go out, and then to share this with the group by one pretending to be a mannequin parading on a catwalk, or standing in a still position, while the partner played the compère, describing what they were wearing. In this way, participants invited us to meet the younger version of themselves, and sometimes startled us all into taking another look at them, as when George, an elderly carer, preened his remembered Elvis haircut and swanked in his yellow winkle picker shoes as described by his partner, a male volunteer. This juxtaposition of the person in the past and the present was an important element in maintaining people's sense of self, whether carer or cared for.

Dancing days

We then divided the room with men on one side and women on the other and asked them to show us how a man would ask a lady to dance and how she would respond, whether with dismay or encouragement. Suggestions for chat-up lines were suggested in the group, or people chose their own, and these were tried out as the men crossed the floor, with much laughter, and reflection on how things have changed. Usually men asked their own wives, and some of the resulting dances were very tender. Sometimes the tunes were played by our wonderful 80-year-old pianist who could respond to almost any request, and sometimes the group would hum songs requested by the couple. For many couples it was the first time in years they had danced together, usually because the carer was under the impression that it would not be possible. Sometimes the group leader would stop a couple and ask what they were remembering, before they danced on, and this revealed much remembered elation of their young love, a feeling which spilled into the present as the elderly couples circled the floor together. In this way, the dancing was an aid to memory as well as an affirmation of their relationship.

Wedding day memories

People brought in wedding photographs and recalled much detail about the occasion. Wherever possible, we enlarged these photographs so people could see the faces and dresses more clearly and remember the family members and guests who had attended. Sometimes we invited the group to recreate in a tableau a favourite wedding photo, with group members standing in for the important people in the original photo.

Sessions about weddings always presented a golden opportunity for a whole group improvisations, in which everyone could have a role, whether as bride and groom, parents, best man, jilted girlfriend, vicar, photographer and so on. As the 'bride' walked up the aisle, everyone was asked how they were feeling and they all answered in role, including a delightful lady with dementia, cast as the 'bride's mother' who replied, 'I'm very proud. I hope they'll be very happy. I hope he takes care of her.' These responses, entirely in tune with the pretend situation, were performances and memories at the same time, in that we were jointly acting out a fictional event in the present, but the cast were all calling on many memories of related real life events to inform their parts.

Remembering Yesterday, Caring Today: *John and Pat Pellet remember their wedding*

In the 'wedding scene' there was a feeling of euphoria in the room, like a real wedding, but also absolute hilarity, such as when the 'vicar' struggled through a very rough approximation of the service and then accidentally caught the bouquet tossed by the 'bride'! My colleagues who have recently run the project in Bradford said that they also found this wedding-related session very memorable, both moving and entertaining for all involved – the way the occasion flipped between farce and being deadly serious. For some of the couples who have played the bride and groom, with only a veil to support the action, acting out the scene seems to have really helped them in the present, affirming their relationship and reminding them of their relationship at its strongest. The freedom to pretend in this way conveys to the families a sense that the group meeting is a special time and place where, together, we can make anything happen.

Evaluating the project

The *Remembering Yesterday, Caring Today* project was evaluated as it went along and the overall findings were very positive (Bruce and Gibson 1998; Bruce and Gibson 1999a, 1999b). It proved very helpful to all the families in different ways, reducing the stress felt by carers and helping the people with dementia to trust themselves in social situations. People often came to those sessions looking thoroughly drained and unhappy, the carers, particularly, grey with exhaustion after a sleepless night and worried sick about the future. Most of them left feeling much more positive and happy. It was clear that participants valued the project and did not want the sessions to end. They felt appreciated as members of a desirable social group where they could have fun and laughter with others who understood and shared their situation, often a rare pleasure in the lives of families living with dementia. They were reluctant to lose the contact and support they had gained, so several partners in different countries established reunion groups in which the families could continue to meet on a monthly basis with some ongoing professional facilitation.

At the time of writing, the *Remembering Yesterday, Caring Today* project has run about 20 times in the UK and continues to run in other countries where it is being further evaluated (Thorgrimsen, Schweitzer and Orrell 2002). It has recently been awarded Medical Research Council funding for a trial platform preparatory to a major research project designed to investigate its effectiveness.[37]

Summary

This chapter began by exploring project-based reminiscence work by freelance theatre workers and other artists in care homes and day centres. Theme-based reminiscence sessions, with dramatic improvisation as a key medium of communication, have served as a means of promoting knowledge and skill to care staff and greater social contact among the older participants. The second part of the chapter described a major international project designed to support people with dementia and their family carers through reminiscence, using enactment of 'as if' situations and other creative activities to promote communication and enjoyment.

Conclusion

It has been rewarding to review the many different kinds of reminiscence theatre and drama work described in these pages and to identify how they all contribute towards bringing the past to life with the purpose of enriching the present. Whether through skilled professional performers, or through young people or through older people themselves, reminiscence theatre and drama reflect and reshape memories in ways which shed a new light on them for contributors, players and audiences.

Making theatre and improvised drama from memories links people, times and places. It links the older person with the professional artist to create a form of theatre which has a social and regenerative purpose. It links young and old through explorations of childhood experience past and present and builds mutual understanding and appreciation through joint creative activity. It links older people with one another, and enables them to identify and share common ground and mutual interests. Finally, it links people from different cultures by identifying universal themes in their shared stories and finding ways to express them which cross linguistic and aesthetic boundaries.

Reminiscence theatre is full of surprises. The Good Companions were surprised when they found that they could make a good show with just their own memories, which could touch and stimulate a wide range of audiences. By working with guest directors, and not just with me, they could see that there were different ways of making plays and different ways of conveying their experience without ever losing their dignity. It was exciting watching the older people in this group, most of whom had never acted before, develop into a team of people who were first class communicators performing with a unique sincerity. The formation of the first older people's company at Age Exchange had a domino effect as Caribbean, Chinese and African elders were inspired by performances by the Good Companions to tell their own stories. They were surprised at the positive reception given to the resulting shows, not only by their own communities but also by professionals at conferences and festivals in England and overseas.

Professional actors have been surprised by the special performance opportunities provided by verbatim scripts created from recorded interviews. They have

recognised that such material makes particular demands, especially when supported by a complete music score to be delivered 'live', but that it also yields considerable rewards in terms of audience response and feedback. Drama students
arriving for a lecture or workshop on reminiscence theatre, expecting it to be rather
restrictive and nostalgic, have instead become enthused with a desire to explore the
medium because of the opportunities it offers for their own creative development.

Young and older people have been surprised by one another's receptivity.
Through participating in inter-generational theatre projects, trusting relationships
have developed between generations who would not normally encounter each
other. The creative spin-off, the writing, drawing and drama created by the young
people, has been clear evidence of the impact and value of such encounters. They
have invariably found things in their own lives and their own experience which
relate closely with what the older people have told them, especially when the
subject was concerned with childhood and aspects of childhood. And when
children in a classroom find that it is very exciting to work with a group of elders
who like to sing and play with them, their teachers are surprised into rethinking
how they might involve local older people more actively as an educational
resource.

The use of dramatic improvisation in the dementia field was really the biggest
surprise. Many of the participants had great difficulty in communicating but they
were able to surprise themselves, winning unexpected rounds of applause because
they had done something neither they nor other people thought they could do.
And their carers were even more surprised, having often lost faith and confidence
in their person's ability to relate to others and respond to spontaneous opportunities for humour and social exchange.

The development of reminiscence theatre and drama involves all those concerned in a particularly intense and absorbing way. The older people are motivated
to recover their own memories and the confidence to get to know others through
exchanging experience. The flow of creative energy generated when people work
together to bring stories alive acts as a physical and emotional restorative. It is also
a highly sociable activity, reviving communication and social skills in older people,
even those who may be very withdrawn and isolated. Performing the stories to
others, whether in the form of fully-fledged plays, whether performed by themselves or others, or as re-enacted brief moments within a group, brings recognition
and a sense of being valued.

All of the projects described have involved thinking creatively about how to
bring people together to share experience and to give a voice to those who are not
normally heard in a way which can be life-changing for them and is certainly
life-affirming for everyone.

Notes

1. Charles Parker described the *Radio Ballads* (1958–1964) as 'a form of narrative documentary in which the story is told entirely in the words of the actual participants themselves as recorded in real life; in sound effects which are also recorded on the spot, and in songs which are based upon these recordings, and which utilise traditional or "folk-song" modes of expression'.

2. The residents of Minnie Bennett Sheltered Housing Unit had been enjoying reminiscence sessions for a year or so prior to this, led by Alan Behan, my predecessor at Greenwich Task Force, culminating in the publication of a booklet of their memories in 1981 entitled *When We Were Young* (supported by Help the Aged) which was distributed to other older people through the L.B. Greenwich Meals-on-Wheels service.

3. Nick Sales, director of Medium Fair Theatre Company, draws a parallel between reminiscence theatre and Theatre in Education performances (which often bring out in children star qualities which do not emerge in normal classroom transactions) and reminiscence theatre in an old people's home. He writes: 'Standing up and telling the whole assembly your own reminiscence...changes your status, and consequently your self-image, in a way that could not happen in what might seem a very similar conversation, but one that is contained within the daily run of things, and not lifted onto the special plane of public event' (Langley and Kershaw 1982, p.11).

4. The concept of 'attentive humility' is referred to by Nick Sales, director of Medium Fair Theatre Company, as a crucial attribute for the performer in theatre based on older people's memories in Langley and Kershaw (1982, p.14).

5. Kershaw explores this use of the typical or representative relationship, setting and situation in Langley and Kershaw (1982, p.30).

6. Meccano is a toy construction kit.

7. For a detailed account of the making of a later verbatim Age Exchange Christmas show based on wartime memories, see Chapter 4 in Oddey (1994).

8. Barbara Myerhoff, an anthropologist, recorded the lives of elderly Jewish holocaust survivors in California in her highly influential book *Number Our Days*, which was published in 1980.

9. Arthur Strimling in the USA has been developing over many years a series of inter-generational theatre projects with Jewish elders and young people. See Strimling (2004). In addition to the Roots and Branches story, the book includes exercises, story-telling techniques and practical advice on how to bridge the generations in rehearsal and performance.

10. Frances Rifkin from Banner Theatre has written with great insight about the role the cultural worker can serve when recording the lives of workers in a dying industry in *Corby with Banner Theatre 1979–81* (Rifkin 1981).

> They describe it [their work] to me, as witness, in loving detail and as they speak a whole way, of work and relationships, is revealed. The vivid description of a job they are to lose irretrievably merges with the atmosphere in the Club to create an unforgettable poignancy and poetry. Something they would probably not have said just to each other, a shared knowledge and experience, is revealed to an outsider.

Rifkin captures the sense of urgency which the steel men felt about informing the researchers and their desire to affect the cultural product, in this case a play based on recordings taken during the strike and before the factory closure.

11. The importance of recording vanishing working communities has been widely recognised by community theatre companies, especially in the 1980s, with powerful examples such as *The Northern Trawl* (1984) by Remould Theatre in Hull under Rupert Creed, *The Steel Show* by Banner Theatre in Corby under Frances Rifkin and Pete Yates, with music by Dave Rogers, 1982, and *When The Boats Came In* by Eastern Angles, directed by Ivan Cutting, 1982.

12. Comments taken from feedback forms completed after every show by venues and used by the company to inform future productions.

13. COMMA is an independent organisation which has piloted a very useful computer software package for local history and community groups to archive images, documents, text, sound and film and, if they wish, to put it on the web. Contact via the internet: Comma, Community Multimedia Archives at www.commanet.org.

14. A film showing the process of collecting the memories, scripting them and then putting them into performance of the final production of *Memory Lane* has now been created under the title *Reminiscence Theatre*.

15. This process of telling a personal story to a group, who then reflect it back, has been systematised as Playback Theatre by Jonathan Fox, and is now in wide use as a form of creative recreation and as a therapeutic intervention. See Fox (1986).

16. This is a bilingual English–German book with an account of the 2004–5 European Network project and full-page colour photos of Memory Boxes with accompanying life stories from all participating countries: Czech Republic, Finland, Germany, Poland, Romania, Spain and the UK. Available from the European Reminiscence Network, c/o 15 Camden Row, London SE3 0QA or email Schweitzer@beeb.net.

17. Rado Klose produced a remarkable exhibition of black and white photographs of the groups, together with statements by the older performers, at the 1995 European Reminiscence Network festival, 'A Time To Remember'.

18. Frank Matzke's production for Fahrenheit Theatre, Hildesheim, of *Ohne Ende*, a play about the end of the war in Germany, was an especially powerful piece. It was played by students from Hildesheim University and older people who had fled west to avoid the advancing Soviet armies. Meetings took place at the festival between old and young from the British and German groups and strong friendships were made.

19. These papers contain an examination of the impact on older people from eight countries of participating in reminiscence theatre as described by them in their own words.

20. The Young National Trust Theatre experimented with this approach in the 1970s with much success as a means of bringing to life the history of great houses for visiting school-

children. I had the great pleasure of working with them on such a project and earned my Equity card through so doing!

21. Bonnie Vorenberg states on her website (www.seniortheater.com) that between 1999 and 2005, the number of Senior Theatre companies increased from 79 to 530. See Vorenberg (2000).

22. Founded in 1985 by Dr Joy Reilly of Ohio State University. Joy has subsequently founded Howling at the Moon, an older women's theatre group making shows from their own lives. See Reilly (2005).

23. A written comment sent to me by Sally Knocker and printed here with her permission.

24. Schweitzer (1996) contains interviews with the Good Companions and six other older people's theatre groups from different countries concerning their participation in theatre making about their own lives and about participation in the 1995 international festival 'A Time To Remember'.

25. I had the great good fortune to meet Peggy Pettitt at a festival of creative theatre work promoted by Elders Share The Arts in New York in 1993. Peggy's African-American elders' group, the Pearls of Wisdom, can be heard telling stories: *Pearls Of Wisdom: Elder Storytellers Weave Tales of Struggle and Triumph (Live at Omega Institute Conference on Aging)*. Audio cassette 30 minutes. Available from Elders Share The Arts, c/o National Center for Creative Aging, 138 South Oxford Street, Brooklyn, New York 11217.

26. Susan Perlstein's Elders Share The Arts organisation in New York has many valuable informative publications concerning creative arts and older people, including *A Stage for Memory: A Guide to the Living History Theater Program of Elders Share The Arts*, which is a comprehensive guide to the theory and practice of reminiscence, as well to the ways to use theatre to elicit, enhance and document memories. Based on 25 years of 'Living History Theater' at Elders Share the Arts, c/o National Center for Creative Aging, 138 South Oxford Street, Brooklyn, New York 11217.

27. 'The Place Where I Grew Up' photographic exhibition by Rado Klose in 2004 is now available for touring, details via Age Exchange.

28. Jean Valsler's film, *Long Ago and Far Away*, featuring creative reminiscence work with these groups, is included as a CD-ROM in the publication *Mapping Memories: Reminiscence with Ethnic Minority Elders*, edited by Pam Schweitzer (2004a) and published by Age Exchange. See the Age Exchange website for examples of the stories at www.age-exchange.org.uk.

29. The film of edited highlights of the festival, entitled *The Place Where I Grew Up: A Film of the 2004 Festival*, by Conal Percy, is available from Age Exchange. This half-hour film features extracts from plays created by African, Chinese, Caribbean, Indian and English elders' groups for the festival.

30. Film footage about this lady's life including interviews with her and photographs is viewable on the CD-ROM entitled *Life Portraits* by Lotta Petronella, which is included in the book *Mapping Memories: Reminiscence with Ethnic Minority Elders*, edited by Pam Schweitzer (2004a) and published by Age Exchange.

31. This was part of a joint project with the National Maritime Museum, 'Across the Seven Seas' 2001–2 and the results appear on their website under their community education section, entitled *Raising the Phoenix* as extracts from their stories and brief video clips of the activities described herein. www.nmm.ac.uk/server/show/conWebDoc6836.

32. See Note 28.

33. These Reminiscence Boxes later became part of the service provided by Age Exchange to support care staff and nursing staff wanting to undertake reminiscence with their clients but lacking the time to assemble suitable stimulus material. Eventually there were about 30 such boxes, all focusing on different reminiscence themes, and these boxes were posted out across the country to hard-pressed staff working with elderly people. The service continued for 15 years and for a while had a paid officer, Vanda Carter, who made user notes for each box and informed hirers of training opportunities in reminiscence. Many museums and voluntary organisations now offer a similar reminiscence resources service.

34. Bernie Arigho and David Savill from Age Exchange have recently extended reminiscence project work and arts-based residencies to Norfolk, Somerset and Yorkshire through a grant from the Department of Health.

35. In Schweitzer (1998) see in particular articles by Errollyn Bruce on carers, Yukiko Kurakawa on couple therapy and Bob Woods on reminiscence with people from long-standing relationships in change.

36. Partner countries were Austria, Belgium, Denmark, Finland, France, Germany, Holland, Norway, Sweden and the UK, with some countries running projects in more than one city.

37. MRC trial platform: reminiscence groups for people with dementia and their family caregivers: April 2004–March 2006

> This project aims to prepare the ground for a multi-centre, acceptably powered Randomised Controlled Trial of an innovative approach to reminiscence therapy, which involves the person with dementia and caregiver together, over the course of 12 weekly group meetings. In this project, in collaboration with Pam Schweitzer of Age Exchange, who was instrumental in developing this approach, a treatment manual has been developed, so that in future studies the intervention can be provided in a standardised manner. Outcome measures have been developed, refined and validated; these assess aspects of the caregiving relationship jointly for caregiver and person with dementia, as well as autobiographical memory across the life-span. Three groups for people with dementia and caregivers have been run in different centres, with a control condition in two centres involving groups for people with dementia meeting separately, as well as a treatment as usual comparison. In total, 69 caregiver/person with dementia dyads were recruited for the trial, with 58 completing the treatment period. Patients are mainly in the mild to moderate phases of dementia (average MMSE score 19), and are all living in community settings.

> Quality of life for the person with dementia (QoL-AD) and caregiver stress (GHQ) are the primary outcome measures in this study. The data will allow a power calculation to be carried out, to establish the sample size required for a definitive, large-scale study. The results of the pilot trial will be considerably more substantial than any previous study, and will in themselves shape practice in the field. The outcome measures will allow a new focus on changes in the overall caregiver/patient relationship, rather than on each separately, applicable to a range of psychosocial interventions. The treatment manual will enable the approach to be widely disseminated, if the results prove to be encouraging. (Summary supplied by Professor Bob Woods, University of Wales, Bangor, Research Project Co-ordinator)

References

Age Exchange Annual Report 1995–6. London: Age Exchange.

Armitage, C. (ed.) (1996) *Calling To Mind*. BBC Radio 4 Programme compiled by Cheryl Armitage about the process of creating the *Work in Progress* show, transmitted 25 September.

Basting, A.D. (1998) *The Stages of Age: Performing Age in Contemporary American Culture*. Ann Arbor: The University of Michigan Press.

Basting, A.D. (2001) 'The Time of Our Lives: International Festival of Reminiscence Theatre' (review). *Theatre Journal 53*, 1, 155–157.

Bender, M., Bauckham, P. and Norris, A. (1999) *The Therapeutic Purposes of Reminiscence*. London: Sage Publications.

Bharucha, R. (1993) *Theatre and the World: Performance and the Politics of Culture*. London: Routledge.

Blythe, A. (2005) *Strawberry Fields*. For Pentabus Theatre, Shropshire.

Boal, A. (1979) *Theater of the Oppressed*. London: Pluto Press.

Boal, A. (1992) *Games for Actors and Non-Actors*. London and New York: Routledge.

Bolton, G. (1995) *Drama for Learning: Dorothy Heathcote's Mantle of the Expert Approach to Education*. New Hampshire: Heinemann Publishers.

Bornat, J. (1989) 'Oral History as a social movement: reminiscence and older people.' *Oral History 17*, 2, 16–24.

Bornat, J. (ed.) (1994) *Reminiscence Reviewed: Perspectives, Evaluations, Achievements*. Buckingham, Philadelphia: Open University Press.

Bornat, J. (2001) 'Reminiscence and oral history: parallel universes or shared endeavour?' *Ageing and Society 21*, 219–241.

Brittain, V. and Slovo, G. (2004) *Guantanamo*. For Tricycle Theatre, London.

Brook, P. (1968) *The Empty Space*. Harmondsworth: Penguin.

Bruce, E. and Gibson, F. (1998) 'Remembering Yesterday, Caring Today: Evaluators' Report.' *Conference Papers*. London: Age Exchange (for the European Reminiscence Network).

Bruce, E. and Gibson, F. (1999a) 'Stimulating Communication: Project Evaluation' Part 1. *Journal of Dementia Care 7*, 2, 18–19.

Bruce, E. and Gibson, F. (1999b) 'Stimulating Communication: Project Evaluation' Part 2. *Journal of Dementia Care 7*, 3, 28–29.

Bruce, E., Hodgson, S. and Schweitzer, P. (1999) *Reminiscing with People with Dementia: A Handbook for Carers*. London: Age Exchange (for the European Reminiscence Network).

Buchanan, K. (1996) 'Talk and identity in reminiscence groups.' *Reminiscence Magazine 13*, 3.

Buchanan, K. (1997) 'Reminiscence and social exclusion.' *Reminiscence Magazine 15*, 3–5.

Burnside, I. (1990) 'Reminiscence: an independent nursing intervention for the elderly.' *Issues in Mental Health Nursing 11*, 33–48.

Butler, R.N. (1963) 'The Life Review: an interpretation of reminiscence in the aged.' *Psychiatry 26*, 65–76.

Chapman, C. and Schweitzer, P. (1975) *Theatre-In-Education Directory*. London and Los Angeles: Theatre Quarterly Publications.

Coleman, P.G. (1986) *Ageing and Reminiscence Processes*. New York: John Wiley and Sons.

Coleman, P.G. (1994) 'Reminiscence within the study of ageing.' In J. Bornat (ed.) *Reminiscence Reviewed*. Buckingham and Philadelphia: Open University Press.

Coren, M. (1984) *Theatre Royal: 100 Years of Stratford East.* London: Quartet Books.

Creed, R., Conolly, J. and Meek, B. (1984) *The Northern Trawl.* For Remould Theatre in Hull.

Csikszentmihalyi, M. (1996) *Creativity: Flow and the Psychology of Discovery and Invention.* New York: HarperCollins.

Cutting, I. (1982) *When The Boats Came In.* For Eastern Angles Theatre, Ipswich.

Doolittle, L. and Schweitzer, P. (eds) (1998) *We Want To Speak Of Old Times.* London: Age Exchange.

Fines, J. and Verrier, R. (1974) *The Drama of History.* London: New University Education.

Fox, J. (1986) *Acts of Service: Spontaneity, Commitment, Tradition in the Non-scripted Theatre.* New York: Tusitala Publications.

Friel, B. (1999) *Dancing at Lughnasa.* London: Faber and Faber.

Gibson, F. (2000) *The Reminiscence Trainer's Pack.* London: Age Concern England.

Gibson, F. (2004) *The Past in the Present: Using Reminiscence in Health and Social Care.* Baltimore, Maryland: Health Professional Press.

Gibson, F. (2006) *Reminiscence and Recall: A Practical Guide to Reminiscence Work.* London: Age Concern England.

Haight, B.K. (1998) 'Use of the Life Review/Life Story books in families with Alzheimer's Disease.' In P. Schweitzer (ed.) *Reminiscence in Dementia Care.* London: Age Exchange Publications.

Haight, B.K. and Webster, J.D. (eds) (1995) *The Art and Science of Reminiscing: Theory, Research, Methods and Applications.* Washington, DC: Taylor and Francis.

Hare, D. (2003) *The Permanent Way.* For the National Theatre, London. London: Faber and Faber.

Hare, D. (2004) *Stuff Happens.* For the National Theatre, London. London: Faber and Faber.

Hatton-Yeo, A. (2006) *Inter-generational Programmes: An Introduction and Examples of Practice.* On-line publication via website for Centre for Intergenerational Practice at www.centreforip.org.uk/default.aspx?page=764. Accessed October 2006.

Heiser, S., Trilling, A., Bruce, E. and Woods, R. (2005) 'Powers of persuasion.' *Journal of Dementia Care 13,* 6, 10–12 November/December.

Help the Aged Education Department (1981) *Recall Users' Handbook.* London: Help the Aged.

Hewitt, M. and Harris, A. (1992) *Talking Time: A Guide to Oral History for Schools.* London: Learning Design.

Hohenthal-Antin, L. (2001) *Taking Permission: Elderly People as Theatre Makers.* PhD Thesis: University of Jyvaskyla, Finland.

Jones, M. (2000) *Stones in his Pockets.* London: Nick Hern Books.

Kavanagh, G. (2000) *Dream Spaces: Memory and the Museum.* London: Leicester University Press.

Kemp, M. (1999) 'The Reminiscence Aids Project: Mick Kemp interviewed by Pam Schweitzer.' *Reminiscence Magazine 19,* 3–6 (published by Age Exchange).

Kent, N. (2005) *Bloody Sunday.* For Tricycle Theatre, London.

Killick, J. and Allan, K. (2001) *Communication and the Care of People with Dementia.* Buckingham: Open University Press.

Kitwood, T. (1997) *Dementia Reconsidered.* Buckingham: Open University Press.

Klose, R. (1996) *A Time To Remember: An Exhibition of Photographs and Words.* Produced for the European Reminiscence Network's Theatre Festival 'A Time To Remember', held in London in 1995. Details from European Reminiscence Network: 15 Camden Row, London SE3 0QA.

Knocker, S. (2002) *Alzheimer Society Book of Activities.* London: Alzheimers Society.

Kops, B. [1958] (1991) *The Hamlet of Stepney Green.* London: Oberon.

Langford, S. and Mayo, S. (2001) *Sharing the Experience: How to Set Up and Run Arts Projects Linking Young and Older People.* London: Magic Me.

Langley, G. and Kershaw, B. (eds) (1982) *Reminiscence Theatre.* Theatre Papers Fourth Series No. 6. Dartington: Department of Theatre, Dartington College of Arts.

Larsen, R. (2004) *A Stage for Memory: A Guide to the Living History Theater Program of Elders Share The Arts.* New York: National Center for Creative Aging.

MacColl, E., Parker, C. and Seeger, P. (1958–1964) *Eight Radio Ballads.* London: Topic Records Ltd. (Originally commissioned by BBC.)

Marziali, M. and Topalian, A. (1997) *Older Women Acting: Experiences of Older Women's Drama Groups in Europe and Elsewhere.* Italy: Older Women's Network (OWN) Europe.

Moreno, J.L. (1987) *The Essential Moreno: Writings on Psychodrama, Group Method, and Spontaneity.* (Edited by J. Fox.) New York: Springer Pub Co.

Myerhoff, B. (1980) *Number Our Days.* New York: Touchstone.

Nixon, J. (1982) *Drama and the Whole Curriculum.* London: Hutchinson.

Oddey, A. (1994) *Devising Theatre: A Practical and Theoretical Handbook.* London and New York: Routledge.

Oral History Society Website at www.ohs.org.uk.

Osborn, C. (1993) *The Reminiscence Handbook: Ideas for Creative Activities with Older People.* London: Age Exchange.

Osborn, C., Schweitzer, P. and Schweitzer, A. (1987) *Lifetimes: A Handbook of Memories, Ideas and 30 Laminated Pictures (4 of Each) for Reminiscence Groups.* London: Age Exchange.

Perlstein, S. and Bliss, J. (2003) *Generating Community: Intergenerational Partnerships through the Expressive Arts.* New York: Elders Share The Arts.

Perrin, T. (2005) *The New Culture of Therapeutic Activity with Older People.* London: Speechmark.

Petrukowicz, M. and Johnson, M. (1991) 'Using Life Histories to individualize nursing home staff attitudes towards residents.' *Gerontologist 31*, 102–106.

Phillips, M. and Phillips, T. (1998) *Windrush: The Irresistible Rise of Multicultural Britain.* London: HarperCollins.

Phillipson, C. (1982) *Capitalism and the Construction of Old Age.* London: Macmillan.

Phillipson, C. (1998) *Reconstructing Old Age.* London: Sage.

Quinn, C. (1989) *Honouring Memories: An Evaluation of the Work of the Age Exchange Reminiscence Project.* London: Centre for Policy on Ageing.

Reilly, J. (2005) *Age On Stage: Life-writing Your Monologue.* Kansas: ArtAge Publications.

Rifkin, F. (1981) *Corby with Banner Theatre 1979–81.* Unpublished article.

Rifkin, F. (2006) Unpublished report for Abhay Partnership Project

Rifkin, F., Yates, P. and Rogers, D. (1982) *The Steel Show.* For Banner Theatre.

Rubinstein, A., Andrews, A. and Schweitzer, P. (1991) *Just Like The Country: Memories of London Families who Settled the New Cottage Estates 1919–1939.* London: Age Exchange.

Salas, J. (1993) *Improvising Real Life.* Iowa: Kendall/Hunt Publishing.

Salt, C., Schweitzer, P. and Wilson, M. (eds) (1983) *Of Whole Heart Cometh Hope: Centenary Memories of the Co-operative Women's Guild.* London: Age Exchange.

Savill, D. (2002) *A Time To Share: Powerful Personal Stories for Teaching History and Citizenship.* London: Age Exchange.

Schweitzer, P. (1975) 'Production Casebook No 17 Theatre in Education: Bolton Octagon and "Holland New Town".' *Theatre Quarterly 5*, 17, 74–83.

Schweitzer, P. (ed.) (1980a) *Theatre in Education: Four Secondary Programmes.* Methuen Young Drama Series. London: Eyre Methuen.

Schweitzer, P. (ed.) (1980b) *Theatre in Education: Four Junior Programmes.* Methuen Young Drama Series. London: Eyre Methuen.

Schweitzer, P. (ed.) (1980c) *Theatre in Education: Five Infant Programmes.* Methuen Young Drama Series. London: Eyre Methuen.

Schweitzer, P. (ed.) (1983a) *Fifty Years Ago: Memories of the 1930s.* London: Age Exchange.

Schweitzer, P. (ed.) (1983b) *All Our Christmases: Memories of Christmas Past.* London: Age Exchange.

Schweitzer, P. (ed.) (1984a) *My First Job: Greenwich Pensioners' Memories of Starting Work.* London: Age Exchange.

Schweitzer, P. (ed.) (1984b) *A Place To Stay: Memories of Pensioners from Many Lands.* London: Age Exchange.

Schweitzer, P. (ed.) (1985) *Can We Afford The Doctor? Memories of Health Care.* London: Age Exchange.

Schweitzer, P. (ed.) (1986) *Many Happy Retirements: A Collection of Personal Reflections on Retirement.* London: Age Exchange.

Schweitzer, P. (ed.) (1989a) *Across The Irish Sea: Memories of London Irish Pensioners.* London: Age Exchange.

Schweitzer, P. (ed.) (1989b) *Good Morning Children: Memories of Schooldays in the 1920s and 30s.* London: Age Exchange.

Schweitzer, P. (ed.) (1990) *Goodnight Children Everywhere: Memories of Evacuation in World War II.* London: Age Exchange.

Schweitzer, P. (1993) *Age Exchanges: Reminiscence Projects for Children and Older People.* London: Age Exchange.

Schweitzer, P. (1994a) 'Many Happy Retirements.' In M. Schutzman and J. Cohen-Cruz (eds) *Playing Boal: Theatre, Therapy, Activism.* London and New York: Routledge.

Schweitzer, P. (ed.) (1994b) *Grandmother's Footsteps: Older People Remember their Grandparents.* London: Age Exchange.

Schweitzer, P. (1995) 'Age Exchange: the potential of reminiscence.' In A. Chadwick and A. Stannett (eds) *Museums and the Education of Adults.* Leicester: NIACE.

Schweitzer, P. (1996) *A Time To Reflect: Conference Papers for the European Reminiscence Network Meeting in Hildesheim 1996.* Unpublished paper available from the European Reminiscence Network, 15 Camden Row, Blackheath, London SE3 0QA or Schweitzer@beeb.net.

Schweitzer, P. (ed.) (1998) *Reminiscence in Dementia Care.* London: Age Exchange (for the European Reminiscence Network).

Schweitzer, P. (2002a) *Jubilee: Memories, Photos, a Play and the Story of How it Was Made.* London: Age Exchange.

Schweitzer, P. (2002b) *Age Exchange: The Story So Far, a Twenty Year Retrospective.* London: Age Exchange.

Schweitzer, P. (ed.) (2004a) *Mapping Memories: Reminiscence with Ethnic Minority Elders.* London: Age Exchange.

Schweitzer, P. (ed.) (2004b) *Middle Park: Memories, Photos, a Play and the Story of How it Was Made.* London: Age Exchange.

Schweitzer, P. (2006) *Reminiscence Theatre: Two Films about Making Theatre from Memories.* London: Age Exchange (on DVD).

Schweitzer, P. and Hancock, D. (1991) *Our Lovely Hops: Memories of Hop-picking in Kent.* London: Age Exchange.

Schweitzer, P. and Trilling, A. (2005) *Making Memories Matter.* Kassel, Germany: Euregioverlag.

Schweitzer, P. and Wegner, C. (eds) (1989) *On The River: Memories of a Working River.* London: Age Exchange.

Schweitzer, P. Hilton, L. and Moss, J. (eds) (1985) *What Did You Do in the War, Mum? Women Recall their Wartime Work.* London: Age Exchange.

Shaw, K. (1999) *Brief Journey.* Hampshire: Forest Forge Theatre Company.

Sherman, M. (1979) *Bent.* Derbyshire: Amber Lane Press.

Sim, R. (2003) *Reminiscence: Social and Creative Activities with Older People in Care.* Bicester: Speechmark.

Soball, J. (1989) *Ghetto.* London: Nick Hern Books.

Strimling, A. (2004) *Roots and Branches: Creating Intergenerational Theatre.* Portsmouth: Heinemann.

Summerfield, P. (1998) *Reconstructing Women's Wartime Lives: Discourse and Subjectivity in Oral Histories of the Second World War.* Manchester: Manchester University Press.

Television History Workshop (1985) *Can We Afford The Doctor?* Channel Four documentary on reminiscence theatre process and product, directed by Marylin Wheatcroft, edited by Sharon Goulds.

Theatre Royal, Stratford East (1991) *Black Poppies.* London: Theatre Royal, Stratford East.

Thompson, P. (1978) *The Voice of the Past.* Oxford and New York: Oxford University Press.

Thorgrimsen, L., Schweitzer, P. and Orrell, M. (2002) 'Evaluating reminiscence for people with dementia: a pilot study.' *The Arts in Psychotherapy 29,* 2, 93–97.

Vorenberg, B. (2000) *Senior Theatre Connections.* Kansas: ArtAge Publications.

Wagner, B. (2000) *Dorothy Heathcote: Drama as a Learning Medium.* Stoke-on-Trent: Trentham Books.

Wesker, A. (2001) *Chicken Soup with Barley.* Wesker Plays Vol. 1. London: Methuen.

Witkin, R. (1974) *The Intelligence of Feeling.* London: Heinemann.

Witkin, R. (1982) 'Contributions.' In G. Langley and B. Kershaw (eds) *Reminiscence Theatre.* Theatre Papers Fourth Series. No. 6. Dartington: Department of Theatre, Dartington College of Arts.

Woods, R.T. and McKiernan, F. (1995) 'Evaluating the impact of reminiscence on older people with dementia.' In B.K. Haight and J. Webster (eds) *Art and Science of Reminiscing: Theory, Research, Methods and Applications.* Washington, DC: Taylor and Francis.

Woods, R.T., Spector, A., Jones, C., Orrell, M and Davies, S. (2005) 'Reminiscence therapy for dementia.' *The Cochrane Database of Systematic Reviews, Issue 2.* Wiley: Chichester.

Young, M. and Willmott, P. [1954] (1989) *Family and Kinship in East London.* Harmondsworth: Penguin.

Index

Note: page numbers in *italics* refer to photographs.